A stranger in my own land

An ordinary Englishman's view.

Barry Sheridan.

British Library Cataloguing In Publication Data
A Record of this Publication is available
from the British Library

ISBN 978-1-84685-934-2

First Published 2008 by
Exposure Publishing,
an imprint of
Diggory Press Ltd
Three Rivers, Minions, Liskeard, Cornwall, PL14 5LE, UK
WWW.DIGGORYPRESS.COM

First Edition. 2008.

Dedication

For
Andrew and James.

Contents

Errata.

Page 17 line 33. Amend invasions to invasion.
Page 35 line 31. Insert 'of' after collection.
Page 38 line 2. Insert 'army' after Scots.
Page 205 line 30. Insert 'the' between at and media.
Page 215 line 17. Insert 'been' before trivialised.
Page 238 line 32. Amend seem to 'seems.'
Page 256 line 9. Insert 'have' after campaigns
Page 295 line 20. Insert 'a' before rich.

Foreword

Assuming the reader gets tempted beyond this page, what they will come across is an account of Britain and its people. One written from the perspectives of an average citizen rather than the studious outcomes of a dedicated historian or professional writer of contemporary affairs.

The foundation for these words comes from the effort of a lifetime, the ordinary day to day experiences where knowledge is accumulated and understanding wrested bit by bit. A collective end reinforced by a particular interest in the real story, where this could be found and relied on. Translating this learning and putting it down on paper cannot be said to have produced a book that is unimpeachable, although nothing was spared in trying to make it so.

Before completing this brief introduction, fix one thought in place and keep it until the final page. The author is not ashamed to be English. As far this individual is concerned, the constancy of effort by those with influence to inculcate such feelings has failed, even if they succeeded in debasing life as it once was in these isles.

Barry Sheridan.

Hampshire. England.
31st December 2007.

I know thy errand, I will go with thee.

Chapter 1

A beginning

Human history summarises the events and actions of a species whose sole constant has been its variability. Every civilisation the product of a troubled beginning, a gestation that took time and much effort to deliver the necessary stability and certainties that contribute to a functioning social order. It is later generations who reap the benefits as life settles into the comfort of what becomes well understood principles and traditions. The appearance of immutability that gradually surrounds such established continuities however, is deceptive. For all manner of circumstances can reduce consensus and with it, the ability to endure.

Such is the case for these isles, the last sixty years a time of profound and destabilising change. Radical departures easier to understand if some idea exists of what we are, not just as Briton's, but as humans. A question whose answers cannot exclude a thought or two about the wondrous world of which we are a part.

As it happens, the second of these imponderables provides a logical beginning to these considerations. Taking those of the Christian faith first reveals clear cut belief in the origins of both universe and ourselves. Get hold of a Bible, open it at the beginning of the Old Testament and there before your eyes is the First Book of Moses, Genesis, where chapter and verse tell us how God created the world and all that was in it. This sort of explanation, common to many cultures in various guises, sufficed for centuries until those uncomfortable with having to accept an explanation that relied on blind faith sought to construct a logical set of theories based, at least in part, on careful observation and plausible hypothesis.

The outcome of these efforts have led to the following claims. The universe was created in a spontaneous explosion that scientists refer to as the Big Bang. An event thought to have occurred around thirteen billion years ago, its aftermath bringing into existence space, time and the forces and elements that make up the stars, planets and other bodies that litter the vastness of an ever expanding cosmos. While the precise details are subject to uncertainty, it is agreed that gravity was essential. Its existence acting on the gas, dust and other material present after the Bang, drawing it into clusters of such mass that eventually localised gravity was able to exert sufficient pressure to cause inward collapse. This had the effect of raising internal temperatures to levels that sparked the thermonuclear reactions that turn a lump of matter into a star.

Of the billions and billions of stars thought to exist, one is of particular interest to us, it is our sun. Around its brilliant mass a number of planets, moons, asteroids, comets and other oddities were formed or captured. Our own home, the earth and its moon make up what is known as a binary system, two bodies in close harmony on an endless journey around the sun. Modest components of a small solar system that itself belongs to a great cluster of stars called a galaxy. The one we belong to revealed by that gentle swathe of light splitting the night sky, something we call the Milky Way. Just one of countless such groupings in a universe whose size is beyond comprehension.

Our planet is thought to be approximately four and half billion years old. Its early existence subject to constant change during a time when its outer surface slowly solidified, forming a thin crust made up of large segments called plates. Floating on a molten interior, each plate is capable of moving independently of the others at differing speeds under the influence of thermal currents generated within the core. As they move into or past each other they ride up, slide below or tear along, elevating or depressing parts of the surface. Geologic activity enlivened by substantial volcanic activity and impacts from bits of rock, ice and other lumps that continually rained down from outer space. Indeed it is thought that enough ice ended up here to liberate the liquid that now covers nearly three quarters of the entire globe to a depth of several thousand feet. The final component of what would become the habitable layer of the earth, or biosphere, originating from venting gases that accumulated to form an atmosphere tens of miles deep.

When it comes down to providing a scientific explanation for the existence of life, an elaborate theory was constructed whose principle rests on the spontaneous formation of specific chemical arrangements in whatever atmosphere or liquid existed early in earth's life. In linked sequence over much time, some twenty or so amino acids were formed, these joining together to make up the basic building blocks of all earth bound life, the proteins. This theory concluding by suggesting that once these organic compounds were freely available, repeating random chance brought about a primitive living thing. Development beyond that point depending on mutation (a change) maintaining a flow of subtle alterations, each contributing in some way to the advancement and survival of the life form. Over millions and millions of years this ongoing process is reckoned to have brought about all the life that ever existed on earth, be it an amoeba or a man.

As it stands today, the scientific viewpoint has conquered divine interpretations. Yet, when prodded, it all becomes less certain. To bring meaning to this hesitation, let us briefly consider the work of those physicists unravelling the mysteries of the Big Bang. It being very much a case of work in progress. As their capacities to examine the universe continue to expand, new information demands fresh interpretations and modifications to the general concept. Ongoing development that has seen terms like dark matter and dark energy invented and incorporated to maintain the theory's integrity and plausibility.

Interestingly, it is possible to see similarities between the Biblical and scientific explanations. Both reckon the universe was created, one by a physical event and the other by divine expression. Further agreement existing in the thought that the cosmos has only existed for a limited period, although admittedly they differ substantially as to how long. Science thinking in terms of billions of years while strict adherents to Biblical text reckon it's only a few thousand. Both sides resting their case on the idea that it all appeared out of nothing.

While such interpretations can be dismissed if the reader chooses, it is not quite so easy to maintain that life had spontaneous origins when exposed to cold analysis. Essentially constructed out of the work of Charles Darwin and Alfred Wallace, this invented elaboration has not yet demonstrated in any realistic way how amino acids or proteins, never mind life, could just come into existence. A doubt all the more pertinent when taking a detailed look at what is supposed to be the simplest form of life, a single celled bacteria. An entity that is in fact anything but simple. Adding to these complications are the general uncertainties that surrounds the precise means by which mutation creates enough aggregate change to make a new species. While it might be credible to accept this for certain aspects of a single cell, extending it endlessly until we end up with something as complicated as the human body strains.

Yet, if this theory is correct, the staggering range of earth bound life suggests this mechanism must be common place, perhaps even observable within a handful of generations. After all, life has recovered from past extinction's such as the one 250 million years ago during which it is thought around ninety-five percent of all life at the time was gradually wiped out (the Permian extinction). A similar occurrence dealing a fatal blow to the rule of the dinosaurs some 65 million years back. Making sense of all this requires evidence of the sort that would take the theory forward into proven fact. A solution that must also deal with the realisation that life appears from time to time to have taken major steps forward in complexity without leaving any evidence of preceding linear development.

These legitimate doubts have been conceded by some scientists who have been looking for other answers, one idea finding support being cosmic ancestry. A line of thought advancing the idea that life exists throughout the cosmos (panspermia). It being possible that over the aeons it travelled here locked in the ice that delivered the water or, as a later hitch-hiker aboard a lump of rock or meteorite. While this neatly side-steps the problems of indigenous creation, as well as providing a way of explaining the conundrum of new species. It makes little headway towards explaining how life came into existence in the first place.

As a result of all this scientific consideration and research we have certainly come closer to realising just how elaborate the universe and life actually is. Knowledge that does not make it any easier to answer the question of origins. Indeed it appears more difficult than ever to accept that we are the product of a single physical event out of nothing and a later, highly improbable, succession of convenient accidents. Those adamant this is the only possible interpretation have latterly resorted to aggressive campaigns against those people who feel some behind the scenes intelligence exists. A God, who in some obtuse way has created us for a purpose we are unable to decipher. The heated arguments and debates that surround this issue unable to disguise the fact that every possible explanation demands faith to cover what remains unknowable.

Whether we will ever be sure is frankly impossible to say. Perhaps better arguments or evidence will manifest themselves in the future, providing ways to strengthen scientific explanations. Or then again, perhaps God will reveal himself. Until such a time, peace must lay in honestly saying we do not really know how we came to be here.

Taking on the other question leads us down a path well trodden by earlier philosophers, theologians and thinkers. People who have long been interested in trying to establish what it is that gives us our particular qualities. Modernist revision overturning many established beliefs, not least that, which once held man was possessed by a spirit or soul that went to God on death. In its place is the view that we are little more than an enhanced ape, a conclusion that seems profoundly unsatisfying given our talents.

Beating a pathway to a fuller understanding must begin with conception. While there is no need here to explain the goings on between a man and woman intent on breeding. It is important to acknowledge that this pleasurable overture provides the gift of life, a union that brings together the two halves of our genetic code. Creating in an instant the blueprint of our physical self and the foundation of those three interrelated elements that make up what we might call our inner being. A formless something whose existence is revealed through instinctive behaviours, emotional reactions and of course the intellect that offers the chance for each to think and reason.

At the basic level, nothing is more fundamental to how we act and respond than instinct. Its remarkable role much easier to appreciate if we examine a simpler form like the Monarch butterfly. This frail creature makes its way to and from its winter refuges in Northern Mexico and coastal California to summer haunts along the north-eastern borders of the United States and Canada. Quite how the capability to navigate two thousand miles between these two places ever camc about is unexplainable. Never mind considering how this is transferred from one generation to the next in something that cannot be seen with the naked eye.

Oddly, observed instinctive behaviour in humans appears on the surface to be much more limited, the suckling response of the infant and its audible grumbling when other wants require attention are two examples. Beyond that, as we grow, these in-built behaviours continue to play a vital role, the physical reactions that prepare the body to meet danger a case in point. Entirely automatic responses kick in to release adrenaline as well as maximising blood flow to the muscles. The essential reason is of course self preservation, a powerful influence that also ultimately drives human co-operation and with it the desire to procreate. The latter wholly dependent on the former.

Wrapped around pre-determined instinct is emotion, an interrelated skein of responses and sensations that react and stimulate. Permanently in play, they fertilise and enrich social interaction, their varied unpredictability going a long way towards defining what we think of as being human. It being emotion that allows us to experience the rise and fall of the loves and antipathies that shift and evolve between us. Strangest of all its many dimensions surely related to the telepathic, countless instances existing of a parent sensing that something has befallen a distant son or daughter.

Behaviour however is not simply tied to the contents of our hereditary package. For our natural inclinations can be enhanced or modified by upbringing during those years when the child is reliant on those around it. At the heart of this protracted business are attempts to selectively hone qualities seen as preferable through a mixture of techniques such as persuasion, example and sanction. The momentum generated by this prolonged training gaining additional impetus from the natural tendency we all have to imitate what we find as appealing. While this formative phase is largely complete by the age of six or seven, our character continues to remain responsive, most importantly to the gathering potential of our native intelligence. An uncertain and powerful force capable of subjugating instinct and emotion one moment and being controlled by it the next.

Intellect is, as far as we know, a gift exercised in the mind. Although being precise about what this means is far from easy to explain. It may be a single physical location within the brain, or perhaps the sum of its parts that relies on sophisticated interconnections. Then again, it may be something entirely different. Whatever the truth, we must also consider the fact that the mind has at least two states, one conscious, the other unconscious. Being aware of ourselves and the world around us comes mainly through the conscious. It is also where, during the waking hours at least, our deliberate mental processes appear to take place in response to whatever concerns and interests prevail from one second to the next. Less easy to assimilate are the purposes and roles of the unconscious. It seems possible that various thoughts continue to take place there even though we are not aware of them, just as it's speculated that this is the realm of dreams.

While man's material progress has largely been the result of applying intellect to practical need. Our conscious output is not simply limited to such ends, there is some indefinable inner desire that has been present from the earliest moments of our existence, something partly satisfied by artistic expression. Painting the surrounding world, the crafting of jewellery for personal ornamentation and of course creating music are obvious illustrations of this peculiarity. On another plane altogether has been thinking suggestive of the idea that death is the transition from one world to another. Complex reflection and imaginings that made considerable progress in the relative freedoms of the early civilisations. Times that allowed flexible minds to range over the abstract, the theoretical as well as the practical. The outcome of those efforts frequently disrupted by wars and the periodic retreats from reason that delay or even reverse human progress.

At all times on the very fringes of this intellectual frontier, effort was continually directed towards unravelling our own unfathomable depths. Work that sought to make sense of the turbulent interplay of instinct, emotion and intellect that makes us what we are. Just a part of its many conclusions are invented ways that allow us to categorise and assess people in relation to a spectrum of potential behaviours whose polar ends are marked by the wholly good and the completely bad.

Characteristics commonly seen as good included honesty, self discipline, resilience and concern for others, those suggestive of an uglier side spanning cruelty, greed and indifference. Other attributes exhibit a form of neutrality, the influence they have depends upon the degree to which they are applied, obvious here are ambition and determination. The collective sum revealing how tenuous the certainties are, for we surprise when it is least expected, bewilder when it is unnecessary and endear through compassion when we appear immune from all feeling. While the fact that we can be straight forward about certain things and devious over others acknowledges deeper tussles. Turbulence compounded by the fact that we can and do camouflage or shield our true selves. Not that this is necessarily malicious in intent, though it can be, shyness is a common and innocuous reason, as is lack of confidence.

Weighting all the strands that contribute to the essence of what makes us human produces a reality that is not fixed around some good or bad axis, but is instead centred on uncertainty. Its natural flux needs constant checking by clear imperative or solid principle. When such circumstances are weak, then mankind's direction and progress becomes attracted or even subject to, the frivolous side of intellect with all of its notions of perfectibility and the convincing arguments that are put forward as to why this or that objective can be achieved. A repeating cycle that often begins with the temptation to interfere with what is best left alone, or fix what does not need to be fixed.

However well meant, these endeavours are invariably the work of those as reluctant to acknowledge general human failings as they are of their own. The results of this repeating blindness is, as history continues to show, ruinous. The chances to turn back and reassess the situation when it is clear things are going wrong repeatedly squandered in favour of comfortable deception. Only it seems, when near or total chaos begins to assert its rule, do minds concentrate on genuine substance and reason rather than what is invented to suit our own desires. Unfortunately, it also must be said, that sometimes this rational transformation never comes in time to stave off self induced disaster.

Chapter 2

From distant ancestors to early kings

The murk of an ancestral past does not hide the fact that early Britons arrived from the continent in successive waves over thousands of years. What induced their exodus to here is naturally down to guessing, but the assumption must be one of migration in search of favourable conditions. Having found what was acceptable, these tribes or groups settled as far as we can tell largely independently of one another. A patchwork arrangement that may have been essential due to mutual antagonisms. Surely a fair conclusion given the existence of the ancient hilltop forts, themselves advanced versions of earlier defensive constructions.

Irrespective of the unknowns, we can be sure the people of those times were capable of organising themselves towards a common goal. The substantial earthworks at Danebury in Hampshire and the construction of Stonehenge just two examples of such co-operative ventures. Evidence of other abilities revealed through surviving artefacts that included personal jewellery and other treasured items.

In the final decades before the birth of Christ, the most successful peoples of the Iron Age, the Celts, turned up on these shores. People who with chariot, horse and coinage created space by conquest as others had done before them. Taking over the south east corner of England, they spread west in the short interval before the superior challenge of Imperial Rome arrived. Julius Caesar and two legions making a brief foray, a hundred years passing before they returned in AD 43 to subjugate and civilise England and Wales as provinces of Rome. Peace and prosperity being built and sustained by roads, castles, commerce, justice and the garrisons tramp.

After 300 years of relative peace, Rome's fading strength brought gradual abandonment of its far flung provinces including Britain. Decline coincident with an overall westward shift of peoples on the continent that brought Germanic Saxon's to these shores to add to the problems already facing Roman-Britons from warlike Picts and Scots. Although resisted for nearly two centuries, Saxon aggression eventually overcame the native population, the beaten remnants either surrendering or retreating into the corners of Wales, the far north-west of England or lowland Scotland. Some even abandoning these isles altogether to escape across the seas to distant Brittany.

The Saxon order that took over, flourished between the 6th and 8th centuries, evolving into the seven separate kingdoms known as the 'Heptarchy.' The largest and most strategically dominant of these kingdoms was Mercia, its pre-eminence gaining the respect of its neighbours before indifferent aggressors, marauding Vikings from Norway and Denmark turned up. Arriving first in 789, they kept coming back until the lure of fertile lands tempted many to stay, the bulk of these settling a swathe of central Saxon England that became known as Danelaw.

Viking and Saxon co-existed on what was divided land. Determined races whose approach to accommodation was often solved by reaching for the sword. A tussle for dominance that rumbled on and off with periodic defeats on both sides spaced between times when the business of living took over. A pattern of strife that subsided for a time when all England was unified, a task begun by the Saxon King, Alfred the Great. It being finished by his son Athelstan, during the early part of the 10th century. A man whose contributions were to include the establishment of a single national currency under the provisions of the Statute of Greatley in 928.

Subsequent opportunities presented by this unity were best grasped by Edgar, younger son of Edmund, whose enlightened rule brought administrative and legal overhaul supplemented by reform of taxation and coinage. Fruits that gradually ebbed during the long reign of Ethelred (the Unready), despite his efforts to further administrative reform. The main source of his difficulties, the enduring antipathy between Saxon and Viking. Attempts to secure peace by payment raised through a land tax, the Danegeld, undone following the re-ignition of Danish ambitions after the massacre of Danish settlers early in the eleventh century. An invasions force led by Swegn Forkbeard, king of Denmark, succeeding in temporarily deposing Ethelred in 1013. Reprieve coming when Swegn died the following year, Ethelred regaining the chance to continue his rule before it passed to his son two years later. Edmund the Second's own death after handful of months seeing England united under the firm stewardship of Canute, son of Swegn. A man whose time saw restoration of regard for law and much else during years when once again covetous eyes, Norman this time, cast their stare on these lands.

Canute's own legacy fell to his illegitimate son, Harold, whose short life saw it pass to the rightful heir, Harthacanute, then King of Denmark. The crown moving on again in 1042 to the surviving son of Ethelred, Edward the Confessor. Raised in Normandy, Edward proved pious, more monk than king, ruling as little more than a figure head. The real power being exercised by the intriguing Wessex Earl, Godwine. Following the death of the childless Edward, the Saxon legacy moved towards its final end when Godwine's eldest son, Harold, grabbed the throne, despite it being promised by solemn oath to William of Normandy. An affront that would not go unpunished, though the first challenge that year of 1066 came from the successors of Canute. Aware of the weaknesses of the English defences, they set out to bring England once more under Scandanavian rule. Landing on the north-east coast, the invading forces moved inland and set up camp east of York at Stamford Bridge, where Harold, having marched rapidly to the north, gained tactical surprise and victory.

It was a triumph that opened the door to defeat and loss of the crown. The army raised by William landing unopposed in Sussex. Norman knights reinforced by those of France and Flanders standing side by side with a few descendants of Roman Britons who had escaped to Brittany long ago. Supplemented by mercenaries attracted by the promise of spoil, it readied itself. Made aware, Harold and his surviving forces marched south, briefly halting in London before rushing down to Hastings where they arrived on the 13th of October. Battle joined a day later between the cavalry and archers of William and Harold's infantry. Victory belonging to the men of the Norman banner who proved their mastery in spite of suffering heavy losses. Harold himself falling to a mortal wound from an arrow in the eye.

William's subsequent march towards London demonstrated his ruthlessness as he mercilessly dealt with any who stood in his way or did not pay homage. Awareness of his barbarity soon bringing submission and the English crown, an act confirmed on Christmas Day at Westminster Abbey when the Archbishop of York formally made him King of England. Over the following years his rule was extended by laying waste to the land and people of the north, a period when more than half of the old English nobility joined Harold in the grave. William securing his grip on the throne by having ninety castles built, each manned by the knights personally loyal to him. Guarding the strategic points, they proved an effective check on the ambitions of any who might want to contest his rule. Although William left the old Anglo-Saxon system of local government and law intact, he imposed the Norman feudal pattern of land ownership, where the estate passed whole to the eldest son.

Looking back it's clear the Norman conquest was profoundly significant. For although the origins of us as people stretched back beyond the reach of chronicles, myths and legends. This invasion introduced at a stroke a ruling body that bore little relation or affection for the native stock (sound familiar). Made up of strong, self interested men keen on personal gain, these speculative risk takers held expectations distinctly different from the conquered. A near unbridgeable gulf where king, noble and peasant followed different paths that never met. In the coming centuries our history would flex to these Norman traits, each time leadership became weak, conflicting ambitions would contest for political influence, riches and even the throne itself. Its duplicities employing intrigue and changing alliances in a land where surprisingly, the word would often prove itself the equal of the sword.

With England joined, at least in political terms, to the land of the Norman's. French became the language of the court, reinforcing the distinctions of rank with those of tongue. The long term aims of William served by the unique decision to make a detailed survey of the land, the results filling the 'Domesday Book.' Through it we gain insight into what the country was really like at the time, agriculturally based with few towns or villages. The accurate information this provided allowing sensible decisions to be made over how much tax could be extracted and used to fulfil the king's aims. Not least of which was the intention to continue hold onto lands in France, aims pursued by William until his death in 1087 following a fall from his horse. His legacy, two kingdoms his sons would share. The idea of empire he left intruding into the Tudor dynasty, ambitions that led to conflicts that would see the people of England contesting with those of France for dominance.

Amongst the bounty inherited by William 2nd when he took over England was a re-invigorated church acknowledged for its learning and the work of its stonemasons who built its monasteries and abbeys. It was after all a time of strong faith based on Rome. Strong enough for all

Europe to hear and respond to Pope Urban 2nd call in 1095 to free Jerusalem from the hands of the Seljuk Turks. Whilst these Crusades were a common focus of medieval kings, such ambitions did not deflect the exercise of farsighted abilities as Henry 1st would prove during his reign when he created the 'Exchequer' as means to oversee and audit State accounts. Early recognition of the importance of finance to government, a factor that was to distort our history. Henry's death opening the door for the accession of Matilda (Maude), his daughter, as our first queen. Instead she was elbowed aside by Stephen, who was not the first or last of our monarchs to prove ineffective once they had power.

Stephen's own demise put the throne in the hands of Henry of Anjou, a man of France, who as Henry 2nd became the first Plantagenet king in 1154. Married two years earlier to Eleanor of Aquitaine, his ascension to the throne tied England to substantial tracts of western France, a relationship that prospered. Literate, able as a warrior and widely respected, he laid down those extensions to the old Saxon laws that form the basis of English Common Law. Creating Royal Courts where both criminal and civil cases could be tried before a judge and jury to establish the truth. Although not the jury as we understand it today, this idea, taken from the Frank's, was combined with an open court where accused and witnesses faced cross-examination under appointed, independent judges. Offering greater consistency in the standards of law it was a more than useful addition to the old Anglo-Saxon presumptions where innocence was assumed until the guilt was established.

The stability of Henry's energetic reign left a resilient crown in the hands of Richard the First (the Lion-Heart). It surviving, except for two short interludes, his absence. Yet, such was the appeal of his name that the kingdom stumped up a fortune for his release when he was captured and imprisoned while away on the Crusades. The exercise of authority in his name conducted by others, notably from 1194 by Hubert Walter, then Archbishop of Canterbury. A man who, amongst other things, implemented standard weights and measures, extending this work by employing travelling justices and knights to execute State policy. It being he who put in place the formal record keeping that was used to document day to day government business.

Richard's successor, John, was crowned in 1199. A tireless schemer in pursuit of his own interests, he eventually undermined support amongst the nobility for his rule. Their collective resentments leading to demands he sign the Great Charter of King John, otherwise known as Magna Carta, at Runnymede on 15th June 1215. This landmark document beginning a journey whose ultimate purpose was to limit the absolute power of kings and State (at least until modern times). Its sixty three articles dealing with specific points where authority or right was conceded, something John sought to repudiate shortly after its signing. His death intervening to head off the drift towards open conflict.

What Magna Carta did not do however was to tackle the arbitrariness of the monarchy. Efforts to curtail its frequent excesses featuring prominently during the fifty-six year reign of Henry the Third when the nobility, once more irritated over the king's profligacy, sought to impose restraint. The first plan was drawn up at Oxford with further enlargements put together under the Provisions of Westminster. This constitutional reform included limits on taxation and various other administrative amendments that would collectively check the king's authority. Henry's concession under duress was later repudiated when the Pope released him from his oath in 1261, a step that provoked open rebellion against his rule under the leadership of Simon de Montfort. Captured and imprisoned at Lewes, the king became little more than a vassal. His eventual rescue owed to a split that divided the nobility, one that induced Henry's eldest son, Edward, to turn away from de Montfort. A disagreement resolved by clash of arms, Edward defeating the nobles, firstly at Kenilworth, annihilating their remnants at Evesham in 1265. Nonetheless the principles of reform had been accepted, the main Provisions of Westminster being incorporated into the statute of Marlborough two years later.

The final years of Henry's reign saw peace concluded with France and growing prosperity for England from the wool trade. Wealth that allowed completion of his grand rebuilding of the cathedrals, the consecration of his masterpiece, Westminster Abbey, taking place just before his death in 1272.

Inheriting was the First of the Edward's, otherwise known as 'Longshanks,' king of some three and half million people. The majority peasants whose life had seen little change since Norman times. To their land he would add numerous refinements to State and local organisation during a reign when our future parliament began to play more of a role. Executive and judicial support to the king's rule being conducted through a Great Council, its members made up from the influential nobility. Some of whom were always included, owners of what became known as hereditary right. These Lords were supported from time to time by an assembly of men of lesser status, forming what would later evolve into the Commons. The gatherings themselves known as 'parliamentum's,' a medieval Latin word meaning a talk, meeting or discussion. The power of the Great Council largely based on its authority to control the revenue the crown could extract from the kingdom.

Outlets for Edward's abundant energies included efforts to subjugate the Celtic lands of Wales and Scotland. North and west Wales being largely annexed following two campaigns completed by 1283. Success eluding him in Scotland, where an effective defence was organised by William Wallace. Edward eventually negotiating peace with France so he could direct all his attentions towards subduing the northern foe. Despite victory at Falkirk in 1298, the rebellion endured under Robert de Bruce who became King of Scotland in 1306. Edward himself dying at the head of his army during its march to continue the campaign a year later. Succeeded by his son, the Second Edward, efforts were abandoned for a time, before resuming in 1314. The king's armies suffering defeat at the hands of Scottish pike-men at Bannockburn.

It was Edward's instincts to rely on a few permanent officials personally loyal to him, even so parliament was constantly recalled because of his need for money, in all sitting twenty-five times during his nineteen years on the throne. The control of funding expanding parliamentary influence, allowing some of its nobility to gain much wider prominence. Dissuaded from pursuing union by force due to Scottish resistance, Edward conceded to a truce in 1323. By which time his unpopularity and growing vulnerability were such that the loss of his French possessions to Charles 4th of France incited treachery. It being Edward's wife, Queen Isabella, supposedly in France to negotiate for their return, who combined forces with Roger de Mortimer and other disgruntled elements to return as invaders. The King being seized and later disposed of by murder in September of 1327 at Berkley Castle.

With the power of the throne in the hands of Isabella and de Mortimer, English interests in France were gradually abandoned. As were ambitions in Scotland, who gained full independence following Robert de Bruce's negotiations that led to the Treaty of Northampton in 1328. Effective challenge to these usurpers facing continual delays because of splits and divisions amongst the nobility. Minds only concentrating when the king's uncle, the Earl of Kent, was executed on the trumped up charge of treason. Support gathering around the Queen's son, the young Edward. A carefully planned raid delivering the regicides (the monarch's murderers) into the hands of the officers loyal to Edward, only the conventions of the times sparing Isabella, de Mortimer's fate on the scaffold.

Established on the throne in his own right as Edward 3rd, the young king's reign was to continue in all for fifty years, a period that was to include reviving unrequited ambitions in Scotland. Edward conspiring with the pretender to the Scottish throne, Edward Balliol, against its king, David the Second, son of Robert de Bruce. This support allowed Balliol to gain transitory hold on the throne, but the wheeling and dealing that lay behind all this unhinged success when it became known. Of greater importance were events in France, where following the death of the French monarch without a direct heir, Edward was encouraged to contest the succession through his mother's line. Coincident interference by the Counts of Flanders in England's all important wool trade providing additional momentum to the English nobility's enthusiasm for more aggressive ventures in France.

On such a foundation began that sequence of eight major conflicts known as the 'Hundred Years war.' Its opening gambit seeing Edward assemble a professional army, securing the necessary naval supremacy by annihilating the French fleet at Sluys on June 24th 1340. Further progress was then delayed by the problems of money, an issue that would constrain Edward's endeavours. His army finally getting ashore six years later near La Hogue, forces that wandered around France for a bit before a large chasing French force caught up. Turning to face his pursuers on chosen ground near the village of Crecy, the English gained the first of its major victories against the French, on this occasion over numbers three or four times their own. The Scots, rallying as France's ally, assisted by crossing the English border, meeting defeat by narrow margins west of Durham at the Battle of Neville's Cross. The Scottish king, David 2nd, being captured and eventually held for eleven years until ransomed.

Back in France, following the siege and capture of Calais, the spreading Black Death imposed its own form of peace. A surfeit of dying by disease apparently not enough to reduce tensions, war being resumed in 1355 when an English army commanded by Edward's son, the Black Prince, raided deep into France. Cornered and forced to fight a vastly superior French force at Poitier, the power of the longbow, use of terrain and above all belief gained for England another decisive victory. The slaughter of much French nobility shattering her confidence as conflict petered out without formal end or treaty.

Amongst the Black Death's other contributions to English life was the demise of French as the language of the English court. Not that it helped with money, frequent parliamentary recall continuing to be a necessity, although there was little conscious attempt by the nobles to define or interfere with State policy. Instead the resentments within the country largely fell on the church with its ostentatious wealth and activities of the Papal tax collectors. Sentiments all the harder given the fact that the Papal seat had resided in Avignon, France since 1309.

In 1377 Edward's crown passed to the ten year old son of his own son (the Black Prince). Crowned as Richard 2nd, the duties of rule during his minority fell on his uncle, John of Gaunt. The young king making an early mark at Smithfield during the 'Peasants Revolt' of 1381 when he met the rioting men of Kent under Wat Tyler. An uprising caused by parliament's clumsy decision to impose a poll tax on those least able to pay to fund the war with France. Richard defused the mob by offering the demanded concessions, but whatever the justice, no mercy was subsequently shown once the crisis was passed, the ringleaders being hunted down and executed. Other threats to the king's power were not so easily pushed aside, the Barons, opposing the dominance of his favourites, impeached and executed several during the 'Merciless Parliament' of 1388. A deed Richard would remember, for having declared himself of age in May the following year, he set about obtaining what he had lost. Over an eight year period he reconstructed faith in the throne before moving on his enemies, executing or banishing those he felt responsible.

The opportunity for those affected by the king's actions to even the score came when Richard travelled to Ireland to assert his rule. Henry Bolingbrooke, son of John of Gaunt, having suffered banishment and loss of his fathers estates returned to claim the throne. Richard's hurried return being for naught when he was captured and forced to concede to Henry, ending his days in Pontefract Castle as powerless spectator to a new dynasty, the House of Lancaster. Henry the Fourth's rule beginning with displays of leniency before struggling in the face of widespread disorder. Repeated raids by the French compounded by Welsh rebellions and, following his excursion into Scotland in 1400, a counter invasion by an army of Scots. The Earl of Northumberland, having beaten off the southward advancing Scottish invaders succumbed to the temptation to contest for the throne, the rival armies meeting and slugging it out at Shrewsbury where Henry triumphed. However these upheavals drained the King, his rule lingering on largely under parliamentary advice until his death in 1413.

His eldest son inherited, a strong and able man with a generous streak, one crowned as Henry the 5th. Tempted by disorder in France to reclaim the French throne, he negotiated a deal with the Duke of Burgundy to allow freedom of action. Landing his reorganised army in August 1415, Henry besieged and took Harfleur before marching on Calais, moving about the French countryside until a considerable French army chased him down. The two sides contesting victory on a muddy field near the Castle of Agincourt, where history repeated itself as the English archers inflicted yet another defeat on the French nobility. The fruits of this and his invasion two years later earning Henry the title, Regent of France and heir to its throne. A claim that died with him in 1422, leaving only a reputation for justice and a nine month old son who was to reign as Sixth of that name.

While still a minor, Henry's power was invested in two uncles, the Duke of Bedford taking over as Regent of France while Humphrey, Duke of Gloucester, became Protector of England. It was an era that saw England ejected from a France infused with the spirit of saintly Joan of Arc. While at home, its strength was frittered away by anarchy and civil war, for even when older, Henry displayed little flair for leadership, his hold over the country proving slack and insecure. Periodic bouts of insanity haunted, influence slipping more and more into the hands of his strong willed wife, Margaret of Anjou. The real power in the land dividing amongst the richer nobles who clustered around two poles formed by the Houses of York and Lancaster. Sides that plotted and fought with one another for possession of the throne for over thirty years between 1455 to 1485 in what is known as the War of the Roses. Ascendancy shifting between times of uneasy peace and reconciliation.

Claiming the throne for the 'Yorkists' was the Earl of March, whose defeat of the Lancastrian's at Towton in 1461 enabled him to assume the throne as Edward the Fourth. Later, having married Elizabeth Woodville in secret, he miscalculated his hold on the throne, allowing nepotism to dictate policy, a less than shrewd hand that advanced her family's interests against other more deserving claims. This provoked old friends, including the Earl of Warwick into supporting Henry, Edward ending up deposed and exiled to Flanders where he schemed and plotted. Returning in 1471, his cause was aided by his brother Clarence who fought along his side to inflict decisive defeat on the Lancastrian's in the fog at Barnet. The fleeing remnants caught and finished off at Tewkesbury, Margaret herself was captured, her son killed and Henry himself eventually murdered in the Tower of London.

Much hardened by these experiences, Edward sought to govern without parliament. Introducing controls on expenditure through the King's Chamber, he worked to improve the running of the royal estates to provide income, gaining much from the lands of the vanquished Lancastrian's. Revenue supplemented by charges levied on trade. His hold on the throne being cemented by the sending of representatives to every corner and marrying of several of his children to build alliances. His one brief foray into France ending when he was offered cash to go home, a contribution that helped make Edward the first monarch to leave the kingdom solvent. Though what he could not have foreseen following his own death in 1483 was that it would not his twelve year old son, the crown prince, who would be king. Instead he and his infant brother were slain in the Tower, one of a sordid sequence of acts that allowed Edward's own brother Richard, Duke of Gloucester, to end up on the throne. A reign blighted from the moment it commenced by the taint of grisly deeds, the opposition it provoked bringing his own end on the battlefield at Bosworth against an army led by Henry Tudor.

What was won by fighting found reinforcement by peace and prosperity, the keystones of the twenty-four year reign of Henry 7th, the first monarch of the Tudor dynasty. Seeking reconciliation with opponents and resorting to force only when necessary, he too accepted an indemnity from France in return for peace. Carefully avoiding debt by sensible management, he developed the role of the Council where peers, lawyers, household officials and prelates (high church officials) met from time to time to provide expertise and advice. His administrative reforms bringing a role for those trained in law as carriers of justice to distant parts of the realm. The country's financial interests protected by measures to expand the merchant marine as a way of boosting trading, help also finding its way to encourage shipbuilding and exploration. Foundations Henry used to distance the throne from dependence on the nobility and arms, instead, centring influence on the court itself. Bringing to the fore what was known as the Royal Prerogative, the means to rule without earthly restraint.

Chapter 3

Lust and religion

It was Henry's second son, the eighth to be so crowned, who created the rupture that made his reign one of the most important in English history. The prelude to these dramas were set in motion shortly after his coronation in 1509 when he married the widow of his brother Richard, Catherine of Aragon, under special dispensation from the Pope.

Noted for his dislike of the tedious business of State, Henry devolved most of such duties to the Lord Chancellor, Cardinal Thomas Wolsey. A man whose attention to detail was right for the job, but whose own quest for personal power and wealth were to make him vulnerable. With parliament rarely called, never mind consulted, the Cardinal became the force behind the throne. His grasp and remit reaching out to include direction of the law, primarily through his control and use of the Court of the Star Chamber.

Early on it was squabbles with France and her ally Scotland that drew Henry's focus. Forces under his command securing victory at the Battle of Spurs during the siege of Therouanne. The greater dangers posed by the Scottish army defeated by the Earl of Surrey at Flodden. Henry's longer term martial accomplishments also included the founding of the modern navy, expanding its size and capability. Forging it as an instrument that would later serve the nations maritime requirements and wider ambitions.

Cultured, well educated and deeply religious, the king's reputation as a scholar was derived from his upholding of the Catholic Church against the assertions of Martin Luther in a book he wrote and had published in support of the 'Sacraments.' Winning for Henry wide renown and the title 'Defender of the Faith.' It was rather ironic then that his own actions would divide England from Rome, the cause of that schism being Henry's obsession with a male heir. Central to the king's case was the principle that he could not sire a male child because his marriage to Catherine was a sin, the only infant survivor of their union being Mary Tudor. The solution was divorce. The stumbling block the Pope's refusal to sanction such an annulment. The duty to resolve this issue falling to Cardinal Wolsey, his failure to gain that resolution leading to his own downfall.

Support for the king's cause came readily enough from other corners, one advocate being an obscure theologian, Thomas Cranmer, whose suggested appeal to the universities to determine the rightfulness of the marriage to Catherine made favourable progress. Through their agreement, Henry gained the means to attack the power of the church by imposing reform on the clergy. An idea all the more attractive given the widespread anti-clerical sentiment then extant in the Commons and throughout the land. Resentments nourished by the wealth of the churches and monasteries, the actions of its Ecclesiastical Courts and the constant vexations that accompanied payments of tithes. Charged and found guilty of unlawful jurisdiction, the clergy were forced to pay a large fine as well as acknowledging Henry as supreme head of the Church in England.

During that same year of 1531, the King's flirtation with Anne Boleyn moved towards its climax following a prolonged absence from the court. The banishment of Catherine, setting in motion a drift that disturbed many a mind, including that of Sir Thomas More, who would follow his conscience by resigning his post as Lord Chancellor in May 1532, the office and its considerable influence falling to Thomas Cromwell. After the appointment of Cranmer as Archbishop of Canterbury the following year, Henry at last gained a pliable prelate to his cause. Through him came divorce and formal recognition that his marriage to Anne, conducted in private before his divorce, was indeed valid. Crowned queen on the first day of June, the already pregnant Anne gave birth to a daughter, Elizabeth, on 7th September, 1533.

What turned the widening rift with Rome into an open breach emerged from the legislative reforms announced in March of 1534. The Act of Succession excluded Mary Tudor, the daughter of Catherine, in favour of Anne's children. While the Act of Supremacy demanded every adult swear that Henry was head of the Church in England. While most were to attest, whatever the qualms, a few, sure and determined in faith chose eternity, Sir Thomas More being such a man.

The inexorable roll of events accelerated following the decision to transfer payment of the Annates (a religious tax) from the Pope to the Crown. The logical extension to this coming from the dissolution of the major monasteries, their wealth being looted and swallowed up by the treasury. A process guided by Thomas Cromwell, who had by then become Principal Secretary of a permanent inner body known as the Privy Council, forerunner of today's Cabinet. In spite of the far reaching scale of these changes, there was only one notable upheaval against its flow. Formed spontaneously in the more conservative north, it was known as the 'Pilgrimage of Grace.' Though raising considerable numbers to its cause its end was negotiated, dispersal opening the way to a relentless hunt to capture and then execute the ringleaders. In general however, domestic peace was maintained without police or standing army, only the old enemy, France, sparked fresh conflict, Boulogne being besieged and captured in 1544.

Permanent darkness closed over Henry in January of 1547. From his six wives he left three children, The eldest was his thirty-two year old daughter Mary, Elizabeth was by then in her fourteenth year, while the youngest was Edward, the offspring of his third wife, Jane Seymour. Mary was staunchly Catholic, Edward devoutly Protestant and Elizabeth astutely practical in terms of faith. Their inheritance was be a struggle tainted by more than the consequences of religion. Financial irresponsibility proving more destructive, something that flowed from Henry's need for money and his disastrous decision to debase the coinage by reducing its silver content. Only the steady growth of commerce lit this uncertain scene as a ten year old boy stepped forward to claim his birthright.

Crowned as Edward the Sixth, this child's intense devotion to the Protestant cause increased religious tensions. Assisted, or perhaps guided by Cranmer, the King introduced the first Book of Common Prayer by the so called Act of Uniformity. Following this with a revised edition by further Act in 1552. The critical moment coming from the promulgation of the Forty-two Articles of Religion defining how England was to be turned into a Protestant State. The unease provoked by these steps compounded by social discontent when many a landless labourers found themselves in straightened circumstance as previously open fields and common land were enclosed by fences, hedges or ditches. Strong protests to this trend suppressed by the actions of John Dudley, Earl of Warwick, co-regent with Edward Seymour under the terms of Henry's will.

It was Edward's unexpected early death that exposed the fragility of the situation, John Dudley misusing his influence to subvert Henry's will in favour of his daughter-in-law, Lady Jane Grey. Her time on the throne proving short lived (two weeks), widespread resistance and indignation seeing it handed to its rightful claimant, Edward's half sister, Mary. Passionate for the Catholic cause, this intense and rigid woman's actions soon aroused resentments, her political ineptness illustrated when she married the Spanish king, Philip the Second. A deeply unpopular move given that it involved England in Spain's ongoing war with France, while her revival of the 'Heresy Laws' did little more than create a number of martyrs, including the ageing Cranmer, earning for the Queen the nickname 'Bloody Mary.' Only an early childless death prevented the inroads of Catholicism that might have provoked open rebellion and bloodshed.

This opened the way for the uncontested succession of the pragmatic twenty-five year old Elizabeth, her soul being wedded to the throne on November 17th 1558. Surrounding herself with some of the most able men of the time, including William Cecil, England returned to the Protestant fold with the repeal of Mary's Catholic legislation. Forced to steer a difficult path through contesting forces, peace was sought and made with France the year after her coronation. Elizabeth concentrating on countering the fervour of parliament with its strongly puritan minority and the dangers provoked by the counter-reformation then underway on the continent. Her broad concern for the nation's people marked by the decision in 1563 to make giving to the poor compulsory, manifestations of what would later become the modern welfare State.

While continuing to labour under financial weakness, her reign ran into unwanted complications when Mary Stuart, Queen of Scots, threw herself on Elizabeth's mercy after compromising her own throne. The presence of the Scottish queen stimulating rumours of a challenge to the English throne by an uprising in the still largely Catholic north. As is so often the case, it was outside interference that eased these difficulties Elizabeth being excommunicated and declared a heretic by the Catholic church. Favourable sentiments across the land strengthening efforts to counter the work of Jesuit priests, then active in supporting and spreading Rome's message. A situation that provided plenty of employment for Francis Walsingham's many spies. Religious tensions themselves polarising under the radical influences of the Puritan element within parliament, activities restrained by Elizabeth's circumspect use of the Royal Prerogative. Her hand evident in the wide interpretations that could be applied to the 39 Articles defining the beliefs of the Church of England. Though she was less successful in heading off the extremes that saw non-attendance at church made an offence and conversion to Catholicism treason.

Much irritated by Elizabeth's determined attitudes were the powerful rulers of Spain. Ill feeling incited all the more by the actions of English raiders plundering its far-flung empire and the armed interference in the Netherlands under the Earl of Leicester. The quest for revenge led to the idea of a large fleet capable of carrying an invading army commanded by the Duke of Parma to England. Planning for this ambitious undertaking getting underway early in 1586. The trial and later execution of Mary Queen of the Scots following her association, real or otherwise, in a conspiracy against the English throne adding to the strength of sectarian antipathy. The complex preparations for invasion disrupted for a time the following year when Francis Drake led an expedition to Cadiz, 'singeing the beard of the King of Spain,' if not setting it ablaze.

It was not until 1588, during July, that the great fleet's presence was finally detected off the Lizard's Head to the far south-west. Repeatedly harassed by the English ships throughout the second half of that month, the weather eventually took a hand, unfavourable winds finishing the job by driving the Spanish fleet to the north. Gales and difficult seas condemning many of is occupants to death, if not by drowning, then by thirst or starvation. Victory assured security for the nation and church, though anxieties remained. Spanish interference during the Tyrone rebellion in Ireland was easily contained when its small force was overwhelmed and captured at Kinsale. Nonetheless the need to maintain awareness continued to strain England's frail finances, the lack of investment in the navy leading to its decline, Spain once more gaining total dominance of the Atlantic routes as the century ebbed away.

It is perhaps strange that Elizabeth did not recall parliament more frequently. Out of a total of sixteen sittings during her reign, only a few came during the crucial period between 1588-1601. Signs perhaps of good judgement given the opposition from men like Francis Bacon who spoke out openly in 1593 against tax increases, despite the damage it did to his own position and influence. Instead, Elizabeth chose to rely on selling crown lands and raising loans. One of the final acts of her reign marked by the granting of a Royal Charter to the East India Company in

1600. A decision that set in train happenings beyond her wildest imaginings.

Nominated by Elizabeth as her successor, King James 6th of Scotland, son of Mary Queen of Scots, embarked on a southwards journey into a land much changed by the Tudor dynasty. From his carriage window he might have seen the ruin of monastery and castle, catching the glint from the windows of the great houses built by a new aristocracy of moneyed land owning men. He might too have sensed the vibrancy of London, centre of governmental and commercial endeavour with its culture of learning fed by the new printing presses. Sharp contrasts to the timeless quality of the Parish, where the peasant toiled away as if time had stood still in a land that fell under the hand of the first Stuart King, James the First of England.

Chapter 4

The road to civil war

After Elizabeth's soothing reign, England soon learnt that James's had a straighter approach. His hand proving immediately decisive when he ended the long running war with Spain by agreeing terms under the Treaty of London. Less agreeable was the plot by Catholic malcontents to blow him and the House of Lords to smithereens during the State opening in 1605. Betrayed at the last moment, severe retribution was imposed on the conspirators and the still substantial Catholic community. One architect of the plan, Guido (Guy) Fawkes, is a man whose memory we still celebrate on bonfire night, the 5th of November, every year.

Perceptive regarding the drawbacks of England's antiquated financial system, James encouraged Robert Cecil to negotiate fiscal reform. Offering to accept abolition of his feudal rights to raise money in return for a regular income to pay for government and a single bounty to discharge its existing debt. Parliament's rejection of this proposed Great Contract in 1610 was especially short sighted and unfortunate.

The King also took early interest in the development of commerce and exploration, the very first permanent English settlement in America, Jamestown in Virginia, was named after him. A venture followed by other commercially based colonies up and down the eastern seaboard and in the Caribbean. Interests that brought produce such as tobacco, cotton, molasses, rice and sugar to England. The necessary plantation labour provided in the beginning by indentured servants from the British isles and elsewhere, a force later expanded and replaced by abducted African slaves. On the other side of the globe, the East India Company began making headway, exploiting its charter by negotiating preferential treatment from the then ruler of the Indian subcontinent. An agreement that created decisive commercial advantage over the similar ambitions of France, the Netherlands and Portugal.

Back in Europe, the decision by James to involve himself in the continental conflict known as the Thirty Years war proved troublesome. Initially working as a mediator, he became further enmeshed by providing financial support to Danish forces, even sending a small English force to the Netherlands. Moves interpreted as an act of war by Spain, an alliance between them and the French confronting England. Forced to recall Parliament in 1624 to seek funds, the King was persuaded by the Duke of Buckingham to employ it without regard to parliamentary condition, opening a rift that remained unhealed at the time of his death a year later.

Succeeding to the throne was James's son, crowned as Charles the 1st, this self centred individual soon irritated by electing to marry the French Catholic, Henrietta Maria. Criticism sharpening when the secret clauses and concessions in the marriage contract were leaked, generating hesitancy within parliament over granting money. The sense of grievance deepening when his favourite, George Villiers, the First Duke of Buckingham, was blamed for the failure to regain the Palatinate (a German principality) and the less than successful attack on Cadiz. Parliamentary moves to impeach Buckingham only prevented when the king dissolved its sitting. Forced to raise income to further his aims, Charles chose to bypass Parliament, obtaining money by borrowing against the Crown Jewels and using threats to extort loans. Funds employed to mount an unsuccessful expedition to assist besieged French Protestant Huguenots on the Isle of Re, near La Rochelle.

The impending crisis becoming unmanageable when parliament, recalled for the third time in March of 1628 by a king now desperate for money, proved too irritable to control. Its various complaints collected and presented to the crown in the Petition of Right. While conceded under duress by Charles, Buckingham's murder shortly afterwards, changed the drift of events. The King, having established the legality of the Royal Prerogative, lost interest in arguing with parliament, dissolved its sitting and announced his intention to rule alone. Which is exactly what he managed for eleven years, the key to his success coming from control of expenditure, avoidance of wars and the collection as much revenue as feudal right would allow.

This financial freedom allowed Charles to turn his mind towards religious reform and conformity, leaving little escape for those who disagreed with his ideas. It was this blundering that upset the delicate balance, Scotland resisting with force enough to bring concessions, unfortunately Charles took too long about it and rebellion flared. Without parliamentary funding the ragtag army he dispatched north was drubbed, a success that encouraged the flame in Scottish hearts, prompting formation of its own government and renewal of its traditional alliance with France. Affronted and unable to finance an effective army to bring Scotland to heel, Charles was forced to turn to parliament in April of 1640.

After long years without a voice, the so called 'Short Parliament' sat for just three weeks. A tempestuous assembly characterised by furious debates saw Charles lose patience. Without the money to contest the invading Scots he conceded to a truce that was beyond the crown's capacity to pay. Bankrupted, his hand was again forced into recalling parliament. The subsequent election returning what would become known as the 'Long Parliament,' a hostile assembly whose fevered arguments amidst fears of Catholic plots were fanned by Puritan preachers. Violent moods sweeping aside the results of the king's personal rule. News that his majesty intended use of force to suppress his enemies bringing impeachment and execution of Charles's principle adviser, Thomas Strafford.

With parliament pressuring the King to concede to the abolition of the King's Council, events began to move quickly, even the Lords and Commons dividing. The latter, with its Puritan majority, presenting a document made up of nineteen propositions that sought surrender of the king's sovereignty over church and State. Its overtly republican agenda bringing people, out of reluctance or conviction, to take sides. The distraction of rebellion in Ireland advancing parliamentary authority when for the first time it raised an army for use as it directed. This fundamental shift forced Charles to recognise the die was against him. His flight from Whitehall Palace to the north to raise men and arms to his standard confirming the divisions of a nation increasingly polarised by the influences of religious and republican extremes. Attitudes exploited by Puritan members of the Commons pushing hard to further the Reformation, while those staunchly Royalist resolutely sought to defend and preserve the standing order that placed the Church of England as central with the throne at its pinnacle.

The opening phase of the Civil War began in 1642 with the armies assembling around their standards. Sustaining the Parliamentarians (Roundheads) were funds raised by a sales tax introduced by John Pym, leader of the Commons. Wealthy supporters digging deep to provide the means to sustain the Royalists (Cavaliers). The first clash of arms coming at Edgehill in Warwickshire on the 23rd of October, an inconclusive encounter that saw Charles move to Oxford where he set up his court. Widespread, if strategically unimportant fighting occurring at Grantham, Stratton, Lansdowne and later at Newbury. Hints of the likely outcome of the war occurring at Marston Moor in Yorkshire during July of 1644 where a cool-headed Oliver Cromwell secured victory for the Parliamentary forces and loss of the north for the Royalists. Though the king's supporters earned success at Lostwithiel, the overall situation shifted in favour of parliament following formation of the New Model Army under Sir Thomas Fairfax the following year. Oliver Cromwell being appointed as Lieutenant-General of its cavalry. These forces crushing the Royalists on the 14th of June at Naseby, Northamptonshire, catching and finishing off the remnants at Langport in Somerset the following month. Defeat of the last Royalist force at Stow on the Wold leaving Charles with little option but to surrender himself into the hands of the Scots in May 1646. Parliament raising the money to pay for his release into their hands early the following year.

With the war apparently over, coherent rule collapsed, every extreme wanting a say. Splits in parliament opening between those who wanted to retain the national church along reformed lines and those who believed membership of the State should be nothing to do with any church. Rioting caused destruction to church property and brought attacks on clergy, forcing many out of their living. All the while more radical minds debated the disparities of wealth and restricted suffrage with its condition of property owning. Some voices even suggesting the House of Lords should be abolished, as should payment of tithes and the excise tax.

Making sense of this tumult was impossible, negotiations between king and parliament foundering on mutual suspicions. The only stable force, Cromwell's twenty-thousand strong New Model Army, pledging itself not to disband until justice was done, ideals that included payment of its unpaid wage. To maximise its influence it took custody of the King, placing him under armed guard at Holmby House. While comfortable enough despite being detained, the babble of competing views made Charles sufficiently uneasy to tempt him to slip away into the night, finding refuge on the Isle of Wight where he intrigued with the Scots and others. The outcome of these machinations bearing fruit between March and August of 1648 in what may be seen as the second phase of the civil war. Uprisings in support of the king taking place in

Wales, Kent and Essex, all ruthlessly put down by the army. An invading Scots under the Duke of Hamilton in support of Charles getting mangled at the Battle of Preston.

These events profoundly altered the situation, Cromwell using his grip on the army to influence the decision to hold the king responsible for his actions. A step that irrevocably broke away from the concept of a king being God's representative on earth. With the power of the army at his back, Cromwell, through his subordinate, Colonel Thomas Pride, acted to deny entry in early December to all parliamentary members known to favour a deal with the king, leaving what became known as the 'Rump.' It was they who tried and convicted Charles, signing the execution order on 27th January 1649, the King's head rolling off the block three days later. That same day England declared itself a Commonwealth, hereditary succession prevented by parliamentary action before the decision was taken to abolish the monarchy itself a week later.

With the House of Lords gone, a Council of State was elected in the middle of February with Cromwell at its head. Its lofty ideals and new constitution failing to hide its lack of clear policy, differences of opinion hardly helped by commercial downturn and harvest failures. Problems that did not extend to the army, who, under Cromwell, waded ashore in Ireland in 1649 to ruthlessly deal with the rebellious Catholic Irish and the forces landed by the Papal Nuncio, Rinuccini. Hostilities the following year in Scotland showing further signs of Cromwell's strategic and tactical grasp when he handled a number of hostile groups on both sides of the border. An invading Scottish force commanded by Charles's eldest son, later to be crowned as Charles 2nd, roundly beaten at the Battle of Worcester. Good fortune and a convenient tree all that prevented the capture and probable execution of the future monarch.

Closer to home, corruption's within Parliament exacerbated by sectarian intolerance were making themselves felt. The necessary generation of revenue for the State aggravated by disruption to trade following the passing of the anti-Dutch Navigation Acts which restricted transport of English goods to English ships. Cromwell's timely return to this uncertain situation once more putting him at the centre of events. His critical faculties recognising the 'Rump's' failings when he attended its session on the 20th April 1653. Fed up with its aimless ramblings, he stood and addressed the House, commanding, *'You have sat too long here for any good you have been doing. Depart I say, and let us have done with you. In the name of God, go.'* Ejecting its members and locking the chamber, his action turning England from a republic into a dictatorship at a stroke. His decisive mind looking afresh at promoting what would serve England and her interests, assessing too what might give his rule wider legitimacy.

It was a search that never reached adequate conclusion. Cromwell, who had been an MP before becoming a soldier, initially decided to share power with a number of hand picked Puritan nobles. This 'Barebones Parliament' had a useful interlude before losing the plot by showing a preference for radical ideals that included codification of Common Law, the abolition of tithes and attacks on property rights. Employing a pre-planned early morning sleight of hand manoeuvre this arrangement was brought to an end. Power reverting back to Cromwell who in league with other army members drew up an Instrument of Government that included an office titled, Lord Protector. This written constitution sought to contain and balance the role of Protector with a permanent Council of State. Meeting in September of 1654, its ideas again proved too radical for Cromwell's tastes, even after its more extreme members were expelled. Following minor uprising and hints of plots it was dissolved and the country divided into eleven districts, each under control by a Major-General of the army.

In spite of these headaches Cromwell found time to deal satisfactorily with a number of foreign issues. Resolving the war against the Dutch in 1654, securing Jamaica a year later and enjoying the news that informed him of the destruction of a Spanish treasure fleet off Santa Cruz by one of England's greatest admirals, Robert Blake. Domestically, Cromwell's dissatisfactions remained, although others at the heart of affairs believed they had found the solution when they offered Cromwell the crown. Put together in the Humble Petition and Advice Act, this proposed a return of the monarchy and establishment of an Upper House. Refusing the offer, Cromwell continued as Lord Protector, though his restlessness endured, even to the point of dissolving the friendliest of his parliaments in January of 1658. Actions that perpetuated uncertainties, the success of the republic facing compromise as the rigid application of some of its Puritan philosophies began to foster resentments.

Having won agreement to make the title of Lord Protector hereditary, Cromwell's death in September 1658 elevated his son Richard to office. Working in tandem with his brother he tried to strengthen the civil powers of the office, but proved unable to contain the power struggle that isolated him. Pensioned off, his dispatch saw the parliamentary 'Rump' attempt to regain control over the army, moves strongly contested by one John Lambert, who with others ordered an armed guard around parliament to prevent it sitting. This action split the army and reopened old wounds throughout the land, royalist rebellion and sympathies widespread. Revolts handled easily enough, though the mood remained sour and defiant.

It was at this moment that Sir Arthur Haselrig called for army officers to support the 'Rump,' one of those heeding the cry was the professional soldier George Monck, Governor of Scotland. Efforts by John Lambert to counter Monck by marching his forces north fading as his army melted away. Monck meanwhile, having gained the support of the retired veteran, Sir Thomas Fairfax, waited at the head of his well ordered forces. Finally invited, he moved on a London imbued with royalist spirit, establishing military control in early February 1660. Seeing to it that Parliament reopened to members of the 'Rump' and all those who had previously been excluded, completing resurrection of the 'Long Parliament.' Its final act being to dissolve itself, the following election returning a strongly pro-royalist parliament.

Chapter 5

Restoration of the monarchy

Whitehall Palace was the destination of a long procession that set out from Dover on the 23rd of May 1660. At its head, the king to be, Charles, eldest son of Charles the First and lucky survivor of the earlier fight at Worcester. Although recovery of the throne was conditional on the payment of army arrears, confirmation of land purchases and the granting of pardons. A number of those implicated in the death of his father were brought to book and executed, Cromwell's body being exhumed and violated. Events that failed to undermine the desire for co-operation, parliament agreeing to the payment of an annual sum to the monarch to meet government expenses.

Unfortunately as Charles was soon realise, the Treasury was not always capable of meeting what was promised, causing him to employ George Downing to reform the collection of taxes and the Treasury while casting around for other sources of revenue. Favourable sentiment also supporting moves to hand control of the militia back to the crown under the Militia Act of 1661.

The overall sense of relief at this turn of events did not last long, Charles tainting the atmosphere by choosing as his bride the Portuguese Catholic, Catherine of Braganza. His attempts to gain religious toleration for Catholics and non-Anglicans hitting the buffers when the Declaration of Indulgence, issued in 1662 along with an appeal for parliament to make it permanent, was withdrawn the following year in the face of some hostility. Sentiment depressed soon enough by the Great Plague which began thinning out the population during 1665, an event followed a year later by the disastrous fire that turned much of London into ashes.

Coincident complications coming from further conflict with the Dutch over commercial interests, aggravations that involved Denmark and then France in a set to marked by a number of inconclusive naval battles. This, the Second Anglo-Dutch war added to the general unease, feelings stretched all the tighter when the Dutch surprised a good part of the English fleet at anchor on the Medway and Thames during June of

1667, sinking enough of it to anger and embarrass. A loss that increased the desire for peace, resolution of those feelings finding tangible expression in the Treaty of Breda later that same year. The outbreak of public relief exploited by Charles who sacked his long standing adviser, the Earl of Clarendon, who had made the mistake of making his criticisms of the king's private excesses known.

A bare decade after the restoration, with an undercurrent of animosity abroad in the land, Charles's anxiety over funding drew him into secret negotiations with Louis 14th of France. Agreeing to support French aims towards the Netherlands as well as setting in motion plans for the re-establishment of Catholicism in England in return for an annual indemnity of £200,000 per annum. The fruits of this treaty favouring France, an isolated Dutch facing renewed hostilities in 1672. The English fleet being deployed in inconclusive operations in what was the third Anglo-Dutch war, notably against the skilful Dutch Admiral, Michiel de Ruyter. Strong opposition to the war within England soon compelling a separate peace that left the Dutch to fight on alone.

With doubts over the king's true intentions having spread, the actions of his brother, James, the Duke of York, came into play. Shortly before the restoration he had married Anne Hyde, the Earl of Clarendon's daughter, siring two daughters Mary and Anne. Although both girls were raised as Protestants, the parents converted to Catholicism, the mother just before her death in 1671, the Duke the following year. Free to remarry, James picked a Catholic for his second wife, Mary of Modena.

Aggravating the public sensitivities at this delicate moment was renewed attempt by the King to gain acceptance of religious toleration when he re-issued his Declaration of Indulgence. Parliamentary opposition to the move reinforced by threats against the royal finances inducing its withdrawal, the King finding himself having to accept instead the anti-Catholic Test Act which specifically excluded all Catholics from office. The Duke of York preferring to stand down as Lord High Admiral rather than submit to its provisions. A following of faith and conscience that brought home the realisation that the Duke favoured a return to Catholicism. An understanding that saw opposition coalesce into an alliance whose sole purpose was to ensure he could not succeed to the throne. It was to divide Parliament. On one side the Tories, devout Anglicans who regarded the crown as sacred and the succession inviolate, on the other, their Whig opponents who believed the essential trust of the people would be betrayed if a Catholic succeeded. The leading Whig was the Earl of Shaftesbury, who surrendered office to concentrate on making sure James could not become king.

Crucial to the campaign was the marriage between Mary, the daughter of the Duke's first wife, to William of Orange of the Netherlands. An arrangement that opened a possible protestant line of succession. The very issue of Catholicism spread its anxieties, especially when knowledge of who had taken bribes from Louis of France became public. Widespread fears over French designs proving a decisive factor in the election of a strongly anti-Catholic House following the dissolution of Parliament late in 1678.

With feelings running high, a fabricated plot involving the Pope raised temperatures sufficiently enough for the Duke of York to seek refuge in Flanders until tempers cooled. Absence that did nothing to undermine Whig determination to pass the Exclusion Bill, a movement that drew the king into offering concessions to secure the principle of hereditary succession. These compromises included a limited constitutional monarchy, one so restricted in powers that even the militia would be under parliament. However fair the offer, it lacked the appeal to counter the emotions of the time, Charles dissolving parliament shortly after the Exclusion Bill passed its second reading to prevent it becoming law. A manoeuvre that did not prevent enactment of one of England's fundamental legal protections, the Habeas Corpus Act. A law that, with its later revisions of 1816 and 1862, prevented detention without a public hearing before a magistrate for more than 24 hours, or 96 hours in exceptional circumstance. It was to remain a considerable restraint on the power of the State until subverted by modern government.

The hostile temper of Parliament may have prevented agreement, but others in the land grew uneasy over what was happening. In particular, a mix of Anglican's and Royalist's who saw enough reminders of the recent past to tempt them towards accommodation with Charles. Hoping to avoid another parliament, the King sought to persuade the Privy Council to govern, a novel approach that proved impractical. The succeeding parliament elected in October of 1680 proving implacable, Shaftesbury once more leading support for the Exclusion Bill. Unable to overcome this resistance, the King contemplated ruling alone, though to so he needed money, this he was to obtain from France in return for tacit acceptance of Louis's continental designs.

Reluctant to implement the deal, Charles endeavoured once more to reach accommodation, adding to his previous concessions. Shaftesbury however had set himself upon a Protestant succession and nothing else would do. Confrontation giving way to a different strategy when the King embarked on patient diplomacy, moving against his enemies when the chance came. The attempted indictment of the ageing Shaftesbury only failing when forewarned, he slipped the net, escaping to Holland where natural death was not far away. With intense pressures easing, Charles adroitly played his hand, fortunately escaping a plot that aimed to kill him and his brother. Manipulating electoral privileges to keep the Whigs at bay, he eked a meagre existence while sustaining the fleet and holding to his word with Louis. The mood across the land settling towards acceptance that would allow James to inherit following the King's death on the 6th February 1685.

Crowned head of a Protestant nation was a triumph that went to the head of the Second James. His attempts to forge an absolute monarchy along French lines becoming intimately entwined with his desire to reclaim England for Rome. Ambitions that could only inflame passions as he must have known. Although parliaments early conciliatory decision to supply him with a substantial sum to run his government undoubtedly encouraged. As did the actions of the king's mentor, the self interested meddling Louis, King of France, whose own desire to make his country wholly Catholic saw revocation of the Edict of Nantes and the expulsion of nearly half million Protestants (Hugenouts), many of whom came to settle in England.

The opening gambit in this campaign came when James sought control of central and local government. An early diversion from this quest manifesting itself when the illegitimate son of his father, the Duke of Monmouth, challenged his right to the throne by landing with a small army at Lyme Regis. Moving around the West Country, the Duke raised a credible force before clashing with the Royal Army at Sedgemoor. Defeat and capture ended his challenge, wider retribution to his followers handed out during the Bloody Assizes presided over by Judge George Jeffrey's.

Employing constitutional manoeuvres, the King sought repeal of the Test and Habeas Corpus Acts. When advised against this by the Lord

President of the Council, George Halifax, James acted decisively, replacing him with Judge Jeffrey's. Informing parliament in November that he would not disband the army, nor did he intend to discharge its Catholic officers who had proved themselves worthy against Monmouth. Indicating his intentions to build up the army and navy into a tool that he hoped to use to prevent further rebuff. Its loyalty reinforced by moving more Catholics into its hierarchy.

A cold chill must have descended on parliament when the King refused to confirm that he would not use his Royal Prerogative to set aside Acts of Parliament. Concerns parliament sought to have legally clarified, a challenge James headed off by dismissing its sitting during November of 1685 before judgement could be rendered. Acting with increasing boldness, the king's next target was to rid Catholics serving in the army of the need to take the Test oath, packing the judiciary in order to gain a favourable decision in support of that aim. Further insulating himself from adverse criticism by replacing moderate ministers and advisers with Catholics, James even dismissing the Duke of Somerset when he protested the legality of a reception for the Papal Nuncio, Ferdinando d'Adda. The obvious agitation over the king's high handedness prompting even the Papal Legate to urge caution.

It was at this point, some two years into his reign, that a senior Dutch diplomat under orders from William of Orange arrived as ambassador. While seeking formally to counsel James's against his headlong rush, he privately sounded out opposition opinion, querying the all important attitude of the army. Opinion that was undoubtedly stiffening throughout the land well before James's issued his Declaration for Liberty of Conscience. Initial, adverse reactions failing to deter its re-issuance the following April, a move accompanied by the demand it be read in all churches. Opposition to this call centring around the Archbishop of Canterbury, William Sancroft, one of seven Bishops who appealed to the king to draw back. James however was not interested in compromise by this stage, instead, he ordered their trial for seditious libel. Acquittal leading to tumultuous scenes of public joy, the first sign of open opposition to the King, attitudes that assumed greater importance when the Queen produced an heir, shutting out all hopes of the Protestant succession.

It was a decisive moment as the whole country stirred, with Church, Whig, Tory and vote-less mass combining in mind, if not action, though some strained for it, others were still for waiting. As it was, the doers moved, a group known as the 'Immortal Seven' requesting help from William of Orange. The signatories, the Earl's of Shrewsbury, Danby, Devonshire and Orford with the then Bishop of London, Henry Compton, along with the author of the invitation, Henry Sydney and the Viscount Lumley. Spreading out to drum up support, they worked and hoped, while the recipient of that appeal, a frail body that burned with a fire, recognised the time and prepared.

As the army in the Netherlands grew, the king certainly knew about it, but its purpose proved uncertain. James deciding wrongly, failing to obtain the help Louis could have given. Instead, men under the Orange Banner, Dutch, Scots and English joined with those from the threatened Principalities of Germany and a few Danes, Swedes and French Huguenots to set sail after repeated delays due to poor weather. Landing far to the south-west at Torbay late on in 1688.

Forewarned, James marched with his army to Salisbury, where inexplicably he returned to London, leaving others to speak and, if necessary, to fight in his name. From the distance of centuries only speculation serves to divine the reasons for his retreat, perhaps James had finally become conscious of England's change, its willingness to gather around William. Whatever the reason he attempted to flee, was recognised and returned to a London whose gates were already open to welcome the Orange King. James's subsequent escape, more likely by design, saw him find sanctuary in France, the Protestant succession becoming fact by reason of his abandoning the throne. The stain of regicide and civil war had been avoided.

Chapter 6

Constitutional change

William 3rd and Mary 2nd were jointly crowned in February of 1689. Their reign seeing major constitutional and financial reforms whose outcomes would move the nation away from an absolute monarchy racked by problems over money. Creating in its place a permanent parliamentary system that proved responsive enough to give way gradually to the changing aspirations of her peoples.

The fundamentals of these designs sprung from the minds of king, queen and the great public servants in that year of the coronation. For in spite of the immediate dangers posed by James 2nd's landing in Ireland and Scotland's flirtations with rebellion a month or two later, parliament enacted its first great measure, the 1689 Bill of Rights. Its articles stipulated that the throne was subject to conditions and devoid of divine authority, granting at the same time the right for parliament to operate free from interference by the sovereign. On this solid foundation attempts were made to ease the source of internal religious tensions, the Toleration Bill, a cautious gesture towards freedoms of worship for Dissenters. While acceptance of these measures was not universal, some Tories clinging on to the idea that James 2nd was still the divine and rightful king, they prevailed. Additional bulwarks in the national interest being constructed from the introduction of parliamentary elections every three years, although the right to dissolve its assembly remained with the reigning monarch.

Supplementing these great moves was a complete revamp of England's financial system under the direction of Charles Halifax, Lord of the Treasury. Measures that rectified the long standing difficulties over how government should be funded. The basis of these plans started with the conversion of outstanding royal debt into national debt, parliament raising money from the public to loan back to the king's government. This work gained additional substance in 1694 when the Bank of England was established, its Charter granted on condition that half of its initial capital would be loaned back to the king. Included too was overhaul of the currency and establishment of a professional financial service to support the government. Reforms extended by the crucial introduction of the Civil List, this Act, passed in 1697, voted the crown an income, all other government expenses being paid out of taxes raised by parliament.

Conceding to these fundamental changes in the monarchy are what rightly elevate William and Mary to their place in history. William's diplomacy further assured his place following negotiations that brought about the formation of the Grand Alliance of 1689 that surrounded Louis's France and would, eventually, contain his ambitions. Although success in directing military operations towards that aim proved marginal, the combination of threats to the west, north and east tempting William to divide attention and force, with consequent reverse on all fronts. Learning something from his mistakes, the King concentrated his substantial army in Ireland, extracting advantage under his direct command at the Boyne in July 1690. Finally consigning James's hopes to history the following year when he consolidated control of southern Ireland. Scottish flirtations with rebellion being equally roughly handled in the king's name, notably in the massacre at Glencoe.

These early distractions certainly presented Louis with an opportunity, one he should have exploited further after his fleet gained victory off Beachy Head while William was busy in Ireland. For whatever reason the moment passed and initiative returned to the allies some two years later when the Dutch and English fleets combined to wreck French sea-borne power in the decisive encounter of the war at La Hogue. On land, results remained largely inconclusive, William's capture of Dixmude and Huy topped by recapture of the fortress of Namur. The war itself drifting towards stalemate and end with the signing of the Treaty of Ryswick in the late summer of 1697.

With peace came the chance to progress with further domestic reforms. Historic fears over who controlled the standing army finding resolution in 1698 when William surrendered it to parliament, the later Disbanding Act reducing its size to just seven thousand men. Having earlier conceded to reductions in press censorship, the nations intellectual power expanded, with increasing interest in sciences and the arts. One of the world's greatest scientists, Isaac Newton, building on his pioneering work in the field of physics. His, and other efforts of his contemporaries, creating a surge of progress that would be unmatched until the nineteenth and early part of the twentieth century. This initial impetus a major factor in the later growth of economic and political power that would help elevate England to world dominance.

Integral to that story was Scotland, for William already considered himself King of Great Britain, in effect head of England, Wales and Scotland. His determination to achieve proper political union becoming a fact five years after his death with the 1707 Act of Union. The idea of Union also attracting Louis 14th, the death of the childless Spanish King, Charles 2nd, tempting him to advance the cause of his son, Philip of Anjou, as successor. Claims contested by the Austrian Hapsburg Emperor in a clash that destabilised continental peace, France taking advantage of the situation by assuming control of a line of Spanish held fortresses that had to that point ensured the security of the Netherlands. Resumption of war looked inevitable, especially when Louis announced shortly after the death of James 2nd , that he recognised James's son as the rightful King of England. A deliberate affront given Parliaments recent enactment of a statute that specifically excluded a Catholic succession, the so called Act of Settlement. Further legal changes restricting the freedom of the monarch to leave the country without parliamentary permission, a second denying a foreigner office.

It was at this point that fate took an unfortunate twist, William unexpectedly dying during March of 1702, joining Mary who herself had passed on childless in 1694. This saw the crown pass to Anne, who as the last Stuart sovereign was to show the same devotion to her duties as Elizabeth. Head of a nation of five million people, she led the country into contesting the might of France with her allies in the long war of the Spanish Succession.

Sustained during all the difficult years by the counsel of three notable figures, the Lord High Treasurer, Sidney Godolphin, whose management of the finances allowed prolonged deployment of the army without crippling the economy. Robert Harley who held office as Secretary of State before becoming Chief Minister and more critically, John Churchill, First Duke of Marlborough, whose command of the allied armies demanded diplomatic finesse as much as military skill. The hard won victories of Blenheim and Ramallies along with his skilful defence of the Netherlands worthy of a better peace than the politicians eventually contrived at Utrecht in 1713.

It had been Anne's signature on the Act of Settlement following the death of her own son in 1701 that brought the Hanoverian descendants of James 1st into line as successors to the throne. Her passing in 1714 seeing a fifty-four year old German speaking native, the Elector of Hanover, crowned as George 1st (an Elector was a German Prince entitled to take part in the election of the Holy Roman Emperor). A dynasty whose time marked a new chapter in the growing assertion of parliament and the development of politics. The nation moving beyond the contentions between king and parliament towards a regime dominated by the need to find a consensus out of divided opinions. It was to be a future slaved to commerce, economic expansion creating new interests that needed encouragement and protection. A system of trading based for some time to come on the markets opened by colonial ventures and secured by the Royal Navy.

Chapter 7

Wars and colonies

The eighteenth century was a complex period, a time dominated by frequent wars on the continent and elsewhere. Britain's own fortunes over these ten decades rising from astute handling of affairs, both on the political and economic fronts. Initially however, the future was anything but promising, the ending of those prolonged campaigns to arrest the ambitions of Louis the 14th contributing to domestic turmoil, not least because of the demobilisation of its substantial army. Unwanted soldiers swelling the numbers of unemployed in an economy that needed time to adjust.

This situation had hardly begun to stabilise before fresh complications raised themselves following the death of Louis himself in 1715. The vacant French throne tempting the Spanish, a nation whose expanding ambitions were already drawn to Italian prizes. Contesting these claims brought Britain into alliance with France, the Netherlands and later Austria. Spanish pique prompting her support for the Jacobite cause (supporters of James the Second and his descendants) in the north of England as a means of inciting trouble.

These and other problems weighed heavily on George 1st, his main task centring on finding a political leader up to the challenge, one who could command majority support in the Commons. It was not until the collapse of the South Sea investment scheme in 1721, when thousands lost their money that a candidate equal to the job came to the fore. The level headed Whig, Sir Robert Walpole, being appointed both Chancellor of the Exchequer and First Lord of the Treasury, effectively making him Britain's first Prime Minister.

Once in office, Walpole's attention was taken up with the state of Britain's shaky finances, his success in reducing the national debt by stimulating prosperity slowly easing tensions. Continuously in office, apart from a brief spell when the English speaking George II inherited the throne in 1727, this Norfolk squire managed the nation's affairs with a quiet competence. Only experiencing serious bother when he proposed reform of the excise tax on wine and tobacco.

Once more it was external events that disturbed matters, the decision by Spain to search British ships heading for their colonies for illegal cargoes of slaves triggering domestic outrage. The resulting furore, more to do with potential loss of profit than anything else, saw wilder elements calling for war, which is what they get in excess when the colonial spat referred to as the 'War of Jenkin's Ear' opened in October of 1739, a fight that soon blurred into the wider issues of the Austrian Succession. Strands whose impact merged to derail Walpole's careful calculations, which were mainly based on keeping the peace. A reverse coupled with poor electoral performance prompting his resignation in 1742.

British involvement in the spreading war marked the last time a reigning British monarch would personally lead his forces into battle. This happening at Dettingen the following year when George 2nd, at the head of English, Hanoverian and Dutch elements in the so called Pragmatic army, took on French forces along the lower Rhine. The distractions of this strife providing chances for a renewal of Jacobite ambitions in Scotland, James Edward Stuart (Bonnie Prince Charlie), exploiting the situation in his quest for the throne. Having captured Edinburgh, he bested a small English force at Prestonpans before moving south to capture Carlisle and then Manchester, inexplicably giving up the advance at Derby. The Scots eventually coming face to face with hastily re-deployed English forces under the Duke of Cumberland on Culloden Moor in the spring of 1746. The defeat of Scottish ambitions was total, those who did not die on that bleak battlefield would do shortly afterwards by summary execution.

Following Walpole's demise, power slipped towards the Earl of Wilmington, with much influence coming to rest in the hands of Henry and Thomas Pelham. The uncertainties of the time making it far from apparent who would in fact come to master the affairs of State. The individual who made the greatest mark turned out to be William Pitt the Elder, sometimes called the 'Great Commoner,' later raised to the peerage as the Earl of Chatham. A direct robust character who cut his political teeth castigating Walpole, his aggressive attitude earnt him the King's personal dislike. Despite this drawback, talent and a more conciliatory manner saw entry into high office as Vice-Treasurer of Ireland. Promotion coming quickly when Pitt assumed the position of

Paymaster of the Forces, where his efficient honesty created a formidable reputation and great popularity. Unfortunately his opposition to the king's favoured ideas on the continent led to his dismissal in 1751.

Five years passed before Pitt re-entered office as Secretary of State in the coalition government of Sir Thomas Pelham-Hollies. Mere months passing before he was again at odds with George 2nd, this time over conduct of the war, disagreement leading to dismissal. Fortunately his personal popularity overcame the reverse, pressures for his recall inducing the government to concede and invite him back. His stewardship proving vital as the fighting that began in America merged into Seven Year's war, the prototype world war. Pitt's effective changes to both navy and militia assisting in carrying the war to the French on the European landmass, while being able to get the better of its traditional foe in Canada and India. The end to his time in office coming when the Cabinet failed to support him over his interpretation that Spain's likely alliance with France should be pre-empted. A rebuff that left little alternative but resignation. Events proving the soundness of Pitt's judgement when Spain intervened as he predicted.

National debt, Britain's alone had almost doubled, and general exhaustion are eternal incentives to ending any protracted war. Such was the case here as terms were sought all round. The Treaty of Paris, signed in 1763, containing obstacles to a permanent peace that drew Pitt once more into isolated opposition. His reputation sufficiently untouched to see him back in office in 1766, even if ill health prevented much in way of meaningful contribution before his inevitable final resignation.

Whatever reservations Pitt had over the peace, the military successes behind it were responsible for profound changes. A shifting of the balance of power away from France towards Britain. The confidence flowing through the nation promoting attitudes and endeavour that would see Britain soon gain mastery over the fate of much of the world both politically and commercially. One whose markets were soon to be secured by a global empire unprecedented in human history.

An essential element in the development of this domination was the willingness of the people of these isles to leave in search of fortune or a fresh start. Hardy souls who not only made it in America, but also utilised Elizabeth's grant of a Royal Charter to the East India Company to extraordinary effect. Intended originally as a trading enterprise to contest Dutch and Portuguese interests, this organisation became the virtual government of India. The key to this transformation beginning with a commercial agreement made with the Mughal Emperor, Jahangir, then ruler of most of the sub-continent. Privileges extended in 1634 when the Emperor Shah Jahan allowed access to Bengal, a situation that placed the East India Company in the best position to take advantage of the later fragmentation of the Mughal empire into warring factions. The company's success aided by profits ploughed back into sensible administrative effort and locally raised military forces.

Interestingly this came about despite the East India Company's monopoly being broken by act of parliament in 1694. Its later commercial ascendancy owing much to the leadership of Robert Clive who decisively defeated French ambitions and those of the Bengali Nawab at the Battle of Plassey in 1757. Further military actions and wars followed as the 18th century merged in the next, while these were not always successful, a combination of persuasion, threats and commercial incentives usually proved sufficient to pacify or undermine opposition. Successes that would later induce William Pitt the Younger to pass the India Act in 1784, reorganising the company by creating a Board of Control, allowing government to begin absorbing much of its power.

Elsewhere, as part of this penetration of the east, British exploration, various treaties and more aggressive commercial exploitation saw Britain's influence expanding. Captain Cook amongst the most significant of these explorers, surveyed New Zealand, Australia and other parts, claiming them for the crown and eventual settlement.

In direct contrast to this eastern successes was the developing complexities of events in America, where political clumsiness would lead to a half hearted war and colonial loss. Colonised by the Spanish as early as 1513, its northern reaches were widely settled by the French, especially along the Saint Lawrence seaway in what would become Canada. English success in Virginia was followed in 1620 by small numbers of Pilgrims landing and colonising what they called New England. Later arrivals included the Dutch and Swedes, although the preponderance of people who arrived were Britons, ensuring dominance for the English speakers.

In 1754, what began as skirmishing between French forces and their Indian allies against British and American elements in the area of Ohio blended into the wider Seven Years War. The eventual defeat of France in this long campaign brought a peace deal that fundamentally altered the political situation in America by removing French control and ambition. The Treaty of Paris obliging her to cede the areas settled by native French speakers to Britain. The potential of trouble amongst these people headed off by the Quebec Act of 1774 which secured allegiance by offering privileged circumstances such as the continuance of the French language, Catholic faith and French civil law.

While politically sensible from the English perspective, this concession irritated colonialists to the south. A feeling whose strength drew on the predominant nature of those attracted to the New World. It was after all an arduous undertaking to head for America, would be settlers having to cope with a difficult sea voyage followed by all the problems of wresting a living out of raw land. Requisite to making it were strength, determination, stamina and spirit. Traits that contributed to a rugged independence that naturally wanted to control its own destiny as well as enjoying the fruits of its own labour.

Such people were bound to find their allegiance to a land six weeks away to the east across three thousand miles of water weakening with each succeeding generation. Factors king and parliament neglected when they sought to extract payment for maintaining and garrisoning these colonies. The taxation of imports was tried and resented, its replacement, an equally unpopular Stamp Act, widespread colonial anger prompting the then Prime Minister, the Marquess of Rockingham, to discontinue its use, though he affirmed the power of Parliament to tax. With opinion strong on both sides, William Pitt, now old and variable in mind, noted the dangers with clarity and urged amicable settlement. Unheeded words as duties were imposed on American imports of paper, glass, lead and tea.

Indignation over this move created a situation ripe for exploiting, feelings particularly strong throughout the colony of Massachusetts. Attitudes creating an atmosphere the Prime Minister, Lord North, would poison when he authorised the East India Company to sell tea direct to the colonies without payment of import duties. This was a windfall for those opposed to the crown, a few taking advantage by disguising themselves as Indians, boarding shipping in Boston Harbour and dumping their cargoes of tea over the side. Parliament's response was to pass the Coercion Acts in an attempt to isolate the radicals, instead it served to polish the slope down which the Massachusetts military governor, Thomas Gage, was to slide. Having ordered British troops to

Concord to confiscate arms and detain certain worthies, rebellious elements mobilised a small militia in Lexington, a clash leaving a few dead bodies and the sparks that lit a cause. The colonial militia making the most of the situation by harrying the British soldiers all the way back to Boston. The American War of Independence had found its beginning, the colonies going onto declare independence by renouncing allegiance to the crown on the 4th of July 1776.

Although the conflict was to ebb and flow, with formidable difficulties for the American settlers. It found in the justness of cause and the leadership of George Washington a way of sustaining itself against half hearted British tactics. The decisive psychological breach coming when a British force surrendered at Burgoyne. The subsequent siding by France, Spain and the Netherlands with America adding to Britain's burdens. The effective end coming in October of 1781 with the British surrender at Yorktown.

Chapter 8

Industrialisation and continental woe

Whatever the ramifications of losing the thirteen colonies, they soon passed into irrelevance in the face of fresh threats from across the channel. New antagonisms building in a world that had begun to feel the influences of industrialisation, a revolution that was to fundamentally alter the pace of man's material progress. A story shaped by ingenuity, one of innovative minds feeding off each other, reinforcing and encouraging the development of ideas, methods and techniques that would supply Britain most of all with a head start in the ability to mass produce quality goods cheaply.

While free use of practical intellect was its primary force, several other factors proved crucial, notably the presence of easily worked raw materials such as coal, iron ore, copper and tin linked to the labour necessary to exploit these resources. Equally essential were agricultural improvements to provide the food for those who gave up the land in favour of factory and town. Something that drew on Dutch and local efforts to improve crop yield, indications of a willingness to adapt by borrowing knowledge.

One of the most important steps forward in this movement coming from the generation of power where it was wanted by the use of steam. A technological improvement that freed industry from the limitations of wind and water. The advantages of being a small island also showed itself, rivers and coastal shipping making it comparatively easy to shift bulky material and objects from one point to another. The same routes taking the finished articles to the ships that would transport them to overseas markets.

Nevertheless, the price of this pioneering could be harsh in both human and environmental terms. Long working hours in dangerous places compounded by marginal diet in poor, cramped housing imposed their severity's on the ordinary working man, woman and child. The real beneficiaries were that handful of inventive and astute men who owned and controlled the factories that made them money. Enough to sometimes vie with one another in the building of grand houses in park like surrounds. Other early gainers in the national prosperity were the professions, a skilled crowd so necessary to serving a society with its ever increasing complexities. Some of the broader compensations coming from structural developments that included spacious parks and fine public buildings, chapels and churches.

For the well to do it was a creative period in a vibrant society. One revolving around coffee-houses and clubs, concerts, lectures, theatres and race meetings, activities supplemented by visits to fashionable places like Bath. For those with a sense of adventure and the money, Europe beckoned. A grand tour with its visits to Venice, Paris and Rome prime attractions for those eager to swallow continental culture. Journeys often supplemented by liberal spending on the finest of treasures to fill their great mansions.

In spite of ever increasing wealth easing the spiritual grip, the fresh appeal of evangelical preachers like John Wesley with his radical interpretations and morality left their mark. Society growing ever more refined and well ordered, its careful decencies adding to a deepening sense of what was correct and proper. An atmosphere where a sense of mission took root, especially amongst the landed and wealthy. A class whose sons were sent to be educated in the new public schools where the prevailing ethos instilled a sense of public service, honesty, integrity, patriotism and leadership. One of the foremost products of that system entering Parliament at age of just twenty two, becoming Chancellor of the Exchequer in his twenty-third year. The individual in question, William Pitt The Younger, second son of the Earl of Chatham. A man who proved himself in parliament as a debater with principle, showing rare willingness to support parliamentary reform, the great opponent of his years, the shrewd and clever Charles Fox.

By today's standards it is incomprehensible that support should gather around one so young for the office of Prime Minister. Indeed it took the intervention of the King to overcome Pitt's own reservations. Successfully persuading him to form an administration at the end of 1783 at the tender age of 24. His youth ignored by a public willing to provide him with a decisive mandate in the election a year later, a triumph that would see Pitt hold onto the reins of power for the next seventeen years.

Like many of his predecessors and, one might say successors, the key problem facing Pitt was the national debt, something he tackled by setting up a fund where excess tax revenue was diverted to accumulate until such time as it could be used to clear the State's obligations. While his attempts to gain parliamentary reform were denied, Pitt was successful in reorganising the civil service. Revealing during his time in office a remarkable ability to get his head around the economic realities of the day, recognising the drawbacks of tariffs and their inhibiting influences on economic growth, securing a consensus that ensured their revision.

It was to be events in France, wretched under absolute monarchy, a bloated court and empty treasury that most tested Pitt's judgement. The violence and terror of its revolution bringing prolonged war to most of Europe, straining British energy and resolve to the full. At the core of its revolutionary zeal were aims that sought the abolition of feudalism and the creation of a society based on the rights of man, wealth and merit. Lofty ideals represented by the slogan Liberty, Equality & Fraternity. Principles France struggled with as it descended into chaos, law and order breaking down amidst use of summary justice.

Pitt's instincts were to keep Britain out of it, declining at first to join the Austrian-Prussian-Piedmont alliance that had been established with the intent of restoring the old order by force of arms. However, Pitt's hopes were soon derailed when events took a more radical turn, the execution of Louis 16th adding to the pressures that were to see Britain allying itself as part of the First Coalition formed in 1793 to counter the revolution. Most of the next twenty-two years were spent resisting French ambitions, either on its own or as a member of various alliances. Tricky events that made it essential to maintain and expand both the navy and army. The heavy burdens on the Exchequer solved in part when Pitt introduced a graduated Income Tax in his budget of December 1798.

Remarkably France avoided early defeat despite internal chaos, the introduction of mass conscription enabling it to create large disciplined armies. Forces that circumvented inexperience with great determination and will, eventually gaining a string of epic victories under its masterly general, Napoleon Bonaparte

Compounding Pitt's worries as the 18th century moved to its end were affairs in Ireland, rebellion flaring in 1797. The answer in Pitt's mind was union along the lines of that between England and Scotland, a concept put in place on the 1st January 1801. General sensitivity to what was happening all round convincing the government of the necessity's of suspending Habeas Corpus, strengthening as the same time the laws dealing with treason and sedition. Pitt's own position in this turbulence finally becoming untenable when he tried to gain Catholic Emancipation in return for acceptance of Anglo-Irish union. Opposed by the crown it left Pitt in a corner, one he extricated himself from by standing down.

Succeeded by Henry Addington, a short general peace was brokered between France and Britain under the Treaty of Amiens. Temporary respite ended by the imposition of a naval blockade of continental ports in 1803 in response to the assembly of a French army at Boulogne, forces clearly suggestive of Napoleon's intention to cross the channel and conquer. Pitt's recall to office during May of the following year bringing renewed diplomatic overtures and the formation of the Third Coalition in conjunction with Austria, Russia and Sweden. The threat it posed drawing Napoleon away to the east, the dangers of invasion being relieved when the Royal Navy, under the command of Horatio Nelson, destroyed the combined French and Spanish fleets off Cape Trafalgar on 21st of October 1805. A triumph sharply contrasting to disasters on land as the coalition suffered comprehensive defeat at Ulm and Austerlitz. Its subsequent collapse wearing the final reserves in Pitt's body, his tired frame giving up its ghost early in 1806.

In the short lived administrations that followed, the first under William Grenville, the great work of William Wilberforce to abolish the slave trade reached fruition with parliaments agreement in 1807. A step, given Britain's isolation in opposition to France, all the more remarkable when it is considered that eventually Britain enforced this policy on much of the rest of the world. All but eradicating international aspects of the trade by the middle decades.

Rather more frightening was Napoleon's decision to engage in economic warfare by closing the continent to British goods. As exports fell, industrial unrest and bankruptcies followed, concerns exacerbated by food shortages. It was fortunate that this double edged sword loosened before it affected the nation's capacity to fight. The decisive moment in the war coming in 1808 when Napoleon resolved to conquer Spain. His armies facing universal hostility across the Iberian Peninsula from a populace determined to resist. A small British expeditionary force commanded by the Duke of Wellington successfully campaigning in defence of firstly Portugal, and then Spain, a contribution materially aiding in eventual French defeat. Napoleon himself leaving the scene to deal with renewed threats in the east, especially in Austria, where he again crushed the opposition in a series of typically brilliant actions.

French political and economic ambitions were dealt a further blow when British diplomacy succeeded in making peace with Russia and Sweden, persuasions that led both of these nations into rejecting the Continental System. This opposition to French designs led Napoleon to prepare his forces to march east, which they did at the end of June 1812. Despite reaching and sacking Moscow, the subsequent epic retreat of 'La Grande Armee' during bitter winter weather starved virtually all of it to death. Huge losses that compromised the ability of France to resist mounting allied pressures over the following two years, Paris itself coming within reach of hostile guns. The situation resolved for a time by Napoleon's unconditional abdication to Elba.

Peace did not last all that long, Napoleon reneging on whatever promises he had given, returning to France to raise a new army. At the head of this force he advanced on scratch units assembled under the command of the Duke of Wellington. Opposing units engaging in a sequence of clashes, the most decisive being at Waterloo. Careful British tactics and the slow, but nevertheless, timely arrival of Prussian forces under General Blucher enough to cause breakdown amongst the French ranks, winning the day for the allies.

As if prolonged war with France had not been enough, wide ranging interference by the Royal Navy with American shipping and Canadian support for various Indian tribes combined to exhaust American patience. Irritations leading it to declare war against Britain in 1812. Invading Canada did little for American aims, instead it found itself under naval blockade, also facing a British Expeditionary force that in a sequence of minor actions saw little gained by either side. The burning of part of the capital, Washington, its most remembered action, common sense prevailing when the two sides came together in a peace confirmed by the signing of the Treaty of Ghent in 1814.

Chapter 9

The Victorian era

Tying up the loose ends necessary to make the peace lasting began by banishing Napoleon to the remote island of St. Helena. The avoidance of future resentments by overriding vengeful motives finding widespread support amongst all the powers whose informal liaisons made up the Congress of Vienna. Outcomes that assisted Britain in its later efforts to maintain a balance of power between competing nations. Statesmanship exercised by moves to persuade more countries to move towards constitutional, rather than autocratic rule.

For all this maturity, such were the power of ideas unleashed by the French revolution that affairs across the continent and elsewhere remained unsettled. Britain's success in negotiating these consequences without succumbing to social upheaval due to its continued willingness to be guided by what was necessary in the broader interests. Parliamentary reform allied to industrial supremacy and social progress helping push Britain's fortunes to its peak, beneficial legacies lasting into the twentieth century.

Not that the beginning was all that auspicious, as once more the demobilising of the large armies raised against Napoleon tossed many a soldier into a country already struggling with poor harvests and the overly hasty abolition of income tax. The government finding itself in the predicament of being unable to finance its own activities, never mind service the national debt, which had grown rapidly during the years of conflict. The fight against France estimated to have cost Britain the then staggering sum of £600 million.

These were circumstances offering chances for the seductive voices talking about universal male suffrage, reform of parliament, lower taxation and relief from poverty. Talk that initially led an overly tense government towards repressive measures, a series of six acts passed in 1819 tightening the laws of sedition and libel, further regulating public meetings and preventing overtly militaristic demeanour. This general nervousness seeing clumsy use of the Manchester Yeomanry during a public meeting at St. Peters Field in Manchester that left eleven dead and hundreds injured (The Peterloo Massacre).

As is normally the case, as the economy recovered so matters improved, fortuitously for the unpopular George 4th whose time as Regent saw him first betrothed and then unhappily married to Caroline of Brunswick. Relations between the two proving so poor that she was excluded from his coronation in 1820 to widespread dismay. On the political front, the debates largely centred around the merits of free trade and Catholic Emancipation. Unpleasantness tainting the public scene following the suicide of the primary architect of Britain's foreign policy, Robert Castlereagh.

Stepping into this turbulence was the anti-Catholic Robert Peel who took over at the Home Office, while George Canning assumed the reins of Foreign Secretary. Peel instigating much needed changes to the Penal Code and later, during a second period as Home Secretary in 1929, establishing London's first police force, the Peelers. Across the Channel events in Europe once more tested, Canning's delicate diplomacy much needed to cope with sensitivities over the former Spanish and Portuguese colonies and the issue of self determination for Greece.

It was Canning who took over as Prime Minister in 1827 in what was a Whig-Tory coalition. His death shortly after taking office passing power via Viscount Goderich to the Duke of Wellington. Still high on the political agenda of this new government was the tackling of religious bigotry. Surprisingly, it was Peel, who in spite of long opposition actually presented the bill that would change matters. The repeal of the Test and Corporation Act in 1828 allowing Catholics and Dissenters to finally hold public office. While the Emancipation of Catholics in 1829 allowed those of that faith to take their place in parliament.

With parliament by now the established centre of power, the passing of the crown to William 4th in 1830 was a low keyed succession. His coronation taking place against economic set-backs and political tensions. Rocky circumstances negotiated by the new Prime Minister, Charles Grey, the Second Earl Grey, who already had it in mind to pursue electoral reform. The government he led introducing its ideas in a Bill put before the Commons by Lord John Russell in March of 1831. Despite intensive lobbying the Bill was defeated, forcing Grey's resignation. Re-elected with a solid majority, the measure was once more put before parliament, this time successfully negotiating the Commons before heading off to the Lord's where opposition orchestrated by Wellington ensured its defeat. A third attempt to get the measure accepted coming amidst widening agitation, this too passing the Commons, only to founder on the Lords obduracy, Grey once more resigning.

With Wellington unable to form an administration, the king returned once more to Grey, asking him to put together a government. Acceptance this time being conditional on the promise that should the Lords reject the measure, enough new Peers would be created by the king to ensure its passage. Facing the inevitability of defeat, the Lords conceded, the Reform Act gaining Royal Assent in June of 1832.

While the Act itself only introduced modest changes to the numbers who could vote, as well as redistributing a few seats. It gained real significance from the fact that parliament had responded to pressures for reform, taking it upon itself to do so in the wider interest. Later amendments to the franchise occurring in 1867, 1872, 1884 and 1885, although full and unconditional adult suffrage was not to arrive until 1928.

This sensitivity to political demands was matched by social activism, interests that would see reforms constructed around the realities of human nature. Leading the way was a Royal Commission put together to investigate the workings of the Poor Laws. Headed by Edwin Chadwick, this body examined how different Parishes administered the scheme and what happened to those given money. The conclusions determined that funds supplied without interested follow up undermined the willingness of the individual to provide for themselves. Parliament responded to these findings by passing the 1834 Poor Law Amendment Act which reduced the grounds on which welfare was given. This contributed to a revolution in the attitudes of ordinary people, almost the entire working population eventually making personal provision against hardship by voluntarily payment into what were known as Friendly Societies. A willingness to take responsibility that was supplemented by a remarkable growth in charitable giving by the middle classes.

These developments gained strength as the century waxed, becoming part of the national identity, a moral order that found further expression in the common sense of self sufficiency. Its effects were to last well into the last century, becoming, for a time at least, the foundation for the restrained and disciplined behaviour that was seen internationally as being typical of us as a people.

Coincidentally the government turned its attention towards other obvious iniquities. Amongst them, the gruelling consequences of child labour. Demands reined in by the 1833 Factories Act. Children under the age of nine being banned from working, with limits being imposed on everyone under the age of eighteen. This far reaching legislation was to be strengthened by Grey's successor, William Lamb (Lord Melbourne) whose Municipal Corporations Act created Borough Councils. These locally elected, centrally funded organisations provided the means through which the implementation of government legislation could be ensured. A role that was to undergo both refinement and expansion, especially via the 1888 Local Government Act which set up sixty-two elected County Councils tasked with a range of responsibilities that included managing roads and the local police.

Following the death of William in 1837, a weakened throne passed to an eighteen year old diminutive woman, named Victoria. It was she, with the shrewd help and guidance of her first Prime Minister, Lord Melbourne, and her later husband, Prince Albert of Saxe-Coburg, who created the role it has today. One that is above the politics and daily squabbles, an impartial figure head, symbol of the nation, not its rule. The early years of her reign complicated by economic reverse, a situation handled by an administration put together by Robert Peel in 1841. His actions to stimulate trade prompting reform of import and export duties to go with the re-introduction of income tax to address government funding shortfalls.

His sternest test coming from events in Ireland, where opposition to the Union remained strong, the Irish nationalist, Daniel O'Connell, working tirelessly to get the Act of Union repealed. Efforts stifled, or at least side-tracked, by the disastrous consequences of potato crop failure in 1845, then the staple food of the Irish people. Faced with a population that was bound to starve if nothing was done, attention turned to the repeal of the Corn Laws, a tariff on imported grain that kept prices artificially high. Determined resistance against the duty was matched by the vested interests of those who profited, Peel becoming involved in an arduous campaign that won phased repeal beginning in January 1846.

Such was the severity of the crisis in Ireland that various other measures were added piecemeal in an effort to ameliorate its worst aspects. Included here was the importing of maize, known curiously as 'Peel's brimstone,' various make work projects, use of soup kitchens and strict imposition of the Poor Laws. None of these efforts proved up the task of sustaining the population, substantial numbers choosing to escape starvation by immigrating to America, Australia, Britain, Canada and elsewhere. For those who stayed, malnutrition or disease was often the route to early death, although exactly how many died remains a matter of debate, numbers possibly being as high as one million. As for Peel, the controversy over his actions and stand proved politically damaging, his own party splitting, contributing to the grounds for his own resignation.

This human catastrophe had wide ramifications, not least from the seeding of the idea that government had a duty to implement measures that secured the public's health and wellbeing. Further stimulus to that concern motivated by the cholera outbreak of 1847-48, the first Public Health Act in 1848 a tangible product of this concern. Legislation that set up a Central Board of Health with clearly defined responsibilities.

Not that any simple Act could be a panacea to the complex social conditions of the time. Far too many people lived cheek by jowl in overcrowded housing that created an environment ideal for the spread of infectious diseases. Nevertheless, since the beginning of the 19th century the population of Britain had been expanding. Rough estimations suggest that numbers increased by fifty percent during the first thirty years, with a further rise of twenty-five percent over the next twenty. By 1851 the population of England, Wales and Scotland was nearly twenty-one million, evenly split between those who lived in towns and rural areas.

While it might be thought that industrial employment dominated this landscape, the reality is surprising. Agriculture remained the largest user of labour, with over one and half million men and just under a quarter of million women. Equally important was domestic service, nine tenths of more than a million workers being female. Over five hundred thousand worked in the single most important industry, cotton textile production, with about half that toiling in the woollen industry. Building and general labouring accounted for just over eight hundred thousand, other major employers being milliners, dress makers, seamstresses and hosiery workers. Coal mining, although a vital element in the nation's economy, provided work for just over two hundred thousand people.

Following the repeal of laws that restricted the emigration of working men, many chose to leave these isles, taking their skills elsewhere. A substantial exodus that saw many going to America and Canada, plenty also heading further afield, chancing their fortune to conditions in the distant colonies of Australia, New Zealand and Southern Africa. The land they left was approaching commercial supremacy, an event celebrated by the Crystal Palace Exhibition of 1851 at a time when nearly a quarter of all international trade passed through British ports. The opening of the Suez Canal eighteen years later supplying a further shot in the arm to trade by reducing the time and costs of shipping to the all important Far Eastern markets.

Remarkably, the actual peak of Britain's share of world trade was reached during the early 1870's. Spreading industrialisation on the continent and in America increasing the world's productive capacity, reducing Britain's share as it did so. This loss of dominance would be reinforced by other factors, not least from the failure to invest in the evolving and growing industries such as chemicals. Further complications coming from the spread of price deflation across Europe in the final decade of the century. Circumstances that were to see Germany and France abandoning free trade, part of an overall shift towards protecting established markets by using a mix of import and export tariffs and quotas.

Other ambitions emerged over the second half of the century, hopes that would bring Britain into conflict with those who envied its position. The wellspring of this development was the spread of nationalist feeling across the continent from the 1830's that led to the small principalities of Italy and Germany being welded into larger entities. Modern Italy taking shape as early as 1861, while the ambitions of the great Prussian statesman, Count Otto Von Bismarck, grafted the smaller, western most German principalities onto the powerful militaristic power that was Prussia. A journey that saw it take up cudgels against Denmark in 1864, Austria two years later and France in 1871.

Bismarck's role as Chancellor, which did not come to an end until 1890, was instrumental in Germany adopting universal suffrage, reform of its currency and the nationalisation of its railways. His guidance essential to the rapid development of its scientific base and heavy industries. Progress that increased the desire amongst Germans for a place in the sun, an Empire, a goal remaining out of reach because of the supremacy of the Royal Navy on the high seas. Not that this prevented Germany from achieving economic parity by the final decade of the 19th century, continued expansion leaving Britain behind before the end of that important period. Whilst the dangers of conflicting ambitions seemed to be ameliorated by the close ties between the two royal dynasties, the potential dangers prompted a domestic response, one reflected in the Naval Defence Act of 1889. A Bill allocating substantial additional funding to allow for the largest peacetime expansion of the Royal Navy. Effort that worked towards ensuring the fleet would continue to outgun the combined strength of any other two navies.

Also important during this period was the growing organisation of labour, trade unions finding legal recognition in 1871 though the Trade Union Act. The Employers and Working Men's Act four years later putting employers and employees on an equal footing. While the Conspiracy and Protection of Property Act freed unions from charges of conspiracy when making a strike, adding in the right to peacefully picket. The protective influences of belonging to a strong trade union movement a welcome facet to the hard lives of working people.

Selling the Victorians short.

Modern opinions of Victorian accomplishments and attitudes usually concentrate on the negative, views that typically fail to weight the contributions of the many men and women of that era to all fields of human endeavour. Influences that collectively helped create a nation whose people exhibited for a time some remarkable good qualities. A few of these Victorians making contributions that had influence well beyond these shores, a leaving of indelible marks on the collective story of humanity. Three who stand out politically are Henry Temple (the Third Viscount Palmerston), Benjamin Disraeli and William Gladstone.

Lord Palmerston's career stretched across more than fifty years. A period of service that started when he was offered the position of Chancellor of the Exchequer in 1809, his own choice leading him to take on the lesser post of Secretary at War. An office he held for twenty years during which his perceptive nature and gift for speaking saw his interest drift firmly into the sphere of foreign relations. Crossing the floor of the House, he joined the Whig government in 1830 as Secretary of State for Foreign Affairs. Becoming the architect of policies that sought to contain the conflicting ambitions and tensions then endemic to Europe. His nature and attitudes contributing to considerable successes, in particular when handling relations with France and Russia.

Having been Home Secretary for a short time in the coalition government of the Earl of Aberdeen, Palmerston became Prime Minister for three years from 1855 and then again in 1859, this second term extended by victory in the election of 1865. His death later that same year ending a remarkably long career. Besides foreign affairs, his contributions included the Matrimonial Causes Act of 1857, which removed jurisdiction for such proceedings from the ecclesiastical to the civil courts.

The Conservative Disraeli, son of the writer Isaac D'Israeli, earnt a reputation as a fine debater and a man who gave a populist edge to Conservatism. After serving as Chancellor of the Exchequer he gained the highest office on two separate occasions, briefly in 1868 and for a full term six years later. It was Disraeli who purchased the half share in the Suez Canal in 1875, going onto bestow the title Empress of India on Queen Victoria. His enduring legacy, the organisation he brought to party politics through the introduction of a central office and grassroots bodies under a party manager that remains with us still.

Gladstone began as a Tory, crossing the floor to become a liberal in 1859, when he was nearly fifty. After holding a number of posts, including two stints as Chancellor of the Exchequer, he became leader of the Liberal Party, taking office as Prime Minister at the end of 1868. Interested in administrative reform, he was instrumental in furthering elementary education, part of his general belief in the need to try and improve the lot and condition of the people as a whole. In all he served four times as First Minister until his resignation in 1894 following defeat of his second Irish Home Rule Bill. A cause in which Gladstone had spoken eloquently in favour of for the first time in 1886.

The Victorians were energetic and creative builders, most of the basic infrastructure of the nation was laid down during those fertile years. Sewers, the provision of a fresh water supply, bridges, viaducts, canals, tunnels and many fine buildings are all a part of their legacy. Behind this pioneering effort were some great industrial minds including Isambard Kingdom Brunel, Sir William Armstrong and Joseph Whitworth. Their collective imaginations and effort seeing everything from new types of ship, locomotives and rolling stock, pre-fabricated buildings, hydraulic machinery and other industrial machines and tooling of all kinds in quantities that saw it exported just about everywhere.

Of necessity, domestic production included everything from footwear to foods and soaps to confectionery. Recognisable names to the modern shopper who gained a start in those times include William Lever, Joseph Rowntree, John Sainsbury, Michael Marks and Tom Spencer. Some of these individuals were noted for their strong social conscience and interest in ordinary people. The soap entrepreneur William Lever for example built the model environment of Port Sunlight, a development matched by the Cadbury Brothers at Bournville. Far-sighted entrepreneurs with ideas we take for granted today also included people like Thomas Cook who perceptively realised the opportunities of leisure. Ideas that would create the massive tourist industries of the modern day.

The provision of insurance and other specific financial services is an important part of British economic history that reaches back a long way. Lloyds of London belongs to the late seventeenth century, perhaps as early as 1688 when Edward Lloyd opened a coffee house. A place that would gain a reputation as somewhere those seeking marine insurance could meet with those able to offer it. From this informal practicality grew the specialised financial institutions that became essential as trade flourished. The rapid expansion of industrial age placing Britain at the very hub of supplying this very necessary expertise.

Scientific advancement also accelerated during this period. In every field Briton's, or those attracted to Britain, had a shared interest or took the lead in scientific observations and research, bringing objective assessment to the discovery of new facts. Laying foundations that would evolve into the international co-operative endeavours of the twentieth century.

One such investigator was a Doctor John Snow who identified the source of the cholera outbreak in Broad Street, Soho, in London in 1854. From this understanding, although it was to take time to find universal acceptance, came the remedial efforts that saw major public investment in trying to secure a supply of clean water and take away human waste. A case perhaps of reinventing the wheel, the Romans just one civilisation who had already reached the same conclusions. Steps that proved essential in the work to conquer disease and improve public health. Significant in a different way was the work of Joseph Lister, his experiments identifying effective methods of containing infections caused by operations. The adoption of his methods of rigorous sterilisation and the use of antiseptics, itself based on the pioneering efforts of the great French chemist, Louis Pasteur, proved a major medical advance.

This sort of work and that by countless others saw the formation of a host of societies aimed at encouraging still more in the way of advancement. The Royal Society had already led the way, a body set-up shortly after the restoration of the monarchy in 1660. Adding to this establishment were the Royal Geographical Society, the Royal Historical Society, the Chemical and Faraday Societies, the Society for Analytical Chemistry, the Royal Institute of Chemistry and the Royal Society of Medicine and the Royal Statistical Society amongst others.

This near universal interest in learning was perhaps the most fundamental characteristic of the Victorian era. An intellectual stimulus to rational thinking and reasoning that for a time infused Britain with vitality and confidence. This sentiment communicated itself through out society, debates and lectures along with pamphlets, journals and books spreading knowledge amongst a nation eager to share and learn. Unprecedented levels of public enthusiasm contributing to the expansion and use of public libraries, itself a tradition that reached back to 1653 with the establishment of the Chetham Library in Manchester.

Picking up on this was government, the authorities taking it upon themselves to provide access to learning as a public duty. Accepting the necessities of funding the costs of building and running the schools if required. An obligation that added in training the teachers to handle the syllabus to an acceptable standard. Trends gaining weight once attendance at school became compulsory in 1880, elementary education becoming free eleven years later, the leaving age being raised to twelve by the end of the 1800's.

Chapter 10

Empire and small wars

The central role Britain forged for itself during the 19th century continued to ensure plenty of practice in fighting. While most actions took place during short campaigns against numerically superior, if less disciplined and armed opponents, a few needed extensive deployments. Two major conflicts stand out in which serious military shortcomings were exposed to much scandal. The first of these was the joint Franco-British effort against Russia in the Crimea, the second, the protracted struggle to subdue the Boers in South Africa.

Long sensitive to the expansionist aims of Russia, both in the Middle and Far East, Britain joined with France in encouraging Turkey following a quarrel over jurisdiction of the Holy Places within Turkish ruled Jerusalem. Long entrenched antipathy between the Ottoman Empire and the ambitions of Tsar Nicholas the 1st of Russia were exacerbated by Russian forces following their occupation of the Rumanian principalities, then subject to Turkish rule. This threat brought an Anglo-French forces to the Crimea, a venture in which France was much the major partner.

The contribution of these isles during most of the campaign was severely hampered by both logistical deficiencies and poor command allied to witless indifference to the welfare of the ordinary soldier. It taking domestic uproar and the arrival of Florence Nightingale amongst others to reverse the appalling neglect of the sick and injured.

The roots of the South African conflict at the end of the century involved indigenous tribes fighting for their own land against Dutch settlers who in turn contested with British colonisers. Following the discovery of gold and diamonds on land occupied by the Dutch, everyone's interest perked up. As the squabble descended into war, mobile, well armed and motivated Boer commandos took on the conventional British army. Fluid tactics and accurate rifle fire by the Boers countering the numerically larger British forces. Only when revised strategies were employed that isolated the fighting men from the farming populace they depended on did the balance tip away from the Dutch commandos.

While tactically rational in military terms, the disregard for the welfare of non-combatants taken into custody during the latter phase of the war stains the memories of that campaign, many thousands dying from indifference. Outcomes that again sparked uproar and condemnation in Britain and elsewhere.

Across India and elsewhere in the Far East, including Burma and in the so called Opium Wars in China, British interests and ambitions led to its share of martial art. Little remembered are host of minor rebellions and a few quite considerable wars. Some incited by French interests, others from resentments to British administrative rule and more from clashes brought about by the commercial activities of the East India Company and others. Remarkably most of this trouble was contained without massive commitment of regular British units. Locally raised forces commanded by British officers effectively self policing the land.

Amongst the most difficult were three wars in Afghanistan. The first between 1839-42 seeing the British garrison in Kabul capitulate, its retreat ending in massacre. Other notable conflicts included two hard won conflicts against well organised Sikh forces in the Punjab. Although the delicate balance on the Indian subcontinent only really spiralled out of control when various local resentments came together to incite the Indian army into mutiny during 1857. This loss of control resulted in widespread insurrection with the occasional massacres of European residents, instances that led to ruthless retaliation. Circumstances that saw the government at Westminster move to assume full control of India.

British involvement in Africa was equally remarkable, especially during the latter part of the 19th century when European nations went berserk amongst themselves trying to stake a claim to part of this vast continent. By the time this mania had exhausted itself, Britain had its fingers in Bechuanaland, Egypt, Gambia, Kenya, Nigeria, Nyasaland, part of Somalia, Rhodesia, Sierra Leone, South Africa, Sudan, the Gold Coast, Uganda and Zanzibar.

Inevitably there were instances when the local populations rose up against the imposition or interference of British control. Amongst the most serious of these conflicts were the Ashanti, Kaffir and Zulu Wars. One notable defeat for the British army coming early in 1879 when warriors under the Zulu king, Cetewayo, gained surprise and total victory at Isandhlwana.

Following the purchase of a half share in the strategically vital route provided by the Suez Canal in 1875, Britain found itself entangled with Egypt. Interests that faced challenge from both French and Italian influences in upper Nile valley, a threat answered by the decision to retake the Sudan. A major task force being assembled under the command of Lord Kitchener, one that headed south, following the river. The end coming in a mismatch of technology over bravery, complete victory achieved over the Mahdist forces at Omdurman. A triumph seen as fully avenging the earlier death of General Gordon of Khartoum.

Chapter 11.

Dawn of the twentieth century.

After nearly sixty-four years on the throne, Queen Victoria passed away early in 1901. Her legacy, a nation at the peak of its Imperial power passing to her eldest son, Edward, then fifty-nine. An eminence founded and maintained by a system of government drawn mainly from an aristocratic elite of moneyed or land-owning men, classes raised to think of running the country as a natural right. The governments they formed, compact entities whose authorities were restrained, not only by long traditions, but also by limited, if growing, social responsibilities. The latter ensuring low taxation, the former, contributing to a robust population, one that was both law abiding and robust. The land's economic vitality, while well past its peak, still contributed towards Britain's place as the world's most influential nation.

Of all the factors that brought about the collapse of this old order, none was more influential than the seismic shift in intellectual thought. Its principle component, the emerging belief government had in itself as a means for change. With policy coming to reflect these evolving attitudes, expectations amongst the people adjusted, more being expected of government and less of themselves. By the last decade of what was a remarkable century, the commitment of a large swathe of the population to care for themselves had more or less vanished. Government finding itself saddled with the intractable social problems it inspired, even if the arrogance of those drawn to politics continues to prevent open admission of this fact.

Following the resignation of Robert Gascoyne-Cecil, Lord Salisbury, as Prime Minister on 11th July 1902, authority passed to Arthur Balfour. Momentary fortune blessing this transition, the Boer war finally reached its end, the nation also having the opportunity to welcome the coronation of its new King, Edward the 7th. For the incoming leader of the government, there were issues enough to overwhelm judgement. The struggle over tariffs at home as way of raising revenue to fund government objectives competing with worrying trends overseas, in particular old antipathies with Russia. These reached fever pitch once more when the Russian Baltic fleet mistakenly fired on British fishing vessels in the Dogger Bank Incident. The agitation's of this fading to some extent when the Tsar's fleet, having steamed from one side of the planet to the other, met decisive defeat at the hands of the Japanese at Tsushima. A loss that sparked political convulsions against autocratic rule that derailed Russia's wider aims in the years after 1905.

Nevertheless a general sense of unease enveloped the body politic of these isles, creating forces within the government that loosened the affection for solitary independence. The nation casting around for ways of meeting growing dangers. Supported by the pro-French feelings of the king, these incentives helped steer policy towards resolving certain long standing colonial issues, agreements formalised by the Entente Cordiale in 1904.

Big on the horizon of concerns by this time were suspicions raised by German ambitions. The visible increase in capability of its High Seas Fleet, an instrument forged under the leadership of the German Admiral, Alfred von Tirpitz, an obvious challenge to the sea-borne superiority Britain had grown accustomed to wielding. The inevitable reactions finding tangible form in the decision to design and commission a new class of battleship. The first of these expensive ships, launched under the name Dreadnought in 1906, made all older vessels obsolete.

What followed was an expensive programme that saw two self imposed attempts to rein in the headlong rush by constraining the rate of building these new ships. Neither solicited a favourable response from Germany, anymore than face to face negotiations would do when they were conducted during in 1909. Talks managed on behalf of the nation by Sir Edward Grey, who had been appointed Foreign Secretary in the government formed by Henry Campbell Bannerman when he took over from Mr. Balfour in 1905.

Adding to general anxieties and domestic ferment were the aggressive activities of a growing band of women agitating over their lack of the vote. Formalised in a sense by the London based Kensington Society in 1866, the campaign for the same political rights as men had long drawn substantial support. Amongst early advocates was the English philosopher, John Stuart Mill, who as a Member of Parliament attached an amendment to the 1867 Reform Act that would have corrected this anomaly, insufficient support seeing it rejected. Progress was however made in a more limited way when unmarried women householders became eligible to vote in local elections following the success of an amendment to the Municipal Franchise Act two years later.

The wider struggle for recognition however gained its most determined support when Emmeline Pankhurst and others joined together to form the Women's Social and Political Union in 1903. A watershed in their activities coming when Pankhurst, aided by Annie Kenney, constantly interrupted a speech by Sir Edward Grey at a meeting in London late on in 1905. Unruly reactions seeing both charged and fined, their refusal to pay opening the door for a visit to one of His Majesty's prisons. The first of several visits for Pankhurst, who would be joined in this militancy by her daughters. Activities that raised the profile of a crusade that continued to face high powered opposition, not least from Herbert Asquith.

Despite such distractions, the wider interests in legislative solutions to what were seen as the social questions of the day held political focus. Following the Liberal landslide in the 1906 election, the government of Henry Campbell-Bannerman progressed these aims, an early measure the Trades Disputes Act which removed trade union liability for damage done by strike action. Further legislation seeing the Merchant Shipping Act, its goal, the improving of seaman's lives. While protecting British inventions from exploitation was the purpose of the Patents and Designs Act.

It was the arrival of David Lloyd George as Chancellor of the Exchequer in the administration formed by Herbert Asquith in April of 1908 following Campbell-Bannerman enforced resignation due to ill health that gave this reforming zeal a radical edge. Long a progressive advocate of improving the lot of the ordinary, Lloyd George set about doing just that by creating a pension scheme for people over seventy.

The enactment of the Old Age Pensions Act turned into a major constitutional crisis primarily because of the proposed method of raising the necessary money. With projected budgetary shortfalls already large because of depressed trade and the extra expenses of the ambitious programme of naval shipbuilding. The so called 'People's Budget' of 1909 moved towards direct taxation on income and wealth via a system of graduated income and land taxes supplemented by death duties and monies raised from the sale and profit of property. Funds supplemented by a proposed levy on new cars and petrol. Demands almost entirely directed towards those with the most means, little more than 25,000 people in all.

Presented and gaining the assent of the Commons, the Budget was handed to the Lords who rejected it by 350 votes to 75. Asquith responded by calling a General Election in January of 1910, returning to office with a reduced majority, the balance of power ending up in the hands of Irish Nationalists and Labour Members of Parliament.

Over the months that followed, the objectives evolved somewhat, with Asquith, Lloyd George and their supporters seeking to do more than simply gain acceptance of the Budget. The argument being converted into a general attack on the hereditary powers of the Peers. The specific aims encompassing moves to circumscribe the Lord's authority to reject any financial bill, proposals expanded by also making it an objective that any Bill passed by the Commons three times would automatically become law regardless of any decision taken by the Peers. Measures that also included a reduction in the life of Parliament from seven to five years.

Given the uncertainties over whether or not victory could be attained, Asquith sought assurances from the king that that he would, if necessary, create enough new Liberal Peers to overcome the entrenched resistance of the Lord's. Edward agreeing only if the government won a second election, this was held in December of that year, with virtually the same result. Having secured the support of the minor parties the government was able to prevail, the Peers capitulating. The Parliament Act becoming law the following year, permanently limiting the powers of the House of Lords. Victory relieving a new monarch, George the Fifth, of the contentious duty of having involve himself in the mass creation of peers.

As a consequence of this constitutional reform, power was concentrated still further into the hands of Commons, bringing Britain closer to a unicameral State. Equally important were the financial consequences, the role of income tax assuming a central place in the raising of government revenue. The planned attempts to raise money from a land tax proving too complicated, leading to its abandonment.

Part of the price of this triumph was the promise to the Irish Nationalist's that the government would reintroduce and support Irish Home rule. In honour of that pledge Herbert Asquith put before the House the Third Irish Home Rule Act in April of 1912. Strong resentments to being ruled from Dublin amongst Protestants in the north east raising the distinct threat of violent resistance should the measure succeed. Political expression of that sentiment seen in a petition raised against the prospect. With opinion polarising, opposing sides prepared themselves by raising private armies, a compromise decision agreeing to implement the main provisions of the act by temporarily excluding the six northern eastern counties that had a protestant majority easing tensions. Having gained its third reading in 1914, the Act only needed royal assent to make it fact, a step unexpectedly delayed by the outbreak of the First World War.

Aside from the constitutional dramas social conditions remained very much in the national eye. Further legislation leading to limits being put on working hours for coal miners. Much more subtle was the issue of delinquent children, the moral problems of sending adolescents to adult prisons targeted by the creation of the Borstal system. While a practical answer to the limited numbers who could afford to become a Member of Parliament was answered in part by the award of a salary of four hundred pounds per annum.

Another making a name for himself during in these times of socially conscious politics was Winston Churchill. At the time an ally of Lloyd George, he himself became intimately involved in the establishment of Labour Exchanges to aid the unemployed find work. The National Insurance Bill, one of the founding stones of the modern welfare State, also gaining his support. Initially offering payment during sickness, this benefit was soon amended to cover unemployment as well. The unexpected downside was that the voluntary contributions most already made to Friendly Societies or Trade Union sponsored insurance schemes to cover these eventualities entered rapid terminal decline as people came to believe they could rely on the State. The outcomes of undermining of individual responsibility exposing the exchequer to demands it had not bargained for, ones that have since proved insatiable.

Not that these measures were able to deflect growing divisions in society. With trade union membership and influence having grown, a wave of strikes disrupted the economy in 1911 as resentments over working conditions, wages and much else boiled over. Class struggle was in the air and with it the spectre of revolution, government resolve marked by the deployment of troops onto the streets.

Chapter 12

The Great War

Europe, by the second decade of the 20th century had evolved by ambition and treaty into two sides, the Triple Alliance binding Germany, Austria-Hungary and Italy, while the Triple Entente did the same for France, Russia and Britain. The build up of pressures between the two sides catastrophically unleashed when a Serbian fanatic, Gavrilo Princip, shot Archduke Franz Ferdinand and his wife in Sarajevo on 28th of June 1914. Austria, seeking to exploit the outrage, made demands Serbia could not concede, on this pretext, war was declared. From that point various treaty obligations kicked in with nations mobilising for war. Germany's opening intrusions through neutral Belgium committing Britain.

Germany's plan of action followed the outlines of the analysis conducted by Count Alfred von Schlieffen of the German General Staff in 1905 when he considered a response to war on two fronts. The intention was to hold Russia on the Eastern Front with minimal forces, trading ground for time as necessary while seeking the knockout blow against its main enemy, France. Crucially however, revisions applied to the concept compromised its success, the German attack being arrested by defensive actions conducted by French armies and the British Expeditionary Force during the First Battle of the Marne. Subsequent westward movements as both sides sought envelopment of the other, failing when the contestants reached the sea. The end of manoeuvring opening a prolonged phase of defensive actions that soon began imposing heavy casualties. Stalemate sucking at the expanding strength of Lord Kitchener's voluntary British Army on what was known as the Western Front. Both sides turning to the spade and digging in, constructing increasingly elaborate defences as massed artillery and the machine guns reduced the conflict to the arithmetic of attrition. Men and material being consumed endlessly for nearly four years before the deadlock was decisively broken.

Turkey's early entry into the war on Germany's side increased Russian isolation from her allies. A British expedition that landed at Cape Helles in April of 1915 hoped to open a route through the Dardenelles by knocking Turkey out of the war. It would prove a costly failure when surprise was squandered more than once. British forces were however to go on contesting with Turkey in relatively minor actions in Mesopotamia, as well as inciting, aiding and using the Arab revolt in the Hejaz to harry Turkish units strung out in their garrisons. A situation exploited when a bridgehead was established on the Sinai side of the Suez Canal from where a general advance was made that pushed the Turkish forces out of Sinai, freed Jerusalem and liberated Damascus.

Joining the Allied side in May 1915 was Italy. Facing her, Germany's partner, Austria, combatants that fought a number of difficult but indecisive battles in the high alpine country. Despite the great courage shown by Italian units at great cost, it was not until the middle of 1918 when British and French elements helped out that real progress was made against a weakening Austria.

Russia's essential contribution to the Allied cause was fully compromised by the third year of the war following a number of catastrophic defeats. Her inadequate industrial capacity not up to the task of supplying her armies, while the increasingly fractious and revolutionary politics further inhibited her effectiveness. All influential factors in the revolutions of 1917 and the abandoning of the war. The Russian exit following a separate armistice conceded at the Treaty of Brest-Livovsk crucially presented Germany with the best chance of forcing a decisive result in France.

Following the transfer of major reinforcements from the east, Hindenberg used them in a sequence of offensives early in 1918 that broke through the allied lines. However these were only partial successes, the ability to capitalise on the penetration proving beyond German capacity. Instead, invigorated by the growing strength of America, the Allied counter-offensive gathered, forcing its way through German defences and driving them back towards their own frontier and the realisation that after years of blockade and privation, the will of its people to fight had gone.

Throughout the war the Royal Navy's primary purpose had been to deter action by the German High Sea's Fleet, this was done by holding the bulk of the Grand Fleet in readiness in British Home Waters. Its presence an essential stratagem, the blockading of Germany preventing the importation of essential war materials. It was however distant units of the German navy that gave the Admiralty an early headache and the run-around, notably by the light cruiser Emden in the Indian ocean. The German China squadron also proved dangerous, winning victory at Coronel before they inadvertently ran into Royal Navy battle-cruisers coaling at Port Stanley. Pursued and caught, all but one of the German ships were sunk by the greater weight of fire during the Battle of the Falkland Islands.

Although there were a number of actions between heavy units of the opposing navies in Home Waters, the only major encounter took place at the Battle of Jutland in 1916, an inconclusive meeting leaving the status quo undisturbed. The real threat to Britain coming from the submarine, especially when Germany declared its unrestricted use in February of 1917. Success threatening Britain's very survival by cutting off necessary imports of food and other goods. The effective counter coming when a system of convoys escorted by ships of the navy was implemented later that year.

Much more revolutionary was the extending of the war into the air, with balloons, airships and aircraft all involved in developing what was a new dimension. Throughout the war much emphasis was given to reconnaissance via direct observation and photography. Pilots only arming themselves for self defence, before the aircraft themselves were fitted with machine guns, allowing one to take on another in combat. Later, Zepplin airships and long range aircraft on both sides added to the threat by reaching out to bomb military targets and cities.

What had begun with waves of almost child-like enthusiasm at its declaration ended on the eleventh of November 1918 with a hush. At the beginning of those years a small, proud professional army marched to honour at Mons and obliteration at Ypres. As the Battalions of Pals faced the sobering realities of endless casualty lists, conscription brought a steady supply of khaki clad men from the homes and factories. Over seven hundred thousand of whom would not return to a nation that could never be the same.

What is left, even at the distance of nearly a century, are images of the Western Front with its endless miles of trench and screens of barbed wire afloat a sea of holes infested with rats. Into this hell were poured the men of Australia, Belgium, Canada, England, France, Germany, India,

Ireland, New Zealand, Portugal, Scotland, South Africa, Wales and finally America. Men united in the comradeship of death. Its great battles woven into a tapestry. First Ypres bleeding into Artois, Champagne and Second Ypres, Verdun, the Somme, Arras and Second Champagne. The constant duelling artillery, sniping and raiding adding endlessly to the toll until it became too much for France. Her army turning mutinous for a time in 1917, its shame hidden from watchful German eyes behind the shadow of the Tommy, the Canadian and Anzac, who, in the cold, mud and misery of the Third Battle of Ypres died for the common cause.

Chapter 13

Economic struggles

The twenty-one years between the end of the Great War and the start of the Second proved tumultuous. Economic struggle exacerbated by ill judged domestic policies and external upheaval over which Britain had little control imposing severe social hardships. Events in Ireland proving equally intractable, before a resurgent Germany presented dangers the nation went out of its way to deny for far too long.

For the government, the same National Coalition formed under Lloyd George in 1916 to pursue the war, attention turned towards the need to articulate some vision of the future that made the sacrifice appear worthwhile. This Lloyd George did in a speech to the nation twelve days after the signing of the Armistice when he pledged *'to make Britain a fit country for hero's to live in.'* The sense of mission behind these words gaining its first expression in reform of the franchise. The Representation of Peoples Act passed in 1918 giving the vote to all men over twenty-one and, for the first time, to women over thirty who met certain property qualifications. The age differential and its limiting qualifications consigned to history by the Equal Franchise Act ten years later.

The real headaches could not be solved quite so easily, political promise having to square off against colossal debt. Four years of all out war lopping a large slice off the national wealth, reducing the resource that was needed to embark on much needed regeneration of the nation's ageing industry. Something ignored during the fight out of necessity, industry concentrating its effort on making the steel for the guns and shells along with the textiles for uniforms, efforts that sustained many a decrepit factory. The drastic pruning that came with the peace all the more of an issue as the largest army this nation ever raised was quickly demobilised. It was fortunate that much of a no longer wanted industrial workforce were women, the greater part of whom could at least return to the home rather than face unemployment.

These immediate difficulties were further complicated by the fact that access to the old pre-war markets was no longer guaranteed. The reputation of British goods insufficient to attract trade when compared with the output of modern American factories able to exploit the ascendancy of the dollar. After a brief rally the economy sank into a deflationary phase during the early twenties, unemployment creeping upwards. Hardest hit were the traditional occupations such as coal mining, textiles production and ship building, many collieries and firms remaining so weak, they were barely viable. The additional relief from a non-contributory insurance called the Out of Work Donation, enacted a year after wars end, insufficient to overcome the onset of severe hardship in some areas. A problem all the more severe given the large numbers of men crippled by war injuries.

Facing up to this gloomy scene was the nation's rising political force, the Labour Party, it first chance coming in 1924 when James Ramsay MacDonald became Prime Minister. Only in power for a short period, its chances of re-election for a full term compromised by the so called Zinoviev letter calling on British communists to work towards revolution. A probable forgery, its existence was leaked to the media just four days before the election, shifting opinion at critical juncture. Taking over were the Conservatives under Stanley Baldwin, management of the economy remaining the key issue. Crucial here was export performance, something hit when the new Chancellor, Winston Churchill, decided to return sterling to the gold standard at its pre-war level. This move, made on 28th April 1925, overvalued the pound, handicapping the international competitiveness of British goods. (Note: the gold standard fixed the value of paper money against a certain amount of gold metal).

The depth of the crisis really coming home when mine-owners, faced with shrinking market share and marginal costs, sought to impose wage cuts as a way of maintaining competitiveness. Miners reactions were understandably strong, with unrest and lockouts soon following. Sympathy action spread to transport, electricity and gas workers until nearly 3 million were on strike. Governmental response was resolute, the army and navy along with large numbers of ordinary volunteers helping keep the nation running. A face saving formula ending the strike after eight days, the threat of a repeat drawing parliament into enacting the Trades Disputes Act the following year, outlawing both general and sympathy strikes.

Enduring the tough conditions and more than holding their own on the world stage were the up to date industries in modernised factories and plants. Besides the expanding use of electricity, with its ongoing construction of the necessary infrastructure, success also came to firms making motor vehicles or producing chemicals. Significant beneficiaries were the skilled workers, higher wages a sign of what investment in the right fields could deliver for the nation and its people. Even if the work showed all the signs of long term de-skilling, assembly line production often a case of simple, repetitive actions. Although in a world where around a million men and boys endured hard graft in miserable conditions down coal mines, such concerns were an irrelevance. For those lucky enough to be earning more, life had an improved tint, access to better housing and much improved standards of living their share of working at the cutting edge of technology. An agreeable experience as the population rapidly recovered from the slaughter of the Great War.

Labour's second stint in office began in 1929 when Ramsay MacDonald, supported by the Liberal's, formed a minority government. Early popularity achieved through revision of Old Age Pensions and more generous unemployment insurance lost as the effects of prolonged decline in world commodity prices contributed to a collapse in confidence in the world's financial system. The consequences following the collapse of share prices on Wall Street hitting the US economy especially hard, effects that soon rippled out across the globe.

As economic recession enveloped the world, those against free trade gained more of a hearing and influence, part of a world-wide movement that saw governments everywhere imposing tariff's and quotas to protect domestic production and markets. The scale of economic reverse totally dominating the international scene, Britain's own response coming from the formation of a national government with Ramsay MacDonald at its head and Neville Chamberlain stepping up as Chancellor of the Exchequer. The severe deflationary actions the nation instituted causing a run on sterling that led to the abandoning of the Gold Standard.

The peak of this crisis was reached in 1932 when just over a fifth of the total workforce was out of work. Predictably, it was the old industries that suffered the most, areas dependent on coal-mining, shipbuilding, textiles and pottery seeing local levels of unemployment often exceeding thirty percent. With many families facing near starvation, government introduced a Means Tested Family benefit. Other well intended attempts to secure regeneration of employment black-spots via two Bills, the Special Areas Development and Special Areas Reconstruction Acts, proving largely ineffective. For many, the only solution was to move to where they could find work, the exodus from South Wales in particular reaching significant proportions by the end of the thirties. Much of this spare labour finding employment in the expanding modern industries that were themselves beginning to be stimulated by moves to rearm.

While undoubtedly pre-occupied by the depression, the business of government still had other concerns. Time being found to formalise legislative equality between the self-governing dominions of the British Empire and crown. The 1931 Statute of Westminster confirming the political and legal change with the Dominion of Canada and New Zealand, the Commonwealth of Australia, the Union of South Africa, the Irish Free State and Newfoundland.

With the economy getting a boost following the reluctant decision to respond to German rearmament, Ramsay MacDonald stood aside in favour of the Conservative, Stanley Baldwin. The incoming PM facing an immediate constitutional crisis provoked by the decision of the popular King, Edward the Eighth, to seek assent to marry the American divorcee, Mrs Wallis Simpson. Following the refusal of the government to compromise over a proposed morganatic marriage which would have excluded their children from the succession, the King abdicated. The throne passing to his painfully shy brother, later crowned George the 6th.

These distressing events were representative of discontented times, the martial rise of Germany self evident, except that is to the self deluding politicians of Europe. Realities inherited by the Conservative Neville Chamberlain when he formed an administration in 1937. His term as Prime Minister dominated by his unstinting efforts to avoid the breakdown of peace.

While historical assessments of this period justifiably concentrates on the bleak circumstances of the depression and the international tensions caused by Germany. The Thirties were not bad times for everyone, growing numbers of working people gaining their first experience of a better life. Something that included new housing, a substantial long term building programme adding hundreds of thousands of new homes, activity matched by determined efforts to demolish the country's remaining slums. A project later aided by the indiscriminate use of bombs made in Germany.

Chapter 14

The Irish problem

While the Great War held up plans for the implementation of Home Rule in Ireland, it did not stop those thinking and working for something much more. That something being full independence. A goal that had motivated Arthur Griffith's establishment of the political party, Sinn Fein (We Ourselves) in 1905.

With Britain heavily involved on the Western Front and elsewhere, the situation seemed ideal to a small number of Nationalist radicals to try and win this very prize by employing force over the Easter period of 1916. Inadequately planned and supported, its failure was followed up by ruthless British action, the ring leaders being tried and executed, thousands more being arrested following the imposition of martial law. Reactions playing a significant role in swaying support in favour of a Republican agenda.

Worried out of its distractions, the government responded to the attempted coup by moving to get the Act up and running. Lloyd George himself, at the time Minister of Munitions, taking on the task of negotiating with the Ulster Unionist leader, Sir Edward Carson and, the Nationalist John Redmond. These efforts were to come within an ace of succeeding, stumbling only over the proposed partition, in particular the ambiguities of how long it was intended to last, something that proved just beyond the capacity of the two parties to find agreement. A second attempt to work things out in 1917 lacked the necessary support, talks petering out after some months without result.

It was at this critical juncture that events in the war gave a boost to those favouring outright independence. The need for recruits to feed the mincing machine on the Western Front bringing those tasked with providing them to eye Irish stock. Opposed to such conscription were supporters of the Republican side, the Irish Parliamentary party finding themselves losing political appeal because of their continued support for the Allied cause.

The full ramifications of these shifts in attitudes were revealed in the elections held in December of 1918 when those sympathetic to the Republican movement won a decisive majority of the contested seats. The subsequent refusal of these Republican MP's to take their seats at Westminster largely defining later events. Gathering around the leadership of Eamon de Valera in a body they called the Dail Eireann, they declared the independence of Ireland, a move that only drew recognition from the Soviet Union.

Unwilling to negotiate with the British government, opinions polarised, leaving little room to escape from the spiral that led to conflict. The opening rounds of the Anglo-Irish, or War of Independence, beginning in January 1919. On one side was the Irish Republican Army (IRA) under the leadership of Michael Collins, on the other, the Royal Irish Constabulary and both regular and irregular units (Black & Tans and Auxiliaries) of the British army. Using guerrilla tactics, the IRA ambushed, assassinated and attacked property as well as employing propaganda and other forms of psychological warfare. Murder on one side sparking summary executions on the other, brutality leaving no one untouched. The spread of this campaign into the north assuming the sectarian dimension all too familiar to later generations.

The response of Lloyd George's government was to replace the suspended Home Rule Act by the Government of Ireland Act. Ratified at the end of 1920, this proposed splitting off the six mainly Protestant counties in the north from the rest of Ireland. Each part having its own self governing assembly with relations between the two linked via a Council of Ireland handling common affairs under a Lord Lieutenant. The crown reserving for itself issues such as foreign affairs, currency and defence.

It was this arrangement that went into effect, firstly in Ulster, the Northern Assembly gathering on 7th June 1921. Its opening marked by a speech by the king appealing for conciliation between north and south. Helpful words aiding the compromise that allowed Arthur Griffith's on behalf of the Nationalists and Lloyd George for the government to work out a truce during which talks could take place. The Southern Assembly continuing to remain inoperative because of Sinn Fein's decision to maintain a boycott. Heading the Republican team during the subsequent negotiations was Michael Collins, a compromise settlement being agreed and signed in December of 1921. This offered Dominion status to

Southern Ireland along lines enjoyed by Canada and Australia. An arrangement that provided for a constitutional monarchy with two elected houses. While this self governing Free State was less than what Sinn Fein wanted, it was an advance on the Home Rule Act of 1914. Integrated into this Treaty was the option for the north, which already enjoyed Home Rule, to opt out. Much more of a problem however to Republican sensitivities was the wording of the Oath of Allegiance, which continued to make clear that the Free State remained part of the British Commonwealth.

Getting unanimous acceptance of this agreement proved difficult, ratification coming by a split vote carried by narrow margins. The winners, led by Collins, opposed by a faction under Eamon de Valera. The decision to accept being validated by the Southern Assembly, which convened for the first and only time for this specific purpose in January of 1922. Under the terms of the Treaty a provisional government was set up under Collins to transfer power, the six protestant counties of Ireland withdrawing from the arrangement.

Unfortunately the split within Republican ranks proved too big to heal. An obdurate de Valera effectively isolating himself and his supporters when he contested the majority decision. Efforts to bridge the gap between the two sides seeing Michael Collins proposing a revision to the constitution. Unfortunately the selected wording proving rather too Republican for the British government's taste's, who, pressured correction, closing the door to that form of compromise. Deciding the future was the electorate, who in June of 1922 gave majority backing to Collins. This effectively solidified the rupture, opening the door to the tragedy of civil war. The ensuing strife seeing the better armed government of the Free State slowly gaining the upper hand in spite of the assassination of Collins himself and other elected officials. The atmosphere poisoned by murders, widespread economic and material damage, internment and hunger strikes.

Integrated into the agreement was provision for disbanding the Royal Irish Constabulary (RIC), its place taken by separate police forces for north and south. As the general lawlessness seeped into the north, the Royal Ulster Constabulary (RUC), established on 29th April 1922, took on the role of normal policing and the fight against terrorist activities. Supporting it was a part time organisation called the Ulster Special

Constabulary (USC), a body whose three elements were to later prove their worth.

As the overall situation gradually stabilised, the political division caused by the treaty in the south found permanence in two political parties. William Cosgrave taking over after the death of Collins as the head of the Free State. De Valera, who eventually gave up on the use of force, formed Fianna Fail in 1926, inheriting the leadership of the Free State from Cosgrave in 1932. Taking it onwards towards the cherished destiny of full independence, which came in 1948 when Ireland declared itself a republic during the Premier-ship of John Costello.

Chapter 15

Losing the peace

The traumas of the Great War naturally left a widespread desire to avoid its repeat, the most powerful advocate of that attitude, the American President Woodrow Wilson. His behind the scenes diplomacy helping forge the Treaty of Versailles, the document that confirmed the end of fighting and the creation of the League of Nations. Although the American Congress never agreed to US membership, which rather limited its influence. Nevertheless the League's objectives were clear, the promotion of disarmament and the prevention of further war by mediating on issues that might cause one. Part of this internationalisation of authority seeing similar organisations such as the Disarmament Commission, the Health Organisation, Mandates and Slavery Commission's and the International Labour Organisation.

Of all the findings regarding the Great War, none proved more significant to what happened later than the conclusion that Germany alone was responsible. A decision used to justify demands for massive compensation and loss of territory. Faced with political instability and hyper-inflation that disrupted her economy, Germany's default on its obligations was inevitable. The governments of France and Belgium co-ordinating action to occupy the industrial heartland of the Ruhr in 1923 when this finally occurred.

Ramsay MacDonald, who acted as his own Foreign Secretary during his short first term in office, directed considerable energy to fixing the problems caused by the Treaty of Versailles. His agenda topped by the need to end occupation of the Ruhr, something resolved by an Allied Committee formed under Charles Dawes. The agreement, or Dawes Plan, announced during August of 1924, modified reparation repayments to manageable levels as well as allowing for withdrawal of the occupation forces. Terms that were further scaled back under the Young Plan in 1929, with a conditional moratorium on all payments entering the equation during the height of the Great Depression.

In the early thirties a conference held at Lausanne proposed that all reparations be cancelled if the US would agree to write off the war debts of the other combatants. An idea that did not find enough support in America to make it acceptable, although by then Germany was close to arbitrarily defaulting on her obligations anyway. Later analysis revealing that Germany only repaid a fraction of what was due, mainly because commercial loans obtained from the US were re-directed towards making repayments.

Also encouraged by Ramsay Macdonald were proposals for general European disarmament, ideas followed up at the Locarno Conference in 1925. The treaty derived from this work binding Britain, Belgium, France, Germany and Italy into mutual arrangements that stipulated what each would do in the event of aggressive actions. The whole concept of disarmament proving popular enough to see a Disarmament Preparatory Commission put together to investigate the practicalities. Some three years later the 'Kellogg-Briand Pact' broke new ground when it outlawed the use of war between France and the US.

Good intentions aside, disorder and economic chaos dogged nearly everyone during the late twenties and early thirties. Germany sharing in the hardships and mass unemployment, unfortunately finding a solution in extreme nationalism. A path Hungary flirted with before Italy, under Benito Mussolini, demonstrated what organisation and discipline could achieve. An example taken up and improved on by an obscure messianic Austrian named Adolf Hitler. His route to power the result of artful exploitation of German grievances over its surrender and the terms imposed on it by the victors, along with plenty of risk taking and ruthless opportunism.

Once invited into power, he employed a subtle mix of emotional appeal, propaganda and thuggery to ensure he stayed. Rebuilding the economy by harnessing the energy of the entire nation in ways not seen since Napoleonic days. Domestic success and stability winning increased tolerance of his behaviour at home, while abroad his daring met with only appeasement and inaction, even after publicly denouncing the disarmament clauses of the Versailles Treaty and rejecting Germany's responsibility for the First World War.

Emboldened by sycophants, assorted brutes and hangers on within the Nazi party, Hitler set about expanding his domain. His confident risk taking starting with re-occupation of the Rhineland in March 1936, a move that evoked no response worthy of the name from either Britain or France. The outbreak of the Spanish civil war that year providing chances for Germany and Italy to further their creed, military aid going to Franco to counter that provided by the Soviet Union. The practical experiences gained by German units helping develop the tactics that would become so successful barely three years later. Both sides attracting various nationals drawn by convictions to fight, including the likes of the British writer, George Orwell. Passions that did not deflect Britain's official policy, which remained one of pragmatic non-intervention.

Hitler's greatest weapon during this shabby phase was fear, a vulnerability he used to his own advantage to extract repeated concessions. Having bullied Austria into the Anschluss (Connection) early in 1938, his next target was the ethnic Germans of the Sudetenland in western Czechoslovakia. British and French politicians, with a few notably exceptions, proving unusually compliant. None more so than Neville Chamberlain who was instrumental in supplying Hitler with the freedom of action he needed to annex this important area. The indignity of mutely spectating on Germany's later occupation of the rest of Czechoslovakia his reward for this miserable treachery.

Paradoxically this diplomatic low acted to consign whatever lingering affections existed for appeasement in the growing affluence of Britain's expanding suburbs and its remaining slums. Militarily impractical guarantees being given to Poland at the end of March 1939 an indication of a shift in mood. The teeth these agreements needed might have been acquired from Soviet-Russia, if negotiations had been conducted with more interest and urgency. Instead, following the assumption of Soviet foreign policy in the hands of Vyacheslav Molotov, a deal was concluded between Soviet Russia and Germany. A non-aggression pact signed on 27th August 1939 following an earlier commercial treaty. Hidden in the details of these agreements was allowance for the partition of Poland following a planned German invasion. The door to war had opened, British and French weakness having helped push it, the cost of this spinelessness would prove severe.

Chapter 16

The Second Great War

It was that mesmeric individual, Adolf Hitler, who wrote the opening chapter of this conflagration. With the touch of a gambler on a winning streak, he had gone on exploiting repeated British and French failures to check his ambitions until he could no longer see straight.

War's beginning mirrored that of 1914, Germany opening hostilities by seeking rapid knock out blows, this time with more success. Three distinct phases executed in rapid succession seeing Poland, Denmark, Norway, Luxembourg, Holland, Belgium and France all overrun. An overture that left ill-prepared Britain with a bloody nose alone behind its salty moat and dependent on vulnerable merchant shipping. Its shield her stubborn nature, its spear entrusted to Winston Churchill, who knew the nation's survival meant engaging the interest and support of the United States.

The immediate concern was buying time to allow the delicacy of his diplomacy to unfold. Precious space won by some rare vision, the Committee for the Scientific Survey of Air Defence under Sir Henry Tizard helping merge the first radar's and a network of ground observers into an functional entity under centralised command. Control that allowed the immortal Hurricanes and Spitfires of Fighter Command under the command of Air Marshall Hugh Dowding to hand, with a little luck, Germany's first reverse.

Abandoning ideas of a cross channel invasion, Hitler's restless mind turned to where it had long looked, eastwards. Leaving Britain to cope with the Blitz and the frightening dangers in the North Atlantic from U-boat's and surface raiders. German ambitions temporarily delayed by the failures of its ally, Italy, to make progress in North Africa or the Balkans. Intervention by General Erwin Rommel and the Afrika Korps helping sort out the situation in Africa, while Italy's stalled efforts in Greece were quickly resolved as the Whermacht overcame Yugoslavia, Greece and Crete in quick succession. Freed from the inhibitions of danger to his southern flank, Hitler took his great gamble, three massive spearheads plunging forward into Russia on 22nd June 1941. Almost five months of success followed, until the advance ground to a halt just short of Moscow. Bitterly cold winter weather combined with a major Russian counter offensive forcing the Germans back in the first week of December.

A day later, a world away from the freezing cold of the Russian steppe, Japan joined the war. Its ideas of a Greater South East Asia Co-Prosperity sphere pursued by a surprise attack on the American fleet at Pearl Harbour. Awakening, as Fleet Admiral Isoroku Yamamoto, architect of this plan predicted, the sleeping giant of the United States. Four days later on 11th December, the crux of the war was reached when Germany rashly declared war on the United States. Action that brought harmony to the goals of Soviet-Russia, Britain and America. Winston Churchill and Franklin Roosevelt, then President of the United States, meeting to forge an alliance with one aim, total victory. The means of achievement derived from the justness of cause, Soviet-Russia's capacity to fight on in spite of horrendous losses and America's unsurpassed industrial capability.

At the beginning of 1942 matters still looked good for both Germany and Japan. German submarines were sinking unprotected shipping off America's east coast and in the Caribbean, while Rommel was once more advancing towards Egypt. Meanwhile, Hitler's mind was still able to contemplate fresh victories in the up and coming summer offensive into the Caucus with its tempting oilfields. Over in south east Asia, Japanese forces swept all before them, easily overrunning Hong Kong, before invading the Philippines and Malaya, forcing shameful defeat on the British Army at Singapore before occupying Burma. Its southern advance reaching the Solomon Isles and Papua, within striking range of Australia. Only in the air did the allies appear to be able to strike back, British bombers heading east in the night skies to pound Germany's industrial centres and cities.

Behind the scenes however plenty was going on that would contribute towards turning the tide. A vital component provided by the British code breakers at Bletchley, their ability to read encrypted German radio messages creating tactical and strategic advantage, something of particular importance on the North Atlantic convoy routes. A success mirrored in the open spaces of the Pacific where Japanese intentions towards Midway Island were exposed by American ability to read the

Imperial navy's codes. Four Japanese carriers taking up permanent residence on the ocean floor, victims of intellect, carrier borne strike aircraft and that essential bit of luck.

On land, the real change in fortunes began in the North African desert where completion of thorough preparations overseen by General Bernard Montgomery allowed the British 8th Army to attack in overwhelming force at El-Alamein. An offensive that drove the Afrika Korp westwards towards Allied forces whose landings in Morocco and Algeria soon overcame French Vichy resistance. German and Italian forces eventually ended up sandwiched and forced to surrender in Tunisia, late in the spring of 1943.

This loss, hard on the heels of the destruction of the German 6th Army at Stalingrad during February marked the turning point. Hitler's decline into stubborn refusal to trade territory for advantage condemning the efforts of his commanders and armies. Only the refusal of Field Marshall Erich von Manstein to adhere to this crippling lack of flexibility allowed him to manoeuvre and gain the last significant victory on the Eastern front at Kharkov. Any fruits from that action squandered in a delayed set to that July at Kursk. The largest tank battle of the entire war turning into one of attrition, something Germany could not hope to win. Hitler's belated realisation virtually ending Germany's offensive capacities on the Eastern Front.

Back in the Atlantic, the U-boat's once more threatened when as many as a dozen boats gathered together into what were called 'Wolf Packs.' Operational units large enough to overwhelm the convoy and its escorts. The response to this danger coming from a combination of tactics that saw long range aircraft providing cover over the entire Atlantic. Local air support becoming available from small carriers able to sail with the convoy. Improved offensive tactics coming from better short wavelength radar's, the 'Talk Between Ships' (TBS) radio system and improved weapons. Co-ordinated groups of warships specifically tasked with hunting down and destroying the U-boats. What worries remained passing completely as the superbly organised American shipyards began building Liberty ships faster than they could be sunk.

Following its North African success, British and American troops crossed the Mediterranean to invade and conquer Sicily. Italy's early surrender leaving Germany on its own in opposing allied intentions, something it did in a series of well marshalled defensive actions. Even the inspirational decision to land forces well behind German defensive lines at Anzio during January of 1944 disappointed. The opportunity appearing to lack the urgency that would have made it decisive, shades perhaps of Suvla Bay in another war.

The opening of the second front, long demanded by the Soviet leader Joseph Stalin, finally began with the arrival of Allied glider borne forces and paratroops during the night of the 5th/6th June 1944. Under the overall commanded of General Dwight Eisenhower, the main invasion fleet arrived off the French coast at dawn to fight its way ashore on the Normandy beaches. Landings also taking place in Southern France, east of Toulon a couple of months later. On all fronts the allied armies overwhelming firepower chewed up German strength, a slow grinding of gains that remorselessly squeezed the Whermacht out of its occupied territories. The frontline approaching the German frontier by September, the temporary reverse at Arnhem changing nothing anymore than the final German fling through the Ardennes would do, the latter founding on obdurate American resistance.

Whatever obstacles existed to allied progress on the ground, there was little Germany could do any longer to prevent the relentless bombing offensive from hitting its targets day and day. The US Eight Army Air Force, having joined the fray in 1943, flew in by day, delivering precision attacks to supplement the destruction wrought by the blunter area attacks of the night flying RAF. Raids that repaid a thousand times over the treatment once handed out by the Luftwaffe. A campaign that reduced entire cities to total ruin, causing more than six hundred thousand civilian deaths. Only the organisational capabilities of Albert Speer, the remarkable efforts of her people, dispersal of production and the inhumane use of slave labour kept output high enough to service the German forces.

Despite these destructive attacks, Germany's technological leadership remained unchallenged. This was demonstrated less than a week after the Normandy landings when the first V1 flying bomb (a cruise missile) was launched against London. Much more frightening was the V2 rocket (a ballistic missile), the first arriving without warning on 8th September. Attacks that did not end until March the following year. Technical accomplishments matched by the design and production of jet and rocket aircraft and much more formidable, had they come earlier, versions of quieter submarines able to go faster underwater than they could on the surface.

Once American, British, Canadian and Free French forces were across the Rhine, cohesive resistance in the west more or less collapsed. Fighting becoming sporadic, if still bitter in some areas. The advancing troops moving through devastated cities, whatever sympathy this might have sparked quickly suppressed as the concentration camps of Belsen and Dachau gave up their secrets. Discoveries confirming the utter depravity behind Nazi efforts to annihilate the Jews and others. The Soviet army having already found this out for itself following the liberation of the huge Auschwitz-Birkenau concentration complex, just west of Krakow, Poland, during January of 1945.

Whatever the circumstances in the west, fierce fighting went on in the east to the very end. Courageous action by surviving elements of the German army holding against incredible odds, buying time to allow much of its civilian population to flee westwards. A significant part of that evacuation carried out by ships operating on the Baltic sea in an operation conducted under extreme duress.

The end to this malice coming when Soviet forces, having finally penetrated into eastern Germany and the Balkans, mustered its strength for the final attack on Berlin under the direction of Marshall Georgi Zukhov. In this last major action in the European theatre, both Russian and German casualties were horrendous in a battle fought with animal ferocity. Acceptance of the Allied terms that called for Germany to unconditionally surrender finally conceded on the 8th of May 1945.

This left only the need to defeat Japan in the Far East, a nation that even at the height of its power was entirely dependent on shipping to feed its factories and re-supply distant garrisons. Arteries that proved all too vulnerable to interdiction by submarine and mines. This issue was highlighted quite early on when its most distant possession, Guadacanal in the Solomon Islands, was invaded by US forces during August of 1942. A prolonged slugging match eventually won by American marines, not least because of the difficulties Japanese forces had in reinforcing the island. Less successful were early British attempts to get back into Burma, a Japanese counter-offensive arresting progress.

The rest of 1943 was used building strength to sustain the prolonged offensives that would converge on the Philippines from two directions. Landings at Tarawa during November teaching valuable lessons that would also be applied to coming operations. Increasingly isolated from the necessary raw materials, the war turned decisively against Japan during 1944 when the fast carriers and amphibious groups started rolling up the Japanese in the south and central Pacific. While back in Burma an allied force composed of British, Indian, American and Chinese troops under General William Slim began sustained operations that would decisively defeat Japanese forces. Rangoon finally liberated during May of 1945.

At the beginning of 1944 the war finally reached the Japanese Home Island's, long range bombing raids starting from India, before transferring to the more convenient Mariana's Islands. The activities of these aircraft initially directing their attention towards destroying industrial targets before a later change in tactics saw massed raids using incendiary bombs to burn out the cities.

At sea the remaining ships of the once all conquering Imperial Navy met annihilation, firstly at the Battle of the Philippine Sea and later at the huge Battle of Leyte Gulf. Actions that confirmed to even the most die-hard Japanese leader that there was only going to one winner, its by now isolated forces usually electing to fight to the last man. The conquest of the Philippines, Iwo Jima and Okinawa characterised by bitter resistance that extracted a considerable toll on both sides.

The prospect of a bloodbath when Japan itself was invaded was a major consideration in the decision to use the atomic bomb, first on Hiroshima on 6th August and then Nagasaki three days later. A cease-fire finally agreed for the 15th August 1945, unconditional surrender taking place officially on 2nd September aboard the battleship, USS Missouri, in Tokyo Bay.

Chapter 17

The immediate post-war situation

For those of us without first hand experience of what was left at the end of the world's most destructive altercation, vast libraries of film and photographs supplement the countless books written since. From the Atlantic coast to the gates of Moscow, what once were cities, towns or villages were often marked simply by mounds of rubble. The Japanese home islands and much of the rest of the Pacific theatre experiencing similar fates. The wooden structures common to this part of world consumed by fires that left little but ash strewn space.

Providing an accurate death toll of the conflict is not easy, most estimates suggest around fifty million lost their lives. The Russians suffering around two-fifths of the total, as they did in the First Great War. Britain had fewer casualties this time around, slightly less than four hundred thousand service men and women were killed, with an additional sixty-five thousand civilians loosing their lives, mostly during the Blitz.

For the survivors of the wastelands life was often primitive, a struggle to keep body and soul together, especially for the millions of displaced peoples. Within Europe, these included Jews who had somehow managed to escape the maw of industrialised death. Remnants of a people journeying along side those who had fled the fighting, in particular several million Germans who left all they knew in East Prussia to escape the Russian advance. Wretched too were around six million men and women imported by Germany for use as forced labour in support of their war effort. A vast pool of people far from familiar surroundings, facing the legacies of abominable treatment and the insecurities of being in lands full of residual hostility.

Confirmation of the conditions at the time is not yet dependent on recorded media, there are still plenty who can remember and reminisce. People able to tell of the dying from neglect, disease and inadequate diet. Recalling that without a system of money, trade devolved to bartering for the necessities, cigarettes, chocolate, nylons and even sexual favours becoming the currency within widespread inflationary black markets. Industry, what was left of it, lay wrecked or simply unable to supply what was needed for peace, while agriculture limped along, lack of labour or the means to distribute its produce compromising what it could do.

It was a war that changed everything, demoting the nations of Europe and Japan from the ranks of world powers. Even victorious Britain forced to recognise that real power now rested with a previously isolationist America and a newly confident Soviet Union. The conveniences that held together the wartime alliance giving way to differing agendas that were already becoming apparent as the Soviet armies stayed onto become enforcers of a new order. America proving much more interested in the distractions of domestic needs and getting the troops home.

Despite the problems, principled hopes were bright, many resting on the potential of the United Nations (UN). Those behind this body advocates of getting beyond the narrow confines of national interest by creating a forum where the squabbles and tensions between states could be resolved. As the natural successors to the League of Nations, promoters of these ideals were eager to endow authority, both moral and legal, to let the UN arbitrate over international relations. Extensions to these far reaching ends coming when the UN formalised the broader hopes of its architects by setting out a Universal Declaration of Human Rights towards the end of 1948, a year already in fear of new tensions and dangers.

For Britain, the aftermath of the fighting meant facing up to a bankrupt exchequer. The lack of preparation to fight an all out war meant it was not long before urgent help was needed from abroad to continue a fight in which it rapidly became the only opposition to triumphant Germany. While America proved willing, it wanted paying, Britain's spare cash soon running out. By war's end matters were dire, straightened circumstances complicated by its banker, America, turning inwards to deal with its own concerns. Circumstances that made it much more difficult for the nation to shoulder the raft of burdens it faced in a ruined world.

These issues were aggravated by the understandable ambitions of the domestic population to have some tangible reward for what it had accomplished. Desires encouraged by those who sincerely believed this bounty could and should be delivered right away. Behind this belief were the intellectuals, their stature much enhanced by their wartime contributions. Voices having weight and influence that would lead to what proved unrealistic and fanciful. Decision making aided by over-confidence amongst those who ran the show during the war and would do so in the peace. The unquestionable success of central government in unique wartime conditions succeeding in convincing many that it could deliver every need and solve every problem.

Of necessity, before Britain's post-war history can be properly evaluated, there is a need to reflect on the wider change in circumstances the fighting brought about. This look has to consider the role America was to play through its economic and political leadership. Support that would prove essential in sustaining the very idea of liberty as the world fell into the maw of ideological division.

Chapter 18

America and youth

If there was a winner from the misery wrought by the Second World War, it was undoubtedly America. Not only did it transform and lift its economy by sweeping away the lingering memories of the Great Depression, but its central role in helping secure victory supplied unprecedented levels of confidence to its leaders and people. It was this strength that would be harnessed in the prolonged effort to defend democracy. A sense of mission that relied on exploiting the advantages of the market economy, an asset that allowed it to deliver unsurpassed standards of peacetime living for its own population while still bankrolling its many weakened allies under a protective umbrella secured by matchless military might.

It might appear strange then, that it was in America, amidst all the idealism and plenty that human contrariness manifested itself so strongly. Putting down roots that would infect the world with ideas both good and bad. Forces that were to disturb the basis of stable societies, creating in their wake intractable social problems. The ease with which these ideas were to spread throughout the world evidence of our vulnerability as a species to ideas that are not necessarily in our long term interests.

Intriguingly, the early impetus for these changes began from the wholly unintended consequences created by the GI Bill of Rights (Servicemen's Readjustment Act). A Bill passed in 1944 by the US Federal government that offered various benefits, including financial assistance for veterans who elected to continue their education. To cope with the huge demand, colleges and universities rapidly expanded in size. The staggering technological development stimulated by war's necessities introducing extended curriculum's, subjects taught by a mix of tutors old and new, many already influenced by the radicalising ferment of the 1930's. Teachers who naturally encouraged the uniquely matured generation of students cramming themselves into the overcrowded classrooms to consider and reflect on unfamiliar ideas. Not that this appeared to have much in the way of impact, they were after all a student body as markedly different from their forebears as they would be from those who followed.

Succeeding intakes to these institutions were mainly the products of comfort. Youngsters granted unprecedented freedom during their teens by parents eager to indulge their off-spring. Comparative independence augmented by having their own money contributing to the development of self confident generations who set about defining their own trends. Seeking individual expression through differing styles of music, dress and even language. For most, this life still remained within rules set by parents and the wider family, a sense of order supported by the entire hierarchy of society right into government. Restrained demeanour and clear ideals the guiding principles, only those on the very fringes gave any hint of what was to come. Bohemian outlooks earning a few the nickname of 'beatniks,' harbingers of radical youth's rise.

Long before any negative effects showed themselves, the principle gainer from this surge in academic activity was America's economy, its intellectual wants supplied by the ever expanding output of its universities and colleges. A system feeding the growing research and development programmes with productive talent. Year on year this cycle created a burgeoning reservoir of intellect that cemented the decisive economic advantages already enjoyed by the United States. Each successive intake helping drive technological development as well as offering thinking room for those flirting with what was different.

This was already apparent by the time a youthful John F. Kennedy gained the Office of the President of the United States in 1960. His inaugural address, one of history's greater orations, identifying in part with these dissatisfactions. His redress, a call for America to take the lead, a confident cry befitting its status as leader of the free world. Critical scrutiny of that challenge and the hopes he expressed getting lost in the enthusiasms, glamour and sophistication he and his wife, Jacqueline, represented.

As his term in office progressed, day to day dramas weighed heavy, Russian and Cuban collusion reinforcing domestic tensions related to racial and economic segregation. His untimely passing to an assassins bullet merging into a complex period haunted by the expanding war in Vietnam. The television camera, wielded by a politically interested and savvy media, acting as informer, intellectual arbiter and propagandist. Bringing into every living room the ugly realities of death in a distant place. The overtones swamping the public with the sort of contradictions that would in time undermine its ability to sift out the truth.

Strongly attracted by Kennedy's image and his high flown calls was America's youth, perhaps its fair to say much of the world's. While the majority were still comfortable with tradition, a growing band were finding that less than stimulating, some abandoning conventional life and its responsibilities altogether. Amongst the vanguard was a group establishing itself amongst the old Victorian mansions in the Haight-Ashbury neighbourhood of San Francisco. Eventually known as hippies, this laid back crowd with its long hair, brightly coloured attire and anti-establishment ethos would be joined by others who would embrace self righteous violence, storming the campuses and spilling onto the streets.

If the crucible of this movement was America, it was that country where this force earnt its political spurs through support for Civil Rights. A clear cut moral issue brought into sharper perspective by the voice and dignity of Doctor Martin Luther King. Its overdue demands gaining fresh political impetus at the highest levels, initially through executive actions instigated by President Kennedy. Efforts later translated into legislative form under a comprehensive programme introduced by President Lyndon Johnson as part of his Great Society initiative. The political momentum he unleashed accompanied by a widening breakdown of societal restraint. Racially motivated riots by ordinary black people fed up with getting the short end merging into later actions by the pampered offspring of Middle America. The latter's indignation centring on America's involvement in South Vietnam.

The sum of these measures addressed some of the legacies of inequality, segregation and ingrained poverty as well as providing an outlet for anti-war sentiment. What they also indicated was the extent to which circumstances were changing, events reaching tragic highs in 1968 when political assassination deprived America of two of its brightest, Martin Luther King and Robert Francis Kennedy. That same year, French and Czechoslovakian youth took up the cudgels, the former against an ageing and out of touch President, Charles de Gaulle, the latter in helpless frustration as Soviet tanks clanked around Wenceslas Square in the heart of Prague. The wilder elements of this international movement embracing open rebellion, extremes pursued by senseless killing over demands no sane nation could concede.

Yet for all the virulence of protesting youth, there was a strange selectivity to it all. Some wars drawing strong reactions, but not others, just as economic inequality on one continent seemed a cause for concern but was glossed over elsewhere. The most wilful of perversities reserved for the freest of political systems, America's own, which was suddenly portrayed by irrational elements amongst its own population as oppressive and vile. Ungrateful vehemence whose twisted logic would see the cause of legitimate reform hijacked and distorted by fanatics.

The originators of these weird ideas, the source of the Sixties counter-culture, were Germanic in origin. In the early 1920's the Institute for Social Research in Frankfurt University explored extending Marxist philosophy by incorporating social and cultural factors. Many advocates of this thinking leaving Germany for the United States following the rise of National Socialism, bringing with them concepts that ripened, before flowering during the Sixties. Ideals overturning classical liberal thought, replacing it with an intolerant bullying ideology we know today as political correctness.

Hand in hand with this irrationality were creative edges, none more memorable than the blossoming of music. Less inventive was the quest for personal expression, some reaching fulfilment in a psychedelic haze of drugs, others through the pursuit of sexual promiscuity. Foundations for licence whose endorsement by both men and women opened the door to what was once unacceptable. Less obvious were the planting of seeds that sought to inculcate guilt in men in particular and white people in general.

A perverted logic that began by poisoning academia before infecting society as a whole. Its most destructive outcome, the driving of a wedge into the life of the vulnerable. That lower strata of society who might always struggle economically, but normally would find compensations of a sort in family, good example, well defined rules and realistic expectations. Instead, encouraged to cast aside the disciplines of the past by those who should have known better, more and more dropped into a life blighted by helplessness, educational failure, drug dependency, criminal activity and emotional hardship. The entrenching division of society that came to afflict America, Britain and just about everywhere else.

Chapter 19

A bipolar world

The ending of one form of war in 1945 proved just the beginning of another. Its protagonists finding motivations in entirely different concepts of society. On one side, the intellectual appeals of a State governed centrally through elaborate bureaucracy, one where planning, processes and controls were supposed to provide equality of outcome. On the other, freer regimes giving space to the natural realities of human difference, the flowering of its creative energies only loosely constrained.

As far as the latter is concerned, as any examination of human activity past or present shows, that whenever someone grows, catches or invents something it has the potential to attract the attention or interest of someone else. Historically, this natural draw gave rise to the bilateral system of barter, deals being struck by swapping one thing for another, an arrangement serving mutual ends. Over time this process became more formalised, those with something to sell meeting those who wanted to buy in a place called a market. When more than one individual sold the same thing, the competition between them favoured the one with the best goods and keenest prices. Supply and demand proving itself as a self regulatory mechanism that determined price, scarcity driving up the cost, surfeit reducing it. The advent of money made this trading easier, lubricating as it were our innate entrepreneurial spirit, the most industrious and perceptive earning the most.

The mixing of suppliers and buyers in a market brings together those who have decided what products they intend to offer along with those who freely determine what and when they will buy. The correctness of their respective judgements subject to constant testing in an infinitely responsive mechanism that continually adapts to price, product improvement as well as fashions. One that supports a continual search for advantage, anything that gives an edge to the seller provides the chance of increasing market share and profit, just as it benefits the buyer who always wants the best value for money. Eventually the very term market expanded to incorporate the entire field that allows suppliers and buyers to gain access to each. Whether this be via specialised venues such as shops or some other channel like the Internet.

Further natural benefits of this free wheeling mechanism comes from its responsiveness to innovation. Anyone who can demonstrate a practical method or new machine that gives advantage will soon finding those willing to try it. Mechanised production using steam power effectively sold itself because of the flexibility and practical advantages it offered. A fact seized on and put to use by a number of far thinking Briton's and others who led the industrial revolution. The industries they created and those that depended on them turning into money spinning ventures. Even if the price of this early mechanisation was, in the beginning, severe on the workers.

It was in fact the very grimness associated with early industrial life that drew two German writers, Karl Marx and Friedrich Engels, to investigate. Their conclusions forming the basis of a manifesto advocating revolutionary political and economic change. Its foremost tenet requiring the nationalising of all industry and agriculture, the resultant entity would then be directed by a hierarchy who would ensure what was needed would be produced or grown on time in the right quantity and at the right cost. Perfect fairness ensured by dictating how much each worker would be given, the guarantee of sufficiency doing away with the supposed iniquities of the free economy with its petty obsessions and concerns with private property.

When the chance came to put this system into practice things turned out to be more awkward. Those in charge usually being unable to understand what they asking others to do. Inflexible detailed planning making it difficult to incorporate innovation, never mind display the capacity to adapt or respond to consumer wants. As a result, buyers found themselves having to accept what was on offer irrespective of quality or quantity. The primacy of political consideration leaving little room for educated initiative or enthusiasm amongst workers whose lives became locked to industries that all too often proved wasteful and dangerous.

None of this had a chance however until the early part of the twentieth century when the gathering chaos in Russian life presented what was known as socialism with its first chance. A critical factor in gaining that opportunity owed to interpretations Vladimir Lenin applied to the work of Marx and Engels. His practical insight providing a way of translating their theories into a political movement capable of seizing power despite setbacks. The triumph of the Bolshevik revolution in October of 1917 as much his as anyone's. A success that led to the implementation of the command economy under a regime that soon distanced itself from any pretence of interest in humanity, though the full ramifications of this took some time to show.

Soviet Russia's immediate hope was to try and export its success by force, the victorious Russian Red Army invading newly independent Poland in 1919. The intention from there being to expand the revolution into unstable Germany. However the Poles won the day, leaving Russia to endure defeat, loss of territory and a grudge it would avenge later.

It was the early death of Lenin that changed the direction of the revolution, power accumulating into the hands of Josef Stalin. A man who manipulated events to ensure his own position as absolute ruler, sidelining and then exiling Lenin's heir apparent, Leon Trotsky, before having him murdered in Mexico in 1940. Just one death amongst the millions of Russians who were to lose their lives in the deliberately engendered famines and political purges of the 1920's and 30's Ugly consequences consistently denied by many a star struck western acolyte of the communist ideology.

The historic inevitability of world dominance communists thought would be theirs, having been put on the back burner during the war, was to find its big chance in the aftermath of defeat for Germany. The part Soviet Russia played in that monumental conflict elevating it to superpower status, a seat at the top table guaranteed when Britain and America joined with Russia in a Grand Alliance against Germany and its allies. As the war unfolded and events favoured only one outcome, relations between the three, which were in reality only a convenience, began to suffer. Stalin out manoeuvring both Franklin Roosevelt and Winston Churchill at the important meeting of the Big Three at Yalta on the Crimea during February of 1945.

The key issue was Poland, especially in British eyes. After all it had gone to war on its account and remained loyal to the idea of providing its people with the opportunity to chose their own future. For a time it appeared as if Stalin was prepared to concede to free Polish elections from comments made at Yalta and reported in Churchill's memoirs. An essential acceptance, for it was Soviet troops that liberated and occupied its soil, having first stood within sight of Warsaw and allowed the German army a free hand in crushing the uprising of the Polish underground during August of 1944. The future however was to dash whatever hopes were carried away within a fading President Roosevelt and still robust Winston Churchill. Their rendezvous aboard the American warship, the USS Quincy in Alexandria harbour (Egypt) during a pause on the homeward journey was to be their last.

In the few weeks of life left to President Roosevelt, his remaining strength ebbed in a stiffening atmosphere. Though lengthy correspondence flowed between the Big Three aimed a keeping alive the opportunities, Churchill found it frustrating as Russian attitudes stretched the spirit of the Yalta agreements over broadening the Polish government. Events in Romania, where a Soviet inspired government had been installed without consideration to local feeling, furthered worries. Russia's own sensitivities erupting over belated acknowledgement that two secret meetings had taken place without their knowledge between representatives of Kesselring's Italian based German forces and American and British officials in Berne, Switzerland during March. Although nothing was achieved by these German overtures, the explanations provided to Stalin fed his suspicions.

Stepping into this awkwardness was the new President of the United States, Harry Truman, successor to America's great leader, Roosevelt, who died on the 12th of April. Lacking the necessary familiarity, Truman felt his way, his natural decisiveness relieving some of Churchill anxieties when he suggested a joint message to Stalin over the Polish question. A step soon overtaken by events as surviving members of the Polish underground were picked out by the Russians and carted off to meet misery and death in the far flung camps of the Soviet Gulag (a system of harsh labour camps). A duplicity confirming the views of experienced counsellors like Averell Harriman, US Ambassador to Moscow, who had already surmised that Soviet designs meant asserting total control over the countries it liberated and occupied. Growing Anglo-American recognition of this fact reinforced when the Soviet Union declared a provisional government in Austria, the access expected by visiting American, British and French missions to Vienna in line with agreements, hindered or denied.

Subject to so many pressures and with war still raging in the Pacific, US attitudes adjusted to the realities of avoiding any situation that might lead to confrontation with Russia in Europe. The greater neutrality of this position failing to accord with Churchill's own view of the dangers presented by Soviet intentions. Concerns summarised by the British Prime Minister in a telegram to Truman on 12th May, where for the first time mention was made of an iron curtain separating old allies. Clear acknowledgement that what was happening behind this wall was beyond understanding or influence of either Britain or the US. An unpleasant fact, but one that had to be faced, whatever British ideas might be over Poland or anywhere else.

Getting in the way were other considerations, foremost amongst American interests was the need to get Soviet agreement to the establishment of the United Nations. This coming on the 26th of June 1945 when it was signed into existence in San Francisco. By that time the Allied Control Council had been in power in Germany for three weeks and, in accordance with the agreed boundaries, the planned withdrawal of British and American forces into their respective zones of occupation were well advanced. Moves briefly delayed at the request of Stalin until 1st July due to his need to have all his senior people in Moscow for discussions.

Such was the general scene for the final meeting of the 'Big Three' at Potsdam to the west of ruined Berlin in mid July. The leaders, along with the incoming British Prime Minster Clement Attlee, who attended at Churchill's invitation and would take over from him halfway through, met to decide on how to settle matters arising from the defeat of Germany. Besides confirming its demilitarisation, it went on to set the western border of Poland along the Oder-Neisse rivers. More contentiously the conference adjudged that it was in the interests of Europe's future security that Germans living outside of German borders be returned. The mass expulsions conducted to meet this objective resulting in at least a million perishing (perhaps as many as two million), mainly due to starvation and disease. Over the question of reparations, where Soviet demands were severe, Anglo-American insistence that these be limited prevailed, undoubtedly based on the earlier experiences after the First World War. Finally agreed was Russian entry into the war against Japan, an unnecessary move, following the successful test and use of the atomic bomb.

Demobilisation of excess British and Commonwealth forces and, those of the United States based in Europe, was already underway before the Japanese surrender. The unexpected end in the Pacific speeding up a process that would see the bulk repatriated in remarkably short time. By the end of 1946 more than four million British service men and women had been released to return to civilian life, while the substantially larger American army was reduced by nearly ninety percent. At the same time huge quantities of armaments were scrapped, disposed of or mothballed. The Soviet Union being rather more circumspect, its standing army only reduced by about half, leaving in place a capable force of over six million.

Wars end also relegated US interest in Europe and elsewhere in favour of a long neglected domestic agenda. Facing a raft of strikes and aggressive demands by trade unions at home, Truman's plans to convert back to a peacetime economy came under threat. This loss of attention combined with disarmament sucked the vitality out of the Anglo-American alliance at a critical juncture. Although American, British and French forces remained in occupation in Germany, the necessary will needed to bolster their standing fell on Britain who lacked the strength to contest Soviet ambition on her own. Untroubled by the domestic matters so vexing to the west, Stalin was able to weigh the opportunities before him with confidence. Establishing Soviet fief over the areas it liberated while scenting advantage elsewhere.

Britain's importance at this point largely hung on the stature gained from being a victorious combatant. Its rightful position as an occupying power making it responsible for the northern half of western Germany and one of the four segments of Berlin. It was on the front line so to speak, the cost of this relevance proving a significant drain to an exhausted exchequer. Adding to these burdens was the humanitarian crisis then developing in Europe over the winter when famine threatened, a further need it sought to counter. It was opportune that America's internal distractions did not exclude it from providing substantial aid, including the acquisition and delivery of six million tonnes of wheat early in 1946.

A bare month later, on the 5th March, President Truman sat adjacent to Winston Churchill at Westminster College, Fulton, Missouri, where in a speech Britain's wartime leader elaborated on earlier thoughts regarding the changes taking place in Europe. Uttering this prophetic sentence, *'From Stettin in the Baltic to Trieste in the Adriatic, an iron curtain has descended across the continent.'* While insufficient in itself to persuade the President or the American public into active renewal of its alliance with Britain. More aggressive persuasions were not long in coming courtesy of communist hopefuls who took on the standing government of Greece. Using aid supplied by Yugoslavia, Albania and Bulgaria, these insurgents burned with the idea of converting democracies cradle into something less agreeable.

The requirements of a strengthened response finding real urgency when the British government, straining under its own economic difficulties and the severe February weather of 1947 recognised it could no longer support the situation in the eastern Mediterranean. Advising Washington of this fact served to highlight the enduring weaknesses across Europe and the dangers of political instability. To counter this deterioration, President Truman sought authority from Congress on the 12th of March for $400 million to be used to supply economic and military aid to Greece and Turkey. Setting in motion what became known as the 'Truman Doctrine.'

Adding further momentum to US and European interests were further words spoken by Winston Churchill in a speech he gave at Zurich University in Switzerland on 19th of September 1946. Calling for a United States of Europe founded on partnership between France and Germany. One that would bring together those willing to build the future its people would want. It was a call he emphasised still further at the Royal Albert Hall on 14th May of the following year, devoting his thoughts to the ideal of European unity. Including for the first time the idea that Britain might lead in this aim rather than act as well-wisher. It was a call heard and echoed by the US Under Secretary of State, Dean Acheson, who noted that so far, US assistance had kept Britain solvent and prevented starvation across ruined Europe. The long term aim however, ought to focus on establishing a co-ordinated continental economy. In Acheson's mind was the hope that Britain would take a major role in leading it towards this self sufficiency.

These thoughts were echoed by the US Secretary of State George Marshall in a speech at Harvard where he remarked, that it was going to take much longer than anticipated to rebuild Europe, a task the US should lead. This far reaching speech hinted of major aid, its realisation the Marshall Plan, a generous package of credit approved by Congress that helped to promote the needed confidence to assist in the rebuilding of Europe. Offered from the word go to all European nations including the Soviet Union, Moscow's refusal on behalf of itself and its satellites served to reduce internal criticisms within US political circles, which later approved a similar package for Japan.

With the war-time alliance fading into history, perceptive American minds recognised the need to counter the tempting intellectual appeals of communism and the commitment of its adherents. The man most associated with framing such a basis was George Keenan, then head of the US State Departments Policy Planning Unit. He pointed out that the principle aim of US policy should be to deter Soviet expansion by steadfast planning and actions. Going onto say that the attitudes and ambitions of the Soviet Union were unlikely to change until the internal nature of the Soviet system itself changed. Seeking in his reasoning to move America away from the principle of violent response that, owing to near total post-war demobilisation, leant heavily on having the ultimate weapon, the atomic bomb.

Any doubts about the seriousness of the threats were swept aside when Europe was convulsed by strikes and other acts of violence stirred by left leaning elements keen to challenge democracy. Overt Soviet muscle flexing during February of 1948 when it engineered a coup that removed Czechoslovakian freedoms and brought it under its control. Only Yugoslavia, under its charismatic leader Broz Tito, remained independent of Russian fiat. Tensions reaching new peaks over Berlin, the city already divided by wartime agreement between the four powers, lay deep within the Soviet occupied zone, with all road and rail links to the western allied sectors under Russian control. Following the Anglo-American decision to assist in the rebuilding the West German economy, these routes were cut on 24th June. A challenge met by a decision to supply the French, British and American sectors and its two million people by air. A massive Anglo-American airlift sustaining the city until land links were restored nearly a year later.

This event fundamentally altered attitudes, it becoming obvious that economic recovery on its own was not going to be enough. There was a security issue that required a convincing arrangement capable of persuading the Soviet Union of western resolve and commitment. The answer was found in the North Atlantic Treaty, signed in Washington by President Truman on the 4th April 1949. The pact created the North Atlantic Treaty Organisation (NATO), a defensive agreement imposing on its signatories, Belgium, Canada, Denmark, France, Iceland, Italy,

Luxembourg, Holland, Norway, Portugal, Britain and the US the duty to support one another should any be attacked. It came into force on the 24th of August, just five days before the Soviet Union exploded its own atomic bomb.

Awareness of these rising tensions between the two superpowers had already filtered into public conscious over the previous two years. Helping provide an understanding of what was going on were a series of articles by the American journalist, Walter Lippmann, it being he who popularised the term, Cold War. As one decade gave way to another this contest came to involve all manner of methods in pursuit of advantage, including diplomacy, economic temptations, military aid, overt and subtle intimidation, bluff, intelligence gathering and espionage, as well appeals to moral superiority, human rights and even war, often between client states.

Part of this dimension were attempts to hold onto colonial possessions, France facing strong resistance as it sought to re-assert its authority in Vietnam early in 1946. Britain itself coming to terms with an insurrection by Chinese guerrillas in Malaya a couple of years later. As these conflicts bubbled along the greatest of all communist successes occurred in China during 1949, when forces controlled by Mao Zedong (Mao Tse-tung) finally prevailed over the Nationalists in a long running civil war. It must have appeared to Stalin and other communist leaders that the gods were with them, as the scheduled withdrawal of American occupation forces in Korea went ahead despite the telegraphed dangers. The North Korean army taking advantage by marching south across the 38th Parallel during June of 1950. Only fortuitous Soviet absence from the UN Security Council allowed the US to mastermind a rapid response under the flag of the UN. A truly multinational force, including British contributions, spending the next three years in often desperate fighting.

Early defeat was avoided by an amphibious counter stroke planned by General MacArthur. The landing of US marines on the west coast of Korea at Inchon endangering the supply lines feeding the North Koreans offensive causing its collapse. The subsequent northward advance of UN forces itself the stimulus for massive intervention by China that soon pushed the UN forces back into retreat. After difficult fighting the situation was stabilised, settling down into a lengthy stalemate near its original starting point. Heavy UN firepower exacting a constant toll on the Chinese and North Korean forces until an armistice was finally conceded on 27th July 1953.

With the end of the Korean conflict and the defeat of the Malayan insurrection, the US Secretary of State, John Foster Dulles, inspired a number of treaties aimed at containing communist expansion. The Southeast Asia Treaty Organisation (SEATO) brought Australia, France, New Zealand, Pakistan, the Philippines, Thailand, Britain and the United States together. An alliance unable to salvage events in Indo-China where French forces went down to defeat at Dien Bien Phu during 1954 against the communist supported forces directed by Ho Chi Min. The following year, with NATO strengthened by West Germany's entry, the so called Baghdad Pact tied Iraq, Iran, Turkey, Pakistan and Britain into an alliance with the same purpose.

Back in Europe, irritations over Moscow's rule brought tensions to Poland and a major uprising in Hungary. After controlling the situation in Poland, Russian troops and tanks entered Hungary late in October of 1956, crushing the desire of its people for independence. A wretched moment coinciding with conspiratorial involvement of Britain, France and Israel over the Suez Canal in Egypt, a crisis that severely strained Anglo-American relations.

Much less amenable to a military solution was the steady haemorrhaging of people escaping from Soviet dominated east Europe. Almost a quarter of a million were getting away every year, by 1961 nearly 2.7 million had defected. The response of the East German leadership becoming the defining action of the Cold War when, virtually overnight on 13th August 1961, a wall was erected around west Berlin, all ninety six miles of it, a barrier soon extended down the entire east-west German border.

A year later, with tensions still high in Europe, the Soviet leader, Nikita Khruschev, and his Cuban counterpart, Fidel Castro, concluded a secret deal that allowed nuclear capable Soviet missiles to be based on Cuba. From the moment they were detected and brought to the notice of the American President, John Kennedy, on October 16th, intensive internal debates were conducted within the US hierarchy to work out what to do. This was articulated by the President on the 22nd in an announcement to the American people revealing both their presence and the proposed quarantining of Cuba by US naval and air forces. After days of high tensions that brought the world seemingly closer to a nuclear exchange than it ever had been before, a formula was found that allowed for their removal. A nerve tingling drama that sobered all sides and inspired the installation of a direct communications line (the hotline) between Washington and Moscow to help avoid future misunderstandings.

Following French failure in Indo-China, America's President, Dwight Eisenhower, was not alone in expressing concerns about a communist expansion taking over one nation after another, the so called Domino Theory. A worry that saw the commitment of modest support to the then South Vietnamese government. This was expanded by President Kennedy before regular American ground forces splashed ashore in ever larger numbers following the Tonkin Gulf Resolution obtained by President Lyndon Johnson.

Over the last half of the sixties and early seventies strenuous American efforts failed to achieve a military or diplomatic solution despite imposing horrendous casualties on Vietnamese forces. Indeed, inspired by questionable strategy and the toll of escalating American casualties without clear results, public support waned, increasing pressures to find a way out. Influences encouraged by distorted media coverage and interpretation, especially after the abortive Tet Offensive in 1968. South Vietnam failing to survive American withdrawal anymore than Cambodia was to escape from the insanity of the Khmer Rouge rule under the communist fanatic Pol Pot. His attempt to create a agrarian utopia resulted in the deaths of more than one and half million people from starvation and murder.

Despite Soviet persuasion, freedom's yearning did not desert the Czechoslovak people, their desire for it enjoying a brief flourish during the liberalising period known as the Prague Spring. Modest reforms overseen by Alexander Dubcek inducing fear in Moscow. Their answer, two hundred thousand troops and plenty of tanks to snuff it out lest the experiment prove contagious across its sphere of interest. This desperate act began on the night of 20th August 1968, marking the end of communist hopes of domination in Europe. In its place was the forging of a new consensus between the American President, Richard Nixon and the Soviet leader, Lenoid Brezhnev. Leaders drawn by the mutual interests of reducing the costs and anxieties of the Cold War. Genuine, though protracted, negotiations starting in Helsinki and ending in Vienna in May of 1972 delivering tangible gains through the restriction of anti-ballistic missile systems and limits on missile launcher numbers.

This period, referred to as détente, contributed to a reduction in international stress, one later threatened as the seventies drifted beyond its middle years. The culprit was technology, in this case the Soviet mobile ballistic missile system referred to as the SS-20. The accuracy of this new weapon raising fears of a shift in the nuclear balance within Europe. NATO's response was to deploy new ground launched missiles, ironically raising the ire of the politically active domestic populations of West Europe and Britain. Individuals who protested, as they often do, over measures that defend their right to shout.

The eventual outcome of the Cold War was decided by the election of Ronald Reagan as America's President. It was his vision, however impractical, of a defensive shield against nuclear attack, one firmly supported by Britain, the old ally under its sturdy Prime Minister, Margaret Thatcher, that led the two sides into the endgame. They were to find in new Soviet General Secretary, Mikhail Gorbachev, a sense of realism that allowed this latter day Big Three to share thoughts on how to bring the haunting spectre of superpower conflict to a close.

Chapter 20

The arms race

The great schism we know as the Cold War was essentially decided by the costs imposed by the research, design, development and manufacture of ever more deadly weapons. A race whose early stimulus was ironically derived from Anglo-American demobilisation after the end of the Second World War. A decision initially made comfortable by the security derived from American possession of the atomic bomb. By the time that advantage was negated following the successful Soviet atomic test in 1949, political events had moved on. A divided world making the decided conventional inferiority of the US and its allies a matter of grave concern.

Efforts to redress the imbalance started with the demands brought on by the Korean war, old weapons were put back into service alongside a sprinkling of newer variants. The products of necessity fed by accelerating defence spending. Once underway, two factors kept the momentum up, the competitive nature of the ideological contest itself and the lobbies created by what President Eisenhower called the military-industrial complex. The leaders of both superpowers having to cope with the powerful advocacy of their respective armed forces and the companies that supplied them.

The later decision by some democracies to do away with conscription in favour of fully professional forces added to the problems, not least because it condemned itself to permanent numeric inferiority. The decided solution to that problems was to seek offset by superior weaponry, arms serving as force multipliers. The trouble here was the underlying technology to make them more effective came at the price of making the weapons a great deal more expensive. Costs spiralling upwards as added complexity demanded more capable personnel to operate and use them, people that could only be drawn in by paying market rates.

From the well understood threats of the conventional weapons of the day, the dangers scaled upwards as science came to grips with all sorts of horrors, plenty of money refining of the means to kill. Money poured into every area, designing and producing ever more capable aircraft, better ships, heavier tanks, more accurate missiles and so on. Munitions as fiendish as they were deadly. A necessary and expensive adjunct were the improvements sought in intelligence gathering and surveillance using everything from ground based optical and electronic sensors to airborne radar's and even space based systems. Technology merging in with the older well established methods and techniques used by specialised intelligence agencies such as the KGB, the CIA and MI6.

While funding was stifled by other priorities from time to time, both sides remained in the race. Considerable resources being directed towards investigating the potential of nuclear, chemical and biological warfare, the end products having the capacity to threaten all humanity. While the details are beyond this account, some appreciation of its nuclear component is worthwhile, given that this weapon more than any other encapsulated the threats inherent in the Cold War.

Early nuclear weapons relied on nuclear fission, their explosively destructive power derived from the energy released by splitting the atom. More powerful bombs coming when both sides developed devices capable of harnessing nuclear fusion, a complicated process that releases bewildering amounts of energy when two light atomic nuclei are forced together to form something heavier. These awesome thermonuclear (hydrogen) weapons reaching deliverable form by the mid fifties. Later developments even seeing very high radiation cobalt and neutron bombs, although only the latter went into production and deployment for a short period. Intensive development of these devices reduced their physical size and weight without compromising their explosive power.

Interest in nuclear deterrence and the prestigious effects of ownership were factors in Britain's own programme. Its first fission weapon, exploded late in 1952, was followed five years later by successful test of a fusion device. France also proved its technical prowess at the start of the sixties, followed a few years later by China and eventually India and Pakistan. Shrewd suggestion also adds Israel to the list of nuclear capable nations, while Iran would like to be, North Korea having perhaps recently surrendered this ambition.

Over the years the size of the superpower arsenals grew to staggering levels, the use of only a small part easily capable of killing off much of the human race, even if this meant condemning it to slow starvation.

With the command and control organisations so well protected, and the missile systems often deployed at sea in large submarines, retaliation was virtually guaranteed. Such was the principle of deterrence, one based on Mutually Assured Destruction (MAD), a concept recognised and articulated early on by the scientists that led the research programmes which led to these devices in the first place.

As with conventional bombs, the need is to get the weapon to the target. Early nuclear devices were large and heavy, which meant the only way was by aeroplane, improvements adding greater range, faster speed and higher flyable altitude. However, given the successful use of the German V-2 rocket during the war, it was logical for both sides to mount the thing on a missile. German scientists, many of whom were tempted by life in America after the war, were important contributors to this effort in the United States. While German technicians were inveigled, one way or another, into helping the work that saw Soviet Russia leading the way in the race to dispatch a bomb from one continent to another by ballistic trajectory. The Soviet Union demonstrating such a missile in 1957, its lead failing to survive for long as a determined United States caught up and forged ahead. The race entering a new dimension when the Soviet Union tested a submarine launched missile, something taken to its logical conclusion by America when it launched it own version, the Polaris missile.

While indirectly related to the arms race, the most important spin-offs in terms of world prestige was the use of rocket and electronic technology to conquer space. Triggered by the technical triumph of the Soviet's Sputnik, the earth's first artificial satellite, America felt further humiliation on 12th April 1961 when the Russian, Yuri Gagarin, orbited the earth in the Vostok 1 spacecraft. To a world keen with interest an American response was certain, this came when the US President, John Kennedy, committed America to landing a man on the moon before the 1960's was over. Despite that goal, almost all the early accomplishments came out of the Soviet efforts. The concentrated US programme finally catching up and leaving Russia behind, its aims accomplished on the 21st of July 1969 when Neil Armstrong stepped out onto the surface of the moon.

After more than forty years of pouring money into the black hole of military spending the Cold War died. The decisive period had been the 1980's when the enduring ability of the American economy to sustain high levels of military expenditure while still supplying the bulk of its people with a standard of life better than anyone else could enjoy fully exposed the limits of the Soviet economy. The hopes of the Soviet leader Mikhail Gorbachev had for his liberalising measures dashed when they only served to release the pent up forces within the USSR and its satellites. By the end of 1991 that once great empire had simply fragmented, leaving America and its allies without an immediate cause.

Chapter 21

Reconstruction

The framework responsible for the extraordinary burst of human creativity and productivity following six years of demolition was built on a meeting of influential and distinguished minds. The financially able of some forty-four nations gathering at Bretton Woods, New Hampshire during July of 1944 to discuss what would happen when the dying ended. At the head of a queue of problems they were to consider was the need for money to fund recovery and growth.

These proceedings were dominated by two great figures with contrasting visions of how this might be accomplished, Harry Dexter White, chief international economist at the US Treasury and Britain's foremost expert in these matters, John Maynard Keynes. Given the preponderance of US influence at that stage it was not surprising White's concepts largely prevailed in an agreement establishing rules that would govern international monetary affairs for the next quarter of a century. Each founder member agreeing to policies that would allow fixed currency exchange rates. An arrangement underpinned by the US dollar acting as the world's reserve currency, America's commitment reinforced by its decision to link the value of the dollar to gold at the rate of $35 to the ounce.

Freedom of trade was to be a vital ingredient. A significant step along this path provided by the General Agreement on Tariffs and Trade (GATT), twenty three nations in all signing up to its provisions. While elsewhere, in the financial details, were hopes of making all currencies fully convertible with one another, facilitating trade by allowing money to be easily swapped. To oversee and administer these and other far seeing initiatives, two organisations were established, the International Monetary Fund (IMF) and the International Bank for Reconstruction and Development (IBRD-now a part of the World Bank).

The United States own conversion back to a peacetime regime was swift, federal spending falling nearly 90% in the five years up to 1950. The demobilisation of millions of men and women from military duty becoming beneficiaries of generous provisions contained in the GI Bill. An instant market for the products of a peaceful economy. On top of holding more than two-thirds of the world's gold reserves, America's substantial balance of payments surplus allowed it to act as banker to Europe and Japan, with first public and later private capital.

For Europe, the situation was dire, though what the right policies could do was demonstrated by Belgium early on. Overall however, what was really needed was a boost, something to spark confidence. This was to come from a renewal of US interest, its tangible form, the offer of significant material assistance through the European Recovery Programme (ERP), commonly called Marshall Aid. It's perhaps fair to suggest that its key effect was more emotional than anything, the willingness of the world's number one power to extend a helping hand to a group of struggling nations so that they might help themselves provided the confidence that was lacking. For whatever reason the Soviet Union, on behalf of itself and its satellites, refused this generosity, sixteen other nations sharing some $13.6 billion of conditional aid and credit. Funds that allowed imports to be financed, or help extended to allow the rebuilding of the private and national infrastructures around which private consumption could be restored.

These sums however were insufficient in themselves if the right policies were not invoked, nowhere was this more apparent that in defeated Germany. Its subsequent recovery based more on actions taken by Ludwig Erhard, then director of the organisation directing economic policy in the Anglo-American occupation areas, than Marshall Aid. His grasp of the inhibiting effects on economic activity by the wage and price controls implemented by the Allied Control Commission was crucial. Following the introduction of the new Deutsche Mark in 1948 he chanced his arm by scrapping this regulatory framework against prevailing advice. Two years later industrial production had trebled as the hard working Germans got stuck into the task of creating a miracle that left Britain far behind.

Erhard's free market approach depended on several complementary factors. Firstly, the adoption of astute monetary policies by the German central bank which encouraged firms to get out and compete in export markets instead of relying on trade barriers or financial help from an overly protective government. Secondly was the creation within industry of an attitude of partnership between the owners and their workers, ensuring the settling of differences without the sort of rancour that was to derail progress in Britain. Lastly was the availability of labour, initially from the influx of ethnic Germans expelled from other countries, then, as these were absorbed, the pool was constantly topped up by people leaving the land to work in industry. Numbers supplemented later by the steady flow of immigrants escaping from Soviet occupied East Germany and elsewhere.

Well before any of this had any real impact, American incentives for Europe to consider economic integration were in evidence. While national opinions were initially reluctant, this route gained slow favour, beginning with the formation of the Organisation for European Economic Co-operation (OEEC) in 1948. Its original purpose in helping administer the Marshall Plan expanded by setting up the European Payments Union (EPU) to address the constraints in bilateral trade due to currency bottlenecks. The first major step towards supranational integration coming in 1951 with the establishment of the European Coal and Steel Community (ECSC).

Japan's recovery, the other post-war economic miracle, was initially tied to the policies implemented by then Supreme Commander of the Allied Powers, General Douglas MacArthur. His early focus, of necessity, concentrating on getting humanitarian aid to stifle urban starvation before turning towards forming a democratic structure. Early work with Japanese administrators to rebuild the economy using injections of $1.8 billion in a programme not dissimilar to the ERP.

Once again however, it was home grown policies that proved decisive, in Japan's case this came about from the creation of the Ministry of International Trade and Industry (MITI) in 1949. Though different from the German approach, the results were equally remarkable, MITI setting out from its inception to establish intimate relations with industry, allowing it to direct their capabilities in pursuit of national goals. Gaining in influence and authority over the next three years, MITI oversaw regulation of imports and the handling of foreign exchange to Japan's advantage in an economy largely protected from the outside world. Though a policy of low interest loans to targeted businesses identified as flag-bearers for Japanese expansion proved to be its most productive decision. Japan also benefiting from American military spending during the Korean War. The results were amazing, Japan soon leading the world in steel production and shipbuilding, also turning its energies and abilities towards making cameras, watches and much later, automobiles and consumer electronics. Low taxation assisting in its growth, which took off towards the end of the fifties, surpassing Germany as the world's number two in 1968.

The dynamism of general world recovery was beset quite early by worries regarding the underlying stability of the Bretton Woods agreement. Questions being raised in the early fifties as the balance of payments deficits posted by the American economy grew, although its substantial gold reserves and strong trading performance made it easy to dismiss, or at least gloss over these genuine concerns. The vital importance of the dollar in supplying the necessary liquidity to fund the ever expanding international trade expansion checked dissent. Even so, the numbers of dollars and, to a lesser extent, British pounds stockpiling in central banks as reserve assets made a financial crunch likely one day. One positive, the announcement by eleven West European nations that their currencies were now externally convertible striking a blow for Bretton Woods ambitions, Japan following just six years later in 1964.

The timely economic boost provided by the signature of President Kennedy to the largest ever tax cuts in American history during 1961 was soon to face compromise by the expenses associated with the Cold War and domestic social ambitions. Burdens that continued to weaken US ability to underpin the world's financial system. This became fully apparent following the assassination of Kennedy in 1963, his successor, Lyndon Johnson, embarking on large scale social reform. The costs of his Great Society programme meshing with the need to boost military spending as US involvement in Vietnam grew. The rapid escalation of that war over the latter half of the sixties combined with outflows of capital for investments purposes and spending by American tourists abroad bringing the issue to a head.

The collapse of Bretton Woods becoming a certainty when the US realised it was no longer feasible to honour its pledge to redeem dollars for gold. The quantity in circulation was simply too great in spite of co-operation from other countries. A half move towards the end followed British devaluation of the pound in 1967, the coincidental rush to exchange dollars for gold leading the American government to decline to convert privately held dollars into gold. The system coming off the rails altogether following the unilateral decision by President Richard Nixon on 15th August 1971 to suspend all gold convertibility.

While not unexpected, after all the search for a longer term solution had been under consideration since the early sixties, the immediate fix was something of a stopgap measure. Revaluation of the major currencies bringing some necessary realignment, though speculative pressures continued against the dollar. To counter this uncertainty the European Economic Community (EEC) introduced its own system early in 1972. Called the 'European Snake' this agreement tied the European currencies to each other within a set of rules that allowed for small fluctuations of each individual currency, the whole floating jointly against the dollar. It being clear the era of fixed exchange rates based on gold had reached its end, it abandonment coming early the following year in favour of currencies finding their own level.

In spite of the financial strains that would end Bretton Woods, world economic expansion continued apace throughout the sixties. Japan in particular seeing staggering growth, with cars, consumer electronics and cameras penetrating all markets. Europe, even with a lagging Britain, enjoying marked increases in living standards.

What would ultimately unsettle this comfortable picture were events in the Middle East, the fourth Arab-Israeli conflict during October of 1973 bringing rare unanimity to the Organisation of Petroleum Exporting Countries (OPEC). Using their muscle as a cartel, oil prices were quadrupled, with supply denied to those deemed supportive of Israel. This caused a number of problems, most immediate were energy shortages and increased costs for the oil importing nation that fed through into inflationary pressures. Something already evident due to fiscal in-discipline after the collapse of fixed exchange rates. As world demand eased back, unemployment began to rise, economic planners everywhere struggling to deal with stagnant economies. Complexities compounded by OPEC's growing surfeit of petro-dollars. Unable to sensibly spend or invest these vast sums, a solution was found by recycling the money through the banking system, mainly in the form of loans to nations in debt because of the rise in the price of oil, an answer that brought its own grief later.

Despite embarking on financial deregulation, the situation in the US worsened over the seventies, its currency continuing to fall in value despite efforts of an amalgam of Central Banks. Investors ditching dollars in favour of strong currencies such as the German Mark, the

Swiss Franc and Japanese Yen, even buying up gold, silver, real estate or works of art, almost anything rather than hold onto the dollar.

Giving this fragile structure a further good kick was Iran, a religious revolution during 1979 deposing the western orientated Shah. The price of oil once again rising sharply, boosting inflation and helping to further erode confidence in the methods that had to that point been used to manage national economies. Responding to what had by then become a severe crisis, the US government decisively shifted policy that October, adopting a package of anti-inflationary measures that caused interest rates to effectively double over the three years to 1982. A period that saw Ronald Reagan sworn in as US President, it being his administration that set an example by cutting government spending, reducing taxation and easing regulation. While this medicine was ultimately successful, the dollar exchange rates improving, it was unable to halt the steady downward spiral of the US economy and with it the world economies. Total trade failing to grow during 1981 for the first time since the end of the Second World War.

More worrying were the effects this sharp rise in interest rates had to those nations happily borrowing from the pool of petro-dollars to fund their own economic development. Many loans having been taken out at variable or floating interest rates. The cost of servicing this escalating debt simply proving too much for Poland, then Mexico and eventually around thirty other nations by 1984. It falling to the IMF to co-ordinate concessions from all sides to bridge the gaps, a far from easy undertaking for some nations.

The intensity of these pressures impinged directly on business competitiveness, forcing moves towards rationalised structures that improved productivity. Techniques such as just in time manufacturing proving insufficient to overcome high labour costs and the regulatory overheads of the advanced economies. Many companies adapted by concentrating production at a single site, others transferred operations overseas to a country where the labour was cheaper and conditions of business easier.

Unaffected by all this turmoil with its consumer concerns, the socialist empire led by the Soviet Union continued along stuck in second gear. Falling further behind the free world despite all the problems starting to plague the market economies. While able to benefit from industrial espionage and reverse engineering, its own creativity was frequently stunted except in few chosen areas. Adequate enough at housing, feeding and clothing its peoples, the real cream of its effort was swallowed by a bloated military and prestigious ventures that did not always offer tangible return.

Following the death of its indefatigable General Secretary, Lenoid Brezhnev and his short lived successors, Yuri Andropov and Konstantin Chernenko, the new Soviet leader Mikhail Gorbachev sought via modest liberalisation to introduce much needed economic improvements. Unfortunately these steps only served to increase dissatisfactions, unleashing an unstoppable momentum towards economic and political liberty, firstly amongst its eastern empire and then eventually within itself.

It was Hungary that made the real break, simply dismantling its barriers with Austria in May of 1989. By the end of that remarkable year the symbol of the Cold War, the Berlin Wall, was being hacked down by thousands of wildly exuberant Germans. The West German Chancellor, Helmut Kohl, declaring his intention to unify the two halves of Germany. By years end the fruits of victories won in the Great Patriotic War (World War 2) had gone, leaving the Soviet Union on its own to face a destiny that saw internal collapse without major conflict, surely one of history's most surprising events.

Transitioning from a command economy within a socialist empire to a market system proved no easy ride. Starved of investment and left with old, out of date industries, decision making was painful for all concerned. East Germany, bankrolled by its sister, was lucky, for the rest, including Russia and its former dependencies, falling production and wages squared off against rising prices and the inevitable need to struggle for the basics as an alien approach sought to put down roots. It did not appear to matter how it was handled, Poland jumped right in at the deep end while the Czech republic sought incremental change. Hungary managed to achieve a vigorous market economy, success also coming the small Baltic states of Estonia, Latvia and Lithuania, who embraced market reforms with flat rate taxation and much deregulation.

Elsewhere in the world as the last decade of the twentieth century got underway, there was plenty of worry. Central and South America remain troubled, the Latin economies growth out of debt meeting with reverse. Mexico having to devalue the peso and work hand in hand once again with the IMF in 1995, a huge bailout of $50 billion proving necessary.

Argentina remained reluctant to recognise the lessons of its own past, while Brazil experienced further nightmares in 1998 when investor confidence collapsed and capital ebbed away. Only prompt action by the IMF and other international lenders in co-operation with the Brazilian government stabilised things.

Much of Africa remains hopelessly backward despite substantial aid. A raft of aid agencies, charities, governments and Non Governmental Organisations (NGO) providing assistance that has so far led nowhere. Wastage of both funding and human talent seeing one of the richer continents held back by endemic political and economic incompetence.

Instability also reached into the Asian countries, nearly $120 billion from the IMF preventing the deterioration from spreading. Although here the picture was far from bleak, Japan and its free market partners of Singapore, Hong Kong and Taiwan followed by a vibrant South Korea and latterly China. Finally getting on board (at last) is India, its progress accelerating since it junked its extended obsession with socialist policies. Eager to join in are Indonesia, Thailand and Vietnam, the naturally industrious potential of all these peoples, if it can be sustained by political stability, will give the bulk of them the chance of a vastly improved life.

More than halfway through the first decade of the twenty-first century, the economic balance of the world has begun to shift. China, besides becoming the world's factory, has accumulated huge reserves of foreign currency, as has Japan, the United Arab Emirates and Russia. How this money will be used and for what purpose is open to question. Of particular concern here are the huge debts facing America, a factor in the slide of the dollar, its declining value matched by appreciation of the Euro. While Germany can cope, the weaker European economies are struggling, which could well strain continental unity.

It is abundantly clear the populations of the advanced nations are not prepared for economic hardship. Should the American economy slide down, it may well provoke the sort of crisis that could tip the world into a recession. Such a reverse in a more sensitive, crowded and less stable world is bound to be unpleasant for everyone.

Chapter 22

As it was

Victory in Europe Day, at least for those who were there or who have seen film of it, conjures up pictures of frenzied crowds jamming Whitehall, Piccadilly Circus and the open crescent of Memorial Gardens in front of Buckingham Palace. Those unable to get there more than likely sharing the moment in a local street party. Revellers whose efforts made the winning possible, a triumph guaranteeing their chance to decide the future.

They did not have to wait long, the coalition government that had steered the nation through difficult years, in fact since 1931 under various leaders, came to an end when the consensus on which it depended collapsed. Six years of life and death struggle leaving the nation hungry for a brighter future, one the shrewd Clement Attlee and the Labour Party he led recognised and promised to fulfil.

For Britain's wartime leader, Winston Churchill, and the party he represented, victory meant coming to terms with decisive electoral defeat. One of his last acts as Prime Minister summarising how he felt when he stepped down, a dignified statement that expressed his gratitude for the support and kindness he had received over the difficult years when he led the nation as its servant. And what a servant he had been, the one who more than any other had charted a safe course, steering the nation through its greatest ever trial.

Taking his place was a new leader and government, one made up of committed and intellectually gifted men and women. One commanding a parliament whose two Houses, the Commons and Lords, were crowded places where debates gave full rein to the range of talents of its members. Part of a healthy and vibrant democracy with its requisite interested and informed public. A nation whose citizens could look forwards to continuing to enjoy the historic right that allowed one and all to speak their mind. A prize buttressed by the opportunity to do as they pleased unless a law specifically excluded it. Safe in the knowledge that these laws applied to all in equal measure. Those with less charitable ideas having to deal with a police force whose role as citizens in uniform tasked them with protecting the law abiding by apprehending the criminally minded.

The foundations of these rights built on protections that reached back into Anglo-Saxon law, Magna Carta and the 1689 Bill of Rights. Securities enhanced by Habeas Corpus with its sticky insistence that evidence be subject to independent judicial review. The practical and careful system of Common Law which incorporated presumptions of innocence until guilt was established, also protecting the accused by ensuring that guilt was decided by a jury of his peers based on the evidence put before it. A decision reached in an independent court safe from the iniquities of hearsay and multiple trials for the same offence. The right to silence to avoid self incrimination adding further security to those who might be trapped by an incautious phrase. Rules whose collective weight meant the citizen was usually safe from the ever present desire of ruling elite's to throw their weight around.

In that late spring of 1945, the King, George the Sixth, stood as titular head of the nation. Spread out below were the ruling hierarchy, one now incorporating a wider cross section of the nation's blood. The old class structure, whilst still intact, had blurred following the wars impartial demand for talent irrespective of social accident. The imposition of national service plus rationing also acting to reduce the impact and distinctions of rank. One step down from this ruling class were the men and women who continued as the middle ranks, types drawn from the respected professions of academia, banking, teaching, medicine and others. The solid body of the land provided by the ordinary working man and woman, individuals whose lives had only just begun to glimpse the possibilities the future would hold.

The collective character of this mass, for all the variations that might be expected from its divisions, remained remarkably coherent. To the fore was a quiet formality, undemonstrative, disapproving of excitability and overly emotional displays. This holding back, the stiff upper lip as it were, characteristic of an adult world whose duties were clear enough for everyone to know what was expected of them and why. Behaviour remaining closely tied to a need for respectability, something attained through what was seen as proper behaviour.

The basis, the stereotype if one prefers, was the sturdy, self contained man or woman. One whose self restraint and disciplined honesty was matched to a quaint amateurishness that was in turn connected to a strong sense of fair play that seemed to inhibit prompt and decisive action. Often revealed as ambivalence to reality, it seemed that only war was to be capable of stripping it away. Which is what happened, events showing that underneath all this was an innate toughness with both a brittle edge and a ruthless streak. Conflicting traits that generated all manner of confusions, forces that need the firmest of leadership and a constant reinforcement of necessities to keep attention focused.

Despite these reservations, the conduct of the nation was courteous. The queues for everything invariably orderly and patient. That prickly sense of reserve, most often displayed towards strangers, remaining extant despite the common trials stimulating the feeling that we were one. A world where hypocrisy existed of course, plenty saying one thing and doing another, but at least where failure became known, judgement could be rendered against commonly understood virtues and standards.

Equally distinctive was the respect accorded to women, it being quite possible for a female to walk where ever she pleased, her very presence bringing adjustments to behaviour, altering the tenor of language. Part of an order that still prioritised the protection of women and children.

The primary pillar of this society was the married couple, an arrangement respected and supported for its practical contributions to the demands and lengthy complications of raising children. This independent unit mixed the efforts of the man and woman, the civilising warmth of the family a buffer against the uncertainties and hardships of life. When difficulties arrived and help was needed, the instincts were always to turn for help to one's kith and kin. Networks of relations including parents, grandparents, brothers, sisters and in-laws stepping into support, the State having little inclination to interfere in this everyday exchange.

Re-establishing the family's peacetime shape and role was of course subject to individual circumstances. With war still being fought in the Far East, many would continue to face uncertainty over whether loved ones would ever return. For those in Europe who were no longer required, demobilisation could not come fast enough. Joining them in returning home were thousands of liberated prisoners of war, many of whom had been cooped up in poor conditions for several years. Amongst this crowd were those who returned with the physical and mental injuries brought about by conflict. Conditions the medical profession of the time did their best to treat, although aftercare was often down the family, legacies that for some, only death would cure.

When it came to the fortunes of love, there were gainers and losers, husband's losing wives and wives losing husbands. Life however moves forward and amongst the fortunate were those who found romance in dangerous times, love made more intense by the uncertainty. Freed to make plans, many did not hesitate to make up for lost time by marrying and starting a family.

An important factor in this eternal quest was the assembly of fertile men in the lead up to the invasion of Europe. More than a million and half American's and half a million Canadian's along with a smattering of other nationalities forming the invading army. Men at the peak of their physical attractiveness with more money than the average Briton. Temptations aplenty for more than 110,000 British women who choose to wed their allied sweethearts and leave these isles come the peace. People joined by a further exodus over the next few years that saw quite a few tempted to take up the offers to emigrate to South Africa or Australia. Passage could be brought for ten pounds on condition that they stayed at least two years.

Inevitably some of those tempted by wartime romance were already married, creating the socially awkward problems of an child that belonged to someone else. Worse were those circumstances where a transfer of affections had been conveyed by a 'dear John letter.' A few, failing to get that warning, arriving home only to find their place already occupied. Even for the bulk who remained loyal, apart from the occasional mistake, it meant learning to live with one another all over again. Years apart inevitably bringing changes, a case of strangers who were joined by strangers, fostered children returning home from the country, some of whom never could settle.

Adding to all these headaches was a shortage of housing, the necessity of having to share limited accommodation having its drawbacks. While most country districts, smaller towns and villages had escaped physical damage, the concentrated night attacks during the Blitz had made a mess of larger cities like London, Coventry and Liverpool. The later use of flying bombs and rockets contributing to London's woes, psychologically more than physically. Inevitably the bulk of all this damage was inflicted on inner metropolitan areas and suburbs, large numbers of terraced and semi detached houses were wrecked, or at least damaged and in need of repair. While some of these were slum like and scheduled for demolition anyway, aerial bombing proved a poor tool for this task.

The solution, the only one in many cases, was doubling up, many families falling back on sharing with parents or aunts and uncles. Newly wedded couples often beginning their own life together in a cramped single room where they were usually joined by their first baby. Naturally this form of life had its inhibiting effects, although given that people were more used to sharing space with one another at the time, it was generally manageable, even if the constant proximity of people gave rise to occasional frictions.

Help was at hand from the entertainment of the day, radio and newspapers providing the link with the outside world in a way that reflected the understated tone of the day. A positive presentation and the absence of hype easing the affects on the ear and mind. Music and light entertainment remained important, both live and on the radio, most houses having a piano or some sort of musical instrument capable of being played by someone in the family. Conversation and gossip lubricated, people also interacting over board and card games. Other distractions and interests included reading, making or repairing clothes and of course the growing and preparation of food for preservation. Local produce, grown in the garden or on an allotment, a small area of land allocated by the council to those who wanted to cultivate their own food, having played a vital supplement role in the daily diet during the war, a practice that ran on into the peace.

Outside the home, dance halls continued to attract, as did musical events, the theatre and cinema. Sports, having once been important were to be so again, especially football and cricket, eager interest inciting both widespread participation and spectating. Also drawing participation were all manner of organisations from the Women's Institute to various church affiliated bodies, scouts, guides, cubs and brownies and so on. While heading down to the local for pint or two remained a favoured relaxation if funds allowed.

For the children these were salad days, times when they were free to roam about and amuse themselves. The main aim of play was to get outside, whatever the weather, exploring, running around or just passing the day with whatever interested. When adverse conditions forced a stay inside, limited toys were no obstacle to passing a few hours in the time honoured style of bickering alternating with happy play. Pressures were fewer, there being little concern about fashionable clothing, it was enough to be warm and comfortable, most wearing clothes handed down from older siblings.

Time spent at school introduced and contained the young in a disciplined world where doing as one was told was taken for granted. All children being on a short leash during the learning years, sallying out of line might bring forth the slipper or cane. Outcomes invariably seen as justified by parents, the teacher always assumed to be right. If anymore was heard about it then a further clip might be levied for good measure, a time when those immortal words brought dread, *'just you wait to your father gets home.'* So much the ultimate sanction of those receding days.

For most, learning ended at fourteen, except for the academically gifted, although the leaving age was soon to be raised to fifteen. From full time education it was just a short trip to getting a job where the rules were determined by the adults who ran the factory, mine or works. An occupation introducing the youngster to new disciplines where the learning of a trade was the beginning of a journey to self respect and standing. With earnings being modest, it was common to hand over part or all of this money to fund the family home. What was left by way of pocket money usually went towards the everyday requirements of life at the time, cigarettes, or perhaps pipe tobacco, a few beers, perhaps of even a trip to the local dance hall or cinema.

Chapter 23

Britain's early recovery

The attitudes that saw Winston Churchill voted out of office were influenced by a report commissioned by his wartime government colleague, Ernest Bevin, one written by Sir William Beveridge. The object behind the work was to look towards the future, examining the various ways of providing social insurance and making various recommendations based on these findings. While Beveridge was apparently reluctant to accept this task, he knuckled down to it, presenting his ideas towards the end of 1942 to surprising public interest.

Whatever his original brief, the author certainly set his sights high, talking grandly of defeating want, ignorance, squalor, disease and idleness. Circulated widely it found broad favour with the public, the cautionary reminders lost in the zeal of political enthusiasm. Beveridge at least showing himself aware of what can go wrong with such systems when he pointed out that, '*individual initiative and action had to be sustained if dependency on welfare was to be avoided.*' Noting that this was, '*a situation to be avoided because it rots and demoralises.*' Further emphasising what he was worried about by saying, '*that in return for the security provided by the State, the individual needed to make as much of a contribution as they could manage.*'

The money to fund this far reaching scheme was to come from compulsory contributions levied on the world of work, funds that would provide subsistence level welfare against illness and unemployment, in addition to payment of a pension. Furthering government's social ambitions was a White Paper released in 1944 on future employment policy, this making high and stable levels of employment a fundamental aim of the post-war State. The final plank in this comprehensive re-assessment of national welfare needs supplied by a commitment to provide a system of health care funded and run centrally, access being free at the point of use.

Encouraged throughout the war by the Labour party to consider these plans as the way forward, the electorate needed little additional persuasion. Those who needed it getting positive vibes from the clear and hopeful language of Labour's Manifesto, a document that contrasted sharply to the sobering realities of what the Conservatives had to say. Labour's confident offering, sub-titled 'Victory in war must be followed by a prosperous peace,' reminded the would be reader of pre-war failings and the evils of war profiteering. Going onto inciting the belief that it, and it alone, represented a progressive outlook, a party capable of delivering the deserved bounty. The Conservative's own approach was not quite in tune with these hopes. The result was that few really troubled themselves over the decision to vote Clement Attlee into office, entrusting him to deliver through socialism the rewards the British felt belonged to them by right. After all, they had won the war!

From the outset the Labour government set out to honour its manifesto by creating a socialist State. The four points of its compass, full employment, price stability, economic growth and achievement of a surplus on current account balance of payments. These goals reliant on nationalisation of certain key industries as well as the protections of comprehensive welfare. Circumstances were to constrain deliverance, the primary reason being Britain's weakened state, it having gone from the world's greatest creditor in 1939 to that of its largest debtor just six years later. Estimations suggest around a quarter of the national wealth vanished fighting to remain free. With some two thirds of export trade lost or severely disrupted, vital net income from overseas investments had also shrunk by as much as a half. Daunting facts making it clear the task of recovery was going to be far from easy irrespective of promise, delusion or self belief.

Getting in the way were enduring demands on the Exchequer because of the ongoing fighting in the Far East and the need to maintain substantial British occupation forces in Germany. Even the demobilising and repatriation of surplus units imposed overheads, costs that would continue into 1946. A drain that interfered with plans to fix up housing, repair the nations worn infrastructure and stimulate the retooling of factories for peacetime production.

To these predictable burdens came an early shock following the unexpected surrender of Japan. Welcome though wars end must be, the termination of the Lend Lease arrangement within a week by the Americans threw the British government into a spin. A sense of urgency prompting Attlee's administration to seek a loan from the US to cover immediate shortfalls. Negotiated on Britain's behalf by John Maynard Keynes, the United States was persuaded to advance a line of credit for 3.75 billion dollars repayable over fifty years at an interest rate of 2%, the capital repayments scheduled to commence in 1951. A further sum settled Lend Lease debts while Canadians generosity also provided substantial assistance. Although the terms were reasonable in themselves, US insistence that sterling be made a convertible currency in return was to derail stuttering recovery when implemented.

On the domestic front, the Chancellor of the Exchequer, Hugh Dalton, retained food subsidies and rationing, initiating steps to implement the pledge to avoid unemployment black-spots. The real meat of the governments programme starting with the piecing together its comprehensive system of welfare. Having passed the Family Allowances Act, the revolution proper began in 1946 when parliament approved the National Insurance Act. A popular success bolstered by a determined Aneurin Bevan who convinced the medical profession, well most of it, of the merits of the National Health Service Act. Passed by Parliament in July of 1948, this brought nearly twenty seven hundred hospitals and more than twenty thousand General Practitioners under its wing.

The first moves towards implementing State control of industry came in 1946 when private shareholders of the Bank of England were brought out on the 1st of March. Nationalisation embracing civil aviation that August, succeeding years seeing the electricity, coal, Cable & Wireless, transport, gas and finally the iron and steel industries taken over. In all around 20% of British industry with some two million workers ending up in public hands.

All of these industries were run down, substantial investments being needed to repair and modernise. A point made clear by the Chancellor himself when he commented to the House of Commons at the end of 1946 regarding the £941 million stumped up to take the railways into State ownership. Blandly stating that the nation had purchased a poor set of assets, the track and rolling stock were worn out, while the stations were shabby and run down, in fact the whole lot was a disgrace to the nation. Despite this critical summary further large sums were paid out, the coal industry for example being a snip at £164 million. Many of its collieries being small and uneconomic, which made investment to improve productivity neither affordable or practical. While the government understood the need for rationalisation in these areas, indeed it mentioned it in its manifesto, such decisions usually meant closure and unemployment for the men. Given the stated aim of full employment, this was often a non starter.

Less well known, but nonetheless useful during this period were the solid contributions to Britain's recovery by over 400,000 German POW's. Involved in farm work, repairing roads and other projects the last of these men were not repatriated until the end of 1948.

Those eagerly looking for some improvements in daily life faced disappointment, the austere wartime regime enduring, even bread going on ration in 1946 along with potatoes the following year. Bitter winter weather during February and March of 1947 reducing life to a grim round of shortages of fuel and electricity, some areas suffering rotating power cuts. Matters made worse when attempts to honour the convertibility clause inserted into the Washington Loan Agreement led to a run on sterling. Cumulative pressures that saw even the experienced Hugh Dalton caught out by a minor indiscretion that given the standards of the times forced his resignation. His replacement, the unyielding Sir Stafford Cripps. His first actions to address matters prevented the taking of foreign holidays as part of general moves to control the use of foreign currency. It was as well that foreign earnings were supplemented by the sale of commodities from the colonies, Malayan rubber and tin generating more dollars than British exports did in 1948.

Staving off the worst of this gloom was the announcement of Marshall Aid, Britain in fact receiving more than 3 billion dollars, the largest individual share of these generous credits. Also helping was the devaluation of the pound by nearly a third in September of 1949, a step that boosted export competitiveness. Not that any of this could stem loss of support amongst a disappointed electorate. Although Attlee went onto gain a further term at the February election, internal divisions within the Labour party were deepened following the decision to increase defence spending to cover deployments in Korea. The key resignation of Aneurin Bevan and others from the government forcing an election in October which the opposition Conservatives party won.

Although defeated at the polls, Attlee's administration created an enduring legacy, many of its general principles surviving the remaining decades of the century and into the next. The most damaging part of this heritage was to belief that government alone had the vision and judgement necessary to benefit the nation. In making the economy the proving ground for this idea, it could not have chosen a stiffer test.

Attlee's approach centred on manipulating demand, everything from the manufacture of goods to the buying of factory machinery, the building of houses, or the repair of the nations infrastructure was influenced by government action. Overall demand easing when taxes rose and vice versa, this in turn determined productive output and with it the level of employment. Refinements to this mechanism coming from central authority over interest rates, tweaks to hire purchase rules and the influences brought to bear on bank lending.

Alas sluggish economic performance continued to contribute to a dull Britain as the Nineteen-Forties ebbed away. The new decade lit up by the comparative exuberance of the Festival of Britain in 1951. Modest cheer also coming from the scrapping of wartime identification cards the following February. A month when the king, George the Sixth, succumbed to cancer, an event that would see his daughter crowned as Elizabeth the Second.

With Attlee's departure came the return of Winston Churchill, his peacetime term noted for his continuing interest in foreign affairs. Having met an election promise to denationalise the iron and steel industry, his government put in a lot of energy into meeting the housing shortage under the direction of Harold Macmillan. Work that included taking on and accelerating the necessary rebuilding of damaged towns and cities, a process that came to be marked by the unthinking destruction of much of our priceless heritage. Peaking during the following decade, character was replaced by the construction of what was cheap and shoddy.

Ably coping with the demands of increased defence spending with its inflationary pressures while managing to lay aside the dreariness of rationing by consigning it to history in 1954. The intention of the then Chancellor, R. A. Butler, to introduce a free floating pound might well have changed much of what was to come, unfortunately the idea was shelved following opposition from Anthony Eden and others.

The fresh challenges of office imposed great strains on Britain's great wartime leader, who clearly should not have assumed the arduous duties of Prime Minister. His health suffering under the strain of increasing age and a stroke, his long presumed heir, Sir Anthony Eden, finally taking over the reins in April of 1955.

Like his mentor, Eden concentrated on the international scene, his short administration blighted by his own ill health and the influences of misunderstood medication. Factors that might go some way towards explaining the serious misjudgements made following the decision by the Egyptian leader, Gamal Abd al-Nasser, to nationalise the Suez Canal. The conspiracy Britain formed with France and Israel to regain control of the waterway exposing the pound to severe speculative pressures. Forced to seek a bridging loan from the IMF to overcome the run on sterling, the government found American agreement conditional on complying with the UN resolution that called for immediate withdrawal of all troops. Caught in a bind and with little way out Eden caved in, abandoning his allies. The real irony being that all four protagonists had to go cap in hand to the IMF, the $1.3 billion loan supplied to Britain easing its own immediate predicament.

After Eden's expected resignation, power fell to Harold Macmillan, his immediate priority, repairing relations with the US. On the economic front, the growing awareness that Britain lacked industrial competitiveness drew Macmillan's interest. The path his administration elected to follow introducing ever more complex forms of State intervention, he being wedded, as Attlee would later observe, to the socialist ideal (as were most post-war governments).

The main problem that had to be faced at the time was the tendency of the balance of payments to shift towards deficit every time the economy grew. The cause, rising demand for imported raw materials to expand industrial output. The trouble being that the bulk of this increased production tended to satisfy the domestic market rather than go for export where it could earn the nation money. The situation getting more awkward as inflationary pressures due to labour and material shortages came into play, rising prices influencing the workforce to push for a hike in wages. In combination these pressures invariably induced government to dampen demand by increasing taxes, boosting interest rates or squeezing credit.

With hindsight it is possible to see that part of the problem was related to the failure to understand what fiscal tools and methods could be effective in directing the economy. Efforts to acquire that knowledge, a subject examined formally by the Radcliffe Committee, ended up concluding in its 1959 report that monetary policy could only play a subordinate role. Other avenues that might have helped reassess the situation never overcoming the confidence government had in its ability to plan the answer. The country paying a high price for this misplaced judgement as the economy continued to expand and then contract in a succession of boom and bust cycles.

Complicating life still further was the cast in stone national commitment to full employment, so much a triumph of social desire over reality. Locking as it did manpower in old inefficient industries whose condition was always likely to prevent competitive production and reasonable profit. This institutionalising of labour inflexibility stored up trouble for later years, the tensions between management and workers eventually leading to hopeless confrontation. The need for a legally enforceable framework that bound both sides to sensible procedures and rules that promoted the resolution of disputes failing to materialise. Instead, the dangers of freeing one side from responsibility was ruthlessly exposed when less rationale elements within the union movement ran amok in the sixties and seventies.

As if this was not enough, the years after the war showed that exposure to danger had not scrubbed complacency from the nation's fabric. Nor for that matter had wishful thinking or that misplaced affection for individualistic craftsmanship given way to robust industrial sense. The decisions and disciplines needed to rebuild the economy along practical lines were from the word go discarded by a government and people who preferred political idealism to practicalities. While the desire for social benefits overcame the fact that we as a nation could not afford such ideas at the time. Ambitions that diverted money and attention from the urgent need for modernisation and restructuring, decisions that in the long term reduced the ability of domestic manufacturing to compete internationally, the primary avenue for earning our way in the world.

Not that the outcomes were all that severe during the Fifties, victory's afterglow was still bright and there was plenty of headline catching successes in fields such as aviation that still suggested expertise and technological superiority. An able scientific community able to secure reasonably funded for a time achieving much at the leading edge of research and development. The real disappointments stemming from the failure to build an enduring commercial success story on that solid foundation. One notable blunder by the authorities coming from the publication of a White Paper in April of 1957 which concluded the manned fighter aircraft was on borrowed time because the missile was about to take over. A misjudgement that dealt a severe psychological blow to a still strong industry.

However, neither the deterioration in the balance of payments or these other concerns prevented the Conservatives from retaining office in the election of October 1959. A campaign marked by Macmillan's use of the phrase, '*most of our people have never had it so good.*' Indeed there were justifications for the comment, prices were stable, unemployment remained low and growth was better than pre-war days. However, it was already apparent that a resurgent Germany and France were achieving twice the British growth rate with few of its awkward problems. The first hints of a bleaker future for domestic industry occurring in the north when the old textile mills began to close. The inability to compete in former markets owing much to a reliance on worn equipment still powered by steam engines, an unchanging Victorian legacy.

The growing involvement of government in the nitty-gritty of economic control took another step forward when a moderately expansionist budget brought about another round of balance of payment difficulties. Macmillan's administration trying to correct matters by introducing a sequence of measures, starting with credit and hire purchase restrictions. Failure of these moves leading to modest tax increases and finally a wage freeze, initially covering public sector workers, but soon extended to private industry. A formal basis to this latter policy established on the 1st October 1962 when the National Incomes Commission was set up. Sandwiched between these moves were higher interest rates and not for first, or last time, a helping hand from the IMF. In a trend much imitated over later years the government set up a talking shop to determine policy, this one named the National Economic Planning Council (NEDC).

With its application to join the EEC rebuffed by the French President, Charles de Gaulle, early in 1963. Domestic attention turned toward addressing what was become one of Britain's weeping sores, the haemorrhaging of money by State owned industries, in particular the railways. Plans for their drastic pruning presented by Dr. Richard Beeching to widespread public dismay. With popularity ebbing, despite grounds for optimism over growth expressed by the NEDC, an ailing Macmillan handed over to Alec Douglas Home who in turn surrendered office to Harold Wilson when Labour narrowly won the 1964 election.

Chapter 24

Good times

If a moment must be chosen to mark the point when post-war austerity began to recede, then the coronation of Queen Elizabeth the Second on 2nd June 1953 was it. Modest improvements to the financial circumstance blending into a handful of years noted for their peace and sociability. A high point marked by the anthropologist Geoffrey Gorer who felt able to write in the mid-Fifties, *'the English were certainly amongst the most peaceful, gentle, courteous and orderly populations that the civilised world had ever seen.'*

Helping things along was success in overcoming the worst of the housing shortage. The architects and builders, usually local government, authorities who rented property's, the normal method of establishing a home at the time. The immediate post-war expediency of prefabricated units giving way to redevelopment that often involved the demolition of the old terraced streets. The inhabitants ending up being re-housed in the new estates, some even in the new towns that sprung up around London and elsewhere, places with well spaced semi-detached houses built along broad avenues offering entirely new dimensions to life. Homes big enough from day one to receive the washing machines, vacuum cleaners and refrigerators that would soon transform the running of a house from a labour intensive full time occupation into something much easier.

Life still centred on the traditional family. The modest and short lived freedoms of adolescence soon giving way to strictures of adulthood. For young men this meant getting a job, the first step to earning acceptance as a grown up. From there, it was all about climbing up the ladder towards the time when enough was earnt to support and raise a family of their own. The necessary disciplines to what was often an arduous undertaking provided by a no nonsense upbringing, disciplined schooling, perhaps an apprenticeship and in most cases conscripted military service (though that came to an end in 1960). Women had their own route, after the same no nonsense childhood and schooling that also gave way to whatever employment opportunities existed until, for most anyway, they found someone to marry. The arrival of children bringing about a change in circumstance as life steered a course towards full time care of their children and the home.

Dominating the domestic side of sustaining the family was the getting and preparing of food. With little way of keeping food fresh, only 15% of homes had a fridge in 1957, this meant daily expeditions to the local shops, usually small stores divided into specialities such as bakers, butchers, grocers, greengrocers, newsagents, hardware stores and chemists. Easing the chore was the regular and ad hoc deliveries of milk, bread and heavier groceries. Those looking for a wider selection of goods for some particular out of the ordinary need would find the answer in the larger town or city, the only places that could justify a multi-department store or larger specialist outlet.

Adding to this repetitive labour was the hard work necessary to get clothes and houses clean. Toil that involved hand scrubbing and perhaps even boiling heavily soiled items like sheets or towels. A process followed by the physical effort to hand cranked heavy items through a mangle to squeeze out excess water. From there it was out onto the line to dry, unless that is the weather was inclement, when the struggle to get things dry saw damp things hung up inside.

As the decade progressed almost everyone became better dressed. The manufacture of clothing benefiting from a range of new, cheaper, man made fabrics and materials. Women's fashions shifting away from the severely tailored look that was economical in material to one employing differing lines, much fuller with a wider range of printed colours and patterns. The general principles still centring on the smart co-ordinated look, one briefly copied by the young who were soon to forge their own styles. Men's dress remained conservative, the suit the convention, even if the cut and style became slimmer, lighter cloth improving comfort. The everyday wearing of hats for both sexes slowly passing as strict formality eased, a chance matched by the changing fashions of hair, the severe ways of earlier times giving way to highly artistic and elaborate coiffured looks.

Childhood remained just that, a time free of adult concerns and complications. The opportunity to roam and play, be it in the street or open space, unhindered by later worries of traffic and prowling molesters, the main diversions football, cricket, tag, skipping, hopscotch or just running around. When near the seaside, country or a park, water held its enduring appeal, be it splashing about or fishing for tiddlers. The organised side remained that provided by cubs, scouts, brownies, guides, boys brigade or a church affiliated youth club. When forced to be inside there were an expanding range of toys to supplement reading and drawing, electric train sets, Meccano, plastic models, tea sets, dolls and so on.

The street side of the front door continued to act as a common room, one shared by adults who stood to gossip, laugh, argue or just socialise. Organised entertainment's still centred on the cinema, dance halls and coffee bars, television, at the time a real novelty, displaying its drawing power, attentive audiences gathering around the few sets then available.

With more money to go around, heading off on holiday became an annual venture involving all the family. Favoured locations like the West Country, the Isle of Wight and seaside resorts such as Blackpool Southend-on-Sea and Scarborough acting as magnets to the crowds. Camping and picnics were other popular escapes, while holiday camps such as Butlin's provided an economical respite for those with less in the way of spare cash. The travelling to and from was mainly accomplished by bus, tram, coach or train, although more were finding the money to purchase a car. Not that this showed all that much, traffic remaining sparse apart from Bank Holidays well into the later 1960's.

Hints of change to come might have been seen in the determined independence of some youths, but for the most part this was dismissed as high spirits. From time to time one saw a 'teddy boy' or its female equivalent. Girls finding new ways to express their femininity, one passing trend the wearing of skirts supported by masses of petticoats. By the early Sixties this interest in fashion had spread, trendily dressed 'mods' astride their scooters and the leather jacketed 'rockers' riding motorbikes two extremes. Hundreds making their way to the same seaside resorts down on the south coast where much energy was expended squabbling over the same bit of beach with the police.

Most of the evocative memories of those days are triggered by the tunes, a succession of waves that started in America before being adopted by Britain. The advent of the transistor radio supplying a real boost, music becoming portable, reinforcing the jukebox and the gramophone. The evenings of many a Fifties and early Sixties teenager spent listening to the latest sounds fading in and out on a radio tuned to 208 metres on the medium waveband, the home of Radio Luxembourg.

Early rock and roll vying with the smoother sounds of what was considered mainstream, music that found an entirely fresh approach when bands from Liverpool created immortality for that city. Its distinctive accent and creative talent taking on the best and winning.

The national health was a mix, besides war's hidden legacy, many still wrested a living from hard physical toil, work that often held risk of injury and the longer term dangers. Offsetting this were improvements derived from the balanced national diet enforced by wartime circumstance, a situation that ironically improved the health of those who before that time had not eaten well. Absent, well almost, was over eating, it being rare to see anyone at all who was overweight. Contemporary habits continued to expose, not least that of smoking, the taking up of cigarettes or pipe remaining a rite of passage into adulthood. The most important social lubricant remained alcohol, although limited opening hours, lack of spare cash and moral strictures kept its excess more or less in check.

In general terms there was little crime, figures for England and Wales during 1951 listed just over half a million criminal incidents, ten years later this had risen to more than eight-hundred thousand. A statistically significant rise, but total crime levels remained remarkably low given the population. The main deterrent was societal attitudes, a coherent sense that such things would not be tolerated, a belief made visible by the policeman on the beat. A reassuring and preventative force that headed off many a moment that might have led to trouble. Pointless aggression a rarity, apart from in a few well known areas. Public condemnation and the hand on the collar by a policemen sufficient restraint to those keen on making a nuisance of themselves.

It was a world and way of life where few felt endangered, the street might be no more than a gloomy gas lit avenue. But it was safe to walk home, even in the recurrent smog's.

Chapter 25

National foolishness

The incoming Labour government formed by Harold Wilson in 1964 squared up to an overheating economy with its by now familiar balance of payments deficit. The Chancellor, James Callaghan, cobbling together a mini budget that eased public borrowing through various tax increases. Part of the necessary response seeing some three billion dollars worth of international credit secured by the Bank of England from various friendly Central Banks. His first full Budget the following April introducing the corporation tax along with steps to control foreign investments.

Coincident attention focusing on the most important aspect of Labour's economic strategy, the development of a full prices and incomes policy. Intentions aired with the Trades Unions Congress (TUC) and employers organisations during December, a White Paper on the subject being published early the following year. The primary hope here was that TUC involvement in the construction of such a policy would guarantee compliance of the labour movement. The talks themselves being characterised by a friendly approach, reference being made to them taking place at 10 Downing Street (the home of the Prime Minister) over a pint (beer) and round of sandwiches. The subsequent agreement to hold wage increases to 3% becoming known in March of 1965.

Despite the establishment of harmonious relationships with the trade union hierarchy, it proved insufficient to counter shop-floor discontent and the growing tendency of workers to strike. The absence of any mechanism to handle these outbursts showing the folly of Attlee's repeal of the 1927 Trade Disputes Act. The ramifications of this self destructive behaviour leading to international head-shaking and, with it, a reputation for poor industrial performance. While fully aware of the causes, Harold Wilson was not the first to display a lack of nerve by backing off from potential confrontation with the unions. Choosing instead to employ a typically British fudge when it set up a Royal Commission on Trade Unions and Employers Associations (1965-1968) that took a long time getting nowhere.

This retreat from the responsibilities of leadership set the tone for the next fifteen years, a period that saw near total breakdown of labour relations in some industries and the slow strangling of the economy. A shambles whose origins lay in the unreal attitudes that took root in the national psyche over the course of the Second World War. The belief that central planning could accomplish anything hardly a view restricted to Sir Stafford Cripps. Disastrously, even when the full effects of this folly became undeniable, the country and its governments proved unable to combine in will to face facts and do something about it.

For foreign investors, dispassionate spectators to these machinations and turmoil, the attractions of retaining sterling declined, falling confidence prompting the decision to start selling in favour of more stable currencies. The resultant crisis demanded convincing remedies. Vital in supplying them was the IMF, which agreed to a substantial extension of international credit, Britain drawing on some 2.4 billion dollars worth. The Chancellor backing this up with an import surcharge, cuts in public expenditure and a tightening of exchange controls and rules regarding loans. Frenetic activity topped off by a White Paper detailing government plans for future industrial investment.

What all this energetic crisis management did do was create a favourable impression with the electorate, one that delivered a second term to Wilson following a snap election in March of 1966. A triumph dampened almost immediately when the National Union of Seaman ignored ministerial appeal and went on strike that May. The governments declaration of a state of national emergency exacerbated the pounds difficulties, further hurriedly drafted actions being necessary to settle ragged nerves. A crucial component in managing the immediate crisis was assistance supplied through the Bank for International Settlements. An austerity package introduced by the government restricted personal credit and cut public investment, measures followed by the announcement of a voluntary price and wage freeze. The latter becoming compulsory shortly afterwards, a principle sustained into the following year through government jawboning (talking) and TUC vetting.

The general awkwardness and tensions of the day exacerbated by the closing of the Suez Canal during and after the Six Day war between Israel and the surrounding Arab states of Egypt, Jordan and Syria. A dock strike that October keeping the issue of labour relations very much to the fore. Economic difficulties eased by the politically difficult step of currency devaluation on the 18th of November 1967. A move bolstered by further international credit to go with interest and tax rate hikes, limits on bank lending, more personal credit restrictions and reductions in defence spending. Stabilising measures reinforced by radical pruning of planned government spending. The Chancellor judging that limits on pay were going to be necessary, as was legislation to allow dividends to be determined, price reductions ordered and rents controlled.

Not that any of this influenced the irritably of some in the working population who continued to resort to frequent wildcat (unofficial) as well as official strikes. Eruptions that tempted government to once more consider legal reform. Barbara Castle, then Secretary of State for Employment and Productivity, behind ideas laid out in the White Paper 'In Place of Strife.' The threat of strife placing it firmly with the earlier attempt, a rebuff that heralded a retreat to the only tools government could use. Various tweaks to indirect taxation added to minor reforms to income tax levels in the April Budget of 1969. A further White Paper at the end of the year outlining the immediate thinking related to productivity, incomes and prices. The core idea suggesting that wages rises be limited to a maximum of four and half percent.

Following a mildly inflationary April Budget with its tweaks to income tax thresholds and adjustments to various tax allowances on capital outlay, a generally nervy country swapped sides. Looking towards a change of government to alter fortunes, the baton passing to the Conservatives under Edward Heath. His victory owing much to the promises he made to arrest the creep of industrial anarchy.

Few dramas accompanied the new government's first full Budget with its tax and spending cuts. Its mettle really being tested when that most emotive of British firms, Rolls Royce, faced bankruptcy due to technical problems developing a new aeroplane engine. Unable to contemplate the consequences, the government blinked and opened up the public purse to give it some money. A temporary diversion from this and other economic headaches was the introduction of a system of decimal currency in February of 1971. The old pound with its idiosyncratic 240 big old pennies reduced to a hundred smaller ones. Less agreeable were militant union activists whipping up sentiment against the central plank of the governments programme, the Industrial Relations Act, with its proposed pre-strike ballots and mandatory cooling off periods. A million and half workers revelling in their indignation by taking the day off on the first of March.

A few weeks later Iain Macleod, the Chancellor, stood up to present his second tax reforming Budget. Proposing a Value Added Tax (VAT) in place of the Selective Employment and Purchase taxes. A further mini-Budget that July bringing reductions in Purchase Tax rates and other fiscal modifications, significant amongst these the abolition of Hire Purchase restrictions as well as easing Purchase Tax rates and investment rules for industrial equipment.

With the collapse of the Bretton Woods system a month later and the floating of the pound, the Confederation of British Industry (CBI) campaigned for measures to reflate the economy in return for voluntary price restraint. Progress towards that end proved limited, instead they were rewarded by entry into the EEC. An eager Edward Heath accepting terms, conditions put before the House on 28th October 1971 when a majority of 356 to 244 confirmed entry. A notable advocate standout against membership, the TUC.

It was at this juncture that the biggest single challenger to legitimate political authority in post-war Britain played its first card. The National Union of Mineworkers (NUM) voting to strike from January (1972) in support of its pay claim. Effective picketing of coal depots, mines, ports and power stations forcing the Conservative administration into declaring a national state of emergency. Rolling power cuts reducing most of industry and the population to a three-day working week. Six harrowing weeks later the government capitulated, buying peace by conceding to the 22% pay deal recommended by the Wilberforce Inquiry.

This humiliation capped when the decision to enter the EEC currency snake brought unsustainable pressures against the pound, forcing sterling's withdrawal after just six weeks. A minor bright spot in this hapless interlude, the establishment of the voluntary Advisory, Conciliation and Arbitration Service (ACAS) as a way of getting industry and labour together to prevent strike action.

With formal entry into the EEC on 1st January 1973 offering no immediate advantages, the government found itself pulled towards the same regulatory framework employed by the previous government. One that would allow it to determine prices, control pay, dividends and rents over a three year period under a Pay Board and Price Commission. Union opposition to these proposals orchestrated by the TUC drawing a million and a half workers out on a further one day strike on Mayday. The general fragility of the economy given a fresh kick by OPEC's decision to limit supplies of its more expensive oil. This contributed to a sharp rise in the trade deficits that October, an opportune moment for power workers to ripple its muscles, raising the spectre of a return to the three day working. The necessity for action forcing a Mini-Budget in December that announced plans to axe planned expenditure as well as re-introduce Hire Purchase controls.

The final blow to the viability of the Heath administration coming when the miners executive decided once more to pursue a pay claim through strike action. A decision countered by the government going to the country on the platform of who should govern the country. Alas, the electorate could not make up its mind. An indecisive result forcing the Crown to ask the Labour leader, Harold Wilson, to form an administration. He did so without delay, his minority administration entering office by promising to get the country back to work. Doing so by conceding a 35% pay rise to the miners, repealing the Industrial Relations Act and adding further protections to trade union activity via the 1974 Trade Union and Labour relations Act.

This burst marked the high point, other problems proving much less tractable. Rising unemployment, inflation and an ugly current account deficit contributing to what was a bleak outlook. The man expected to deal with this, Denis Healey, taking over as the new Chancellor. His first Budget setting out plans to increase public expenditure, the necessary revenue to allow this generated by increasing income and business taxes topped off by limiting investments. Political life getting its modern edge when money was channelled to the Building Societies to prevent the unpopular raising of mortgage rates.

Following high level discussions between senior figures in the TUC and government, voluntary wage restraint gained a new look under the so called 'Social Contract.' Additional budgetary measures that July targeting inflation and struggling industry, in particular through assistance for structural investment. The fanfare given to the White Paper, 'The Regeneration of British Industry' with its plans to widen State ownership overlooking the obvious, it being publicly owned industries that continued to loose the most money.

As it was, the ever astute Harold Wilson capitalised on the dramas of his first few months in office, calling a snap election on the 10th of

October 1974 that delivered a narrow, overall majority. A result that provided the chance to develop ideas of improving export performance by relaxing price controls, adding recommendations that the Bank of England should bias lending towards business. In tune with this more aggressive involvement in was the effective take over of the loss making motor manufacturer, British Leyland, following an agreement to supply funding from the public purse.

Whatever hopes accompanied such moves, most were knocked sideways by spiralling wage claims, especially amongst public sector workers, the miners alone garnering a wage hike of around 30% in April of 1975. Concessions that had to be paid for by raising taxes, a deflationary Budget the following April introducing a rise of two-pence in the pound on basic rate of income tax and a 25% rate of VAT on luxury goods. Some sign of realism finally coming through with plans to reduce the subsidies given to nationalised industries, the aim being to phase them out altogether the following financial year.

With inflationary pressures climbing dangerously, stimulating in turn higher wage demands, the fiscal priorities were adjusted in an attempt to get this destructive ratcheting under control. The methods intended to surmount this problem outlined in the White Paper, 'The Attack on Inflation.' Plans that would limit pay rises to a maximum of six pounds per week effective from that August. Arresting the steady rise in unemployment a task given to the National Enterprise Board. State directed investments, subsidies and increased public ownership intended to create the additional jobs that were needed. Getting in the way of this ongoing fantasy was the obvious decay in big firms like British Leyland, which was shortly to announce record losses.

Quite out of the blue in this increasingly difficult situation, the Prime Minister, Harold Wilson, resigned on the 16th March 1976. Power transferring to James Callaghan who assembled his team for the last act in this depressing tale. It being his administration that finally, if tentatively, turned towards the approach that would help remedy Britain's malaise. Recognition of this was first delivered in the budget of the 6th April 1976 where it was stated 'the money supply should not be allowed to fuel inflation.' Although it was not made clear how this was to be done, the eye catching headlines given over to announcement of conditional tax cuts should the TUC agree.

With inflation at the centre of concerns, government plans were detailed in the White Paper 'The Attack on Inflation: The Second Year.' The nitty-gritty concentrating on further controls on pay matched by changes to the means employed to contain price rises. Unfortunately external events dictated action as sterling struggled under heavy international pressure. Forces that led to cuts in public expenditure while for the first time, specific targets were set for the money supply.

To cope with the pressures on the pound, help was sought once more from the IMF, a huge medium term loan of nearly four billion dollars being agreed with the Treasury. With domestic interest rates already reaching crisis levels of 15%, the Chancellor responded with another mini-Budget that lopped still more from government spending. Further treatment for a stressed out pound coming at the beginning of 1977 from the Bank of International Settlement. A support package supplemented by budgetary measures that reduced income tax levels, put controls on dividend levels and through the Price Commission, kept a watch on the prices of goods to go with the by now normal restraint on pay.

The final eighteen months of the Labour administration involved elaborate paper planning dovetailing in with further fiscal adjustments. The gradual narrowing of monetary targets to control the amount of money sloshing around in the economy as a way of controlling inflation gaining in importance. Further strategies being detailed in the White Paper labelled 'Winning the Battle Against Inflation' published in July of 1978. Although by then the headline inflation rate had fallen from its peak of over 25% in 1975 to about ten percent.

Masked by all these political shenanigan's was the growing importance of price and quality if market share was to be maintained in an increasingly competitive world. Previously safe domestic markets coming under threat as consumer began to see better value for their money in imported goods. Yet oddly, Briton's remained surprisingly indifferent to the condition of their own industry. Manufacturing, which has long been the main way of earning our way in the world continuing to decline. Its fate ultimately determined by the inability to produce quality products at competitive prices that someone wanted to buy. Combinations of perpetual State interference, high tax regimes, small profit margins, indifferent management and the reckless trade unions too big a burden.

By the late 1970's it was difficult to see how this might be cured, attitudes on all sides were simply unprepared or unable to respond to these national failings. That public sector workers left rubbish to pile up in the street when they demonstrated one more time over pay during the winter of 1978-79 was simply representative of nation that had denied economic sense for far too long.

Chapter 26

Radical medicine

Inheriting this chronic situation was a determined group under a new Prime Minister, Margaret Thatcher, Leader of the Conservative Party and victor of the May election. Her administration's objectives aimed squarely at permanent fixes to perpetual ills, not only by deregulating the economy through the removal of the State's grip, but also encouraging greater individual involvement and sharing of the national wealth.

Accomplishing this end required the dismantling of the elaborate controls that had been built up over the years, mechanisms that inhibited or cosseted just about every aspect of economic life. Replacing this insular blanket were policies that sought to create a non-inflationary environment where industry was expected to compete. It being accepted that this meant job losses, although it seems improbable anyone foresaw the severity of the resultant collapse. Misjudgements based on a failure to take into account the rapidly evolving competitive needs of the international markets and deep decay of most of Britain's industry.

A vital member of the team behind this revolution, Geoffrey Howe, moved in as Chancellor of the Exchequer. His first Budget, presented on 12th June, introduced the monetary measures and interest rates that continued the task of imposing long term control over inflation begun by the previous administration. This taking the tentative measures of his predecessor to their conclusions, doing away with the regulatory frame that had sought, without much success, to control the economy.

Cuts in public spending were accompanied by reductions in personal taxation, the emphasis shifting towards taxing spending rather than income. Controls on dividends and mortgage lending were removed, a liberalising philosophy soon extended to the removal of foreign exchange controls. Plans also being outlined to levy VAT at a single rate. Longer term thinking regarding the cutting of government expenditure were examined in a White Paper published that November. The Budget the following year reinforcing the initial moves made towards indirect taxation.

In a case of unfortunate timing, rising world oil prices and contracting international trade combined with these shifts in policy to bring about a 15% fall in manufacturing output within a year. With tight money and spending regimes in place to harness inflation, which would continue towards its peak of over twenty percent, the marginal condition of many industrial enterprises were fully exposed, their bankruptcy and attendant redundancies signs of what was to come.

It was against this backdrop of international market forces that the Chancellors third and most contentious budget was announced. His decision to raise taxes and cut public spending during what had become a recession breaking with the economic conventions and orthodoxies that had dominated for about fifty years. Condemned by just about every economic expert who considered themselves an expert, none were more put out than these very same experts when the economy showed unexpected resilience and adaptability over the coming years. Shades of Ludwig Erhard, if thirty plus years too late. With pay settlements moderating, productivity improved, helping ease inflation back into single figures by early 1982. The economy getting a boost from the rising income from North Sea oil, which helped offset the escalating costs of social welfare as unemployment rapidly moved beyond three million.

Considered essential by this government as well as previous administrations was the need to circumscribe trade union power. With opposition becoming muted by recession and rising unemployment, a series of measures tackled this vexing issue a step at a time. The first reform became law in 1980, with further measures passed in 1982, 1984 and later in 1988. Amongst the restraints introduced were secret ballots before a strike could be called, limits on closed shops, at least 80% of the workforce having to vote for any such agreement to be binding, the outlawing of secondary picketing, sympathy strikes and the making of unions legally responsible for their own actions.

Another equally important facet of the Margaret Thatcher's first term were moves to breaking up the monopolies enjoyed by nationalised industries. At the head of what would become a queue was British Telecommunications, a monolith introduced to commercial pressures from Mercury in the provision of its services. Some welcome popularity in this programme gained from the measure that allowed sitting council house tenants to purchase the property they were in at half the market value. The interest this drew clear enough as over 800,000 people took advantage of the chance by the end of 1984.

Not that this step on its own could offset the widespread feeling amongst the public fed up with having to take its medicine. Conservative morale gaining little from the Chancellor's gloomy assessment of the economy during his 1982 budgetary statement. One that announced only modest increases in personal allowances, child and unemployment benefits, matched by the usual raising of duties on tobacco, alcohol and petrol. What seemed to be an unstoppable downward slide in popularity ending in electoral defeat only halted when an equally unpopular bunch of rulers, the military Junta of Argentina, won temporary acclaim for itself by exploiting old grievances, invading and taking over the British administered South Georgia and the Falkland Islands. This delivered a lifeline to the Prime Minister, one she quickly grasped, authorising a task force to assemble and head south and win them back. A remarkably narrow victory bringing an equally remarkable turnaround in national sentiment in her favour and a further term in office. A success, if truth be known, that also owed something to the adoption of a near suicidal political Manifesto by the Labour party.

As world output began picking up in 1983, dragging a lagging domestic economy with it, hopes rose that the worst was over. Thinking that ran against the ambitions of the new leader of the NUM Executive, Mr Arthur Scargill, who led all but the Nottinghamshire miners into contesting the government's decision to close twenty uneconomic coal-mines. In a bitter political struggle lasting 362 days, the shock troops of the labour movement fought a well prepared administration willing to tough it out. The miners eventual climb down sounding the death knell, not only for their industry but, also for the hard working honourable communities they inhabited.

It was in many ways the defining moment of the Eighties, one that conveys much sadness, even if it was essential the nation and its government won the day. Once more public attitudes were surprisingly ambivalent to the underlying dangers, repeating its folly of the 1930's when the nation stuck its head in the sand rather than face up to unpleasant realities. Besides the human costs of this struggle, there were other penalties, financial ones, with around one percent knocked off the national output along with a need to borrow an extra two and three quarter billion pounds to cope with the losses. The recovery from this action signalled by a new Chancellor in his 1984 Budget which brought forward the idea of tax reform. National Insurance and investment income surcharges were done away with, while various adjustments were put in place affecting tax allowances, corporation tax, stamp duty and transfer tax.

Longer term plans to privatise publicly owned assets made a cautious start when BT was floated during November that same year. Encouraged, the new Chancellor, Nigel Lawson, employed this success to secure the principle and continue. British Gas being sold at the end of 1986, followed by British Airways, Rolls Royce and the British Airports Authority the year after that. Towards the end of the decade British Steel and the water and sewage utilities also entered the private domain, while the electricity industry, British Rail and British Nuclear energy went on the block in the nineties.

The peak of Margaret Thatcher's Premier-ship came in the mid-Eighties, conditions in 1985 allowing the Chancellor to raise tax allowances by a substantial amount, removing a large number of people from the burdens of having to pay income tax. Reforms supplemented by changes to the way National Insurance contributions were assessed. The following year he was also able to reduce the basic rate of income tax, boosting interest in saving and investments by way of tax free incentives in what was called Personal Equity Plan's (PEP). Capital Transfer Tax, which took over from Estate Duties in 1975, was replaced by Inheritance Tax, redefining the rules applying to transfers of wealth on or shortly before death.

Arguably the most significant of this era's deregulatory moves came on the 27th of October 1986 when the Stock Exchange was set free. This placed the onus on London to maintain itself as one of the world's leading financial centres, something it was to do, becoming a major factor in turning Britain's fortunes around in the post-industrial era. This so called Big Bang was accompanied by the liberalising of the Building Societies, reform freeing these high street institutions to turn themselves into limited companies. Most if not all, going onto to develop banking and other specialist financial services.

As the economic boom took off, an event closely associated with Nigel Lawson's term as Chancellor. An expanding service sector reduced unemployment, low inflation and easy credit inciting a rise in house prices and a surge in demand for imported consumer goods. The headlines of the day largely free of coverage of strikes, industrial aggravation largely collapsing, less than four million days being lost per annum on average between 1985-89 compared with the peak in the early Seventies of over fourteen million. The Budget in 1987 following the June election that delivered a third term introduced further reductions in taxation and the expected sums government planned to borrow. The basic rate of income tax stepping down to 27%, duty on petrol and inheritance tax also coming in for beneficial adjustment.

Disturbing the general optimism was the results of easy credit stimulating the economy a little too much, its first hiccup coming on the 19th of October 1987 when stock markets around the world endured severe readjustments in what was called ‘Black Monday.’ A shock that upset all the European economies, adding to Britain’s problem of record trade deficits. Over-demand kicking in to drive inflation back up, the necessary brakes being applied by interest rates hikes, an unwelcome step for those who had taken on a big mortgage.

Even though the circumstances had taken a turn for the worse, the 1988 Budget cut the basic rate of income tax to 25%, with the higher rate being reduced to forty percent. Actions that provoked a stormy session in the Commons, some MP’s losing self control, forcing the Deputy Speaker to suspend the House. Tempers barely cooling a year on, when Nigel Lawson’s sixth and final Budget had to contend with the consequences of his earlier actions.

Opposition to government, which had long sought a cause around which it could gather, scented blood over the unpopular replacement to the rating system, the Poll Tax. A major campaign against its introduction flourished, reaching its peak with a major demonstration at the end of March 1990. This disturbed the government equilibrium, forcing the new Chancellor, John Major, in his only Budget that year to alter the qualification for income support for Poll Tax payers to sixteen thousand pounds. Further offset coming the following year when Norman Lamont, who took over as Chancellor from John Major, announced a rise in VAT to 17.5 percent, most of the revenue generated by this measure directed towards reducing the Poll Tax by £140 via the Community Charge Reduction Scheme.

Behind these reverses, were other frictions that took time to reveal themselves. The catalyst for open revolt related to Europe where profound ideological differences separated those who ardently believed in European integration and others much more sceptical over what this meant in the long term. While acceding to the economic justifications behind the 1985 Single European Act, the Prime Ministers instinctive suspicions and rejection of the EEC's overtly Federalist agenda brought her into conflict with senior figures of her own party. Leading this opposition was Geoffrey Howe, who in a speech given to the Commons on 1st November 1990 following his resignation as Deputy Prime Minister, openly questioned Mrs Thatcher's attitudes to Europe.

This is a story with some of its roots in the differences of opinion that surrounded British membership of the European Exchange-Rate Mechanism (ERM). First established without Britain, this system of fixed exchange rates held great appeal, especially given the low inflationary record and enduring strength of its central pillar, the German Mark. It being understandable that this record, so different from the British experience, should result in temptations to copy it in some way in the hope of emulating its success. Indeed this had been a factor in Nigel Lawson's fiscal strategies when he informally tracked the ERM.

Recommendations to join had in fact been sponsored by the Chancellor as early as 1985, Mrs Thatcher's vetoing the idea. Nevertheless pressure for membership continued and very much against her instincts, she was persuaded by Cabinet. Britain signing up in October of 1990. A fateful decision because Germany's own interest rates were by then facing pressures brought on by the burdens it assumed following Helmut Kohl's, the West German Chancellor, decision to bankroll reunification with its eastern half. Influences that would eventually expose the pound to severe international pressures, forcing its ignominious withdrawal.

The decisive rupture that sealed Mrs Thatcher fate came when her leadership was openly challenged by Michael Heseltine. Having failed to win on the first ballot, she unexpectedly resigned, supporting John Major who took over as PM on the 20th November 1990. A difficult moment as economic reverse once more dominated events, inflation and unemployment heading up. A situation that crushed the housing boom, forcing many householders into negative equity, many owing more than the house itself was worth.

These awkward circumstances appeared to swamp whatever good the Prime Minister's might have gained from his personal initiatives in creating the Citizens Charter and National Lottery. Yet, despite the injuries, John Major overcame the pollsters predictions and won a term in his own right in the election of 1992. His easy charm and willingness to get out on the street to meet people overcoming the negatives. A high turnout, nearly 78%, giving him a majority of 21 seats.

A bare five months into his administration however, disaster struck. Membership of the ERM combined with high domestic inflation making sterling a tempting target for speculative attack. Despite interest rates hitting 15% and the squandering of billions of pounds in its defence, relentless international pressure orchestrated by financiers such as George Soros, forced Britain's withdrawal on 16th September (Black Wednesday). An experience that is now seen positively, mainly because it finally forced government into facing up to its fiscal responsibilities.

The aftermath of this debacle was severe, widespread private and business bankruptcies tainting the Conservative Party's reputation in spite of the next few years seeing soundly based recovery. Kenneth Clarke, who took over the mantle of Chancellor, orchestrating a halving of the budget deficit, a reduction in inflation rate to just two percent and steadily falling unemployment. The Poll Tax also consigned to history in favour of the Community Charge, a banded property based system that came into force in April of 1993. Additional revenues generated by his decision to bring in the Insurance Premium tax, which acted as a form of VAT on insurance policies.

Memories of the Conservative years are of course dominated by the dramatic collapse of un-competitive industry, a shakeout more or less over by the mid-Nineties. The concentration of traditional industry in the north, with its largely male dominated manufacturing or mining, meant unemployment took on a distinct north south divide. Many of these skilled men finding few alternatives, their primary qualification rarely appropriate for service sectors opportunities such as retail and office based roles. Work generally better suited to women with its emphasis on patient endurance, use of a computer terminal or shuffling paper. A major factor in the dramatic expansion of women into the workforce over the Eighties and Nineties. A time of evolution that was to see nearly three quarters of the working population involved in what had become a service based economy.

Yet as has been shown since, given a stable environment with up to date technology and modern techniques, British workers are perfectly capable of holding their own against anyone else. Even if those who have proved this are foreign owned firms such as Honda, Nissan and BMW. Organisations that brought with them the management styles able to capitalise on changed attitudes wrought by ugly realities. Nissan's Sunderland plant a case in point, this being one of, if not the most productive motor assembly centre in Europe. Not far behind is the Honda plant in Swindon. The irony in all this is drawn from the fact that those who lost the Second World War on the battlefield would eventually teach the victors how to run a business.

Chapter 27

Stability the aim

For once in its post-war history, a change of British government did not present its successor with a wretchedly difficult economic situation. Manageable public debt, low inflation and comparatively small levels of unemployment along with stable world commodity prices helped the domestic situation, even if an overvalued pound put some strain on unit labour costs. The incoming Labour administration under its leader, Mr Tony Blair, essentially free to develop its agenda without the distractions of day to day crisis.

With a Prime Minister more interested in the big picture, the real responsibility for delivering on the governments financial commitments fell to the occupier of 11 Downing Street, Gordon Brown, the new Chancellor. The necessity of earning a reputation for financial probity starting with the stated aim of staying within Conservative spending limits during its first two years in office. Prudence gaining further kudos when operational independence was handed to the Bank of England by providing it with the power to autonomously set interest rates to meet government inflation targets. Moves supported by the declaration that public borrowing would fund investment and not current spending. A strategy supported by a pledge to control national debt to sensible levels, freeing of financial policy from short term politicking, one finally independent of Labour's historic commitment to the interests of organised labour and the principle of nationalisation.

In his ten years as the principle architect of British economic policy, Gordon Brown delivered eleven budgets. His tenure in office recognised for the inventive measures he employed to raise government revenue and the affection he was to display in allocating this largesse to State run entities.

The broad sweep of the Chancellor's first Budget set an enduring tone, favoured targets for generating revenue were the duties on tobacco, alcohol, petrol and vehicles. Stamp duty proving another productive source, the introduction of a graduated scale seeing later adjustments to garner more money from the ever rising price of houses. Further contributions to the government coffers coming from a windfall tax on the privatised utilities and, much more contentiously, the abolition of the dividend tax credit on pensions funds. A measure netting the government somewhere between five to seven billion pounds a year at the unintended consequence of undermining private pension funding. Many final salary schemes being wound up over the following years as the financial commitments grew too large. Balancing this early taking was a little giving, the outstanding budgetary deficit was cut still further, as was the cost of domestic fuel and power, while businesses in general benefited from a reduction in corporation tax.

Labelled as a budget for work, Gordon Brown's second introduced one of his key concepts, that of tax credits. The Working Families Tax Credits scheme was amended several times before being superseded in the 2003 Budget by two separate measures, the Child Tax Credit and the Working Tax Credit. The former, a means tested benefits supplementing universal child benefit, the latter a way of boosting income for those on a limited wage. Helping fund this transfer was the decline in financial support for marriage, the married couples allowance further restricted, its abolition announced in the 2000 budget for everyone except for those over 65 years of age.

Typically, even good ideas were changed, an example here was the unnecessary tinkering with incentives to save. PEP and TESSA saving accounts being replaced by the broadly similar Individual Savings Accounts (ISA). Revisions also coming to direct personal taxation in 1999 with the introduction of a new starting rate of ten percent for income tax, one complemented by a reduction in the basic rate to 22%. Less welcome, although broadly expected, was the decision to get rid of Mortgage Interest Tax Relief, this coming into effect from April the following year. National Insurance contributions also facing adjustment.

More controversial was the sale of four hundred tons of Britain's gold reserves, some two thirds of the entire amount. Auctioned off against Treasury advice, it was disposed off in several tranches between 1999-2002 during a time when the price of gold hovered around a twenty year low.

The turn of the century and the early years of the new millennium marked the turning point in Labour's programme. Having secured a reputation for reasonable financial responsibility, it reverted to type by embarking on ambitious spending plans, ploughing very large sums into the public sector. Money that reversed the chronic under-funding that had long characterised most of Britain's public services at the cost of failing to examine how this funding was spent. Integrated into this effort was expansion of Private Finance Initiatives (PFI), here too, a lack of oversight was see the potential benefit to the public squandered as contracts were often poorly negotiated. Indeed so contentious did this policy become that it was relabelled as Private-Public Partnerships (PPP) in an attempt to deflect emotive negativity symbolised by the term PFI.

Efforts to encourage business came from new rules applied to investment in research and development. The primary beneficiaries small, medium and loss making companies, larger organisations getting attention later on. A further curiosity at the time was the Child Trust Fund, the Exchequer setting aside money for each child at birth, although for what precise purpose is hard to determine. Efforts to help those at the other end of the age scale, in this case those over eighty, getting additional assistance towards covering winter fuel costs, help extended in the 2004 Budget when council tax payments were eased for pensioners.

Accompanying this major expenditure was a substantial increase in those employed by the State. An awareness of the apparent and hidden costs seeing the Chancellor undergoing a modest conversion somewhat later when he sought retrenchment by announcing the merging of Customs and Excise with the Inland Revenue. Modest cutbacks in certain Civil Service positions matched by plans to move some departments out of London.

Adding to the national burdens were the costs imposed by the second Gulf War in Iraq. An extra three billion pounds being diverted to the defence budget to go with £240 million for humanitarian aid. Equal demands coming from the substantial deployment of British forces into the difficult terrain of Afghanistan. Overall the perceived dangers from international and domestic terrorism incited by these involvement's addressed by major boosts in financial support to the police and intelligence services.

Interfering with the continued optimistic assessments for the domestic economy was the sustained rise in the price of oil. The global economy slowing, a recession that lingered into 2005, an event that did not prevent the Organisation for Economic Co-operation and Development (OECD) noting in its summary of the British economy that the situation remained reasonable. GDP continued to grow steadily, if not spectacularly, with productivity up to that of Germany, even if it remained some way behind France and the US. Inflation, unemployment and the budgetary deficit all remaining at controllable levels.

Fiscal policy in 2006 followed the same general path, with additional tax credits for children along with the provision of free off-peak bus travel for pensioners and the disabled. While the ongoing campaign against tax fraud and avoidance was emphasised and strengthened. Widespread concerns over global climate change, which had already seen the implementation of a tiered system of Vehicle Excise Duty based on its carbon dioxide emissions, was extended into other areas of environmental concern. Duties being applied to air travel to go with a landfill tax and aggregate levy.

As government revenue steadily increased, where and how it spent the money became a matter of concern. Especially over the issue of waste, something exposed by various sharp eyed critical souls who sparked the government into initiating its own review under the stewardship of Sir Peter Gershon. His report identified potential savings of over £21 billion over coming next two to three years, including a reduction of some 80 thousand civil service posts. These relatively low expectations contrasted sharply with the opinion of the European Central Bank which reckoned waste was four times that per annum, a figure the Tax Payers Alliance concurred with. An interesting and unrelated aside at the time was the final repayment of Britain's wartime debts to the US. A sum of £46.9 million being handed over some fifty-five years after the deal was negotiated.

In his final budget before taking up residence next door as Prime Minister, Mr. Brown turned towards articulating a need to simplify the tax system he was mainly responsible for making into a bigger mystery than it was already. A statement that ran along side a modest reduction in the rate of corporate tax to 28% and a peculiar rise in the taxation of small businesses. Much of his final statement devoting space to future planned spending on the health and education, the criminal justice system and the police as well as transport. Ensuring that while he had taken up residence at Number 10, he was in fact still at Number 11.

Any assessment of the past ten years must conclude that the economy has continued to do reasonable well, even with government increasing its take of the national income. Growth being inline or slightly above the laboured Euro-zone average to go with reasonable inflation rates and tolerable official employment figures. Much less justified is the differentiation developing in funding allocated per head of population. Wide variations now exist within the weakening Union, the main beneficiaries of this have been Scotland, Wales and Northern Ireland at the expense of England. Regional differences within England itself revealing a decided north south split in who gets what, smaller variations at the local level appearing to align with known political allegiances.

Chapter 28

Creating a social revolution

Civilisation sustains itself over the long term by broad agreement on principles and standards whose appeal is such that a sufficient mass of one generation is prepared to pass its lessons onto the next. If anything threatens the support necessary to keep that creed common, then ultimately social cohesion must weaken. It proved unfortunate for Britain that it came under the spell of those whose actions were to achieve just that over the final four decades of the last century.

Tracing the origins of what is particular to Britain in an era that has seen world wide changes takes us back to the moment when sharing knowledge became easier. The advent of the printing press freeing mankind from what had been until then, a major constraint on human progress. The ability to put ideas on paper helping stimulate that surge of originality which defined the Renaissance. A period during which Britain emerged from the shadows of its own ignorance under the guidance of writers such as Thomas Hobbes, John Locke, Adam Smith and later, John Stuart Mill. Their work instrumental in the birth and sustaining of that period known here as the Enlightenment. Work that inspired classical liberal thought, the bedrock that raised Britain to world eminence, the Pax Britannica whose peak came late on in the reign of Queen Victoria.

Ironically it was at the very height of this power that the seeds of its end germinated. Those responsible were mainly German thinkers, individuals who held humanity up the light, drawing fresh conclusions on its condition, finding in the harshness of early industrialised life appeals that would resonate amongst Briton's then and now. A crowd whose instincts the Austrian born political economist, Friedrich Hayek wrote of when he stated that, *'intellectuals are drawn to visions and ideas, as well as to systems which accord them a greater share of influence and power.'* Which is precisely what socialism was to offer as it entered mainstream life on the way to becoming the dominant belief system of twentieth century Britain. A movement that drew moral authority from historic inclinations, in particular the principle of welfare which had established itself during the long ago reign of Elizabeth 1st when she imposed a duty on Parishes to care for the poor. Periodic reforms of these same laws just a part of an ongoing interest in the plight of the less well off.

Unfortunately for Britain, this compassionate regard evolved into self righteous political, economic and social interference. Its actions applied without rigorous assessment of human frailty, analysis of cost or examination of consequence. The product being plain enough. The nation of today is no longer the well mannered law abiding place of fifty years ago. That has been lost. In its place is a patchwork of the good and not so good. A land whose majority still strives to live a decent life, even if they are forced to do so under the hand of those disinterested in responding to ordinary concerns.

Unlike some revolutions, the beginnings were comparatively benign. The 1967 decision to decriminalise homosexual acts between consenting adults aged twenty-one and over a broadly welcomed step. Supporting that fundamental change was revision to the law on abortion, one intended to offer termination of pregnancy in sanitary conditions, protecting the mother from the risks of back-street butchery. The debate surrounding this measure with its fine talk of rules against it becoming a last ditch form of birth control proving not much more than a smokescreen as events would prove.

The comparative ease with which these groundbreaking rules were accepted fed into the momentum that would sustain a conveyor belt of change. A process often covered by ruse and subterfuge. Public resistance bringing retreat until attention was diverted or attitudes had grown tolerant enough to accept. Not that what went on ever revolved around a single idea, as one area of custom or sense was discarded or changed, another came into focus. The torchbearers for this crusade have been women, modern feminism providing the means through which the most damaging action, the attack on the traditional family, could be launched. It is with this issue that this examination begins.

Chapter 29

Modern feminism and the attack on the family

The reforms concerning the provision of abortion marked the opening shots in a prolonged campaign to alter attitudes regarding women. The objective of this effort was to equalise the relative roles and contributions made by males and females. An end that was to take little account of personal preference or inclination.

A significant justification for the need for radical change rode atop revised interpretations of past society, the view establishing itself amongst the influential was that past life had permanently disadvantaged females and modern society needed to supply a corrective. The solution to this was to remove the distinctions that had until that point largely determined life. An important element in the necessary policies to achieve that end was to deride the roles that had traditionally fallen to the woman. Ideals that appealed, as they had for some time, to radically inclined females who felt constrained by conventional society.

A major stumbling block to these particular ambitions however was the instinctive pull even gifted women experience for children. The emotional satisfactions of motherhood often bringing prolonged or, even permanent retreat from any further involvement with paid employment. Traditionally because a man and woman joined forces, usually he earning and she caring, a practical arrangement generally cemented through marriage. Whatever advantages were associated with this structure, it was seen in lofty intellectual circles as a restraint on female fulfilment.

As communist philosophy understood from its genesis and western intellectual thinking came to fully appreciate later, nothing keeps the ruling hierarchy at bay so much as a man and woman supporting each other in the business of living. This symbiotic relationship, greater than the sum of its individual halves, acts as a closed loop keeping out other interests. Its greatest contribution to the traditions and stability of society being the influence it exercises over its offspring's formative years. As Mikhail Gorbachev amongst others pointed out, control of the population becomes easier, for a time anyway, when this sanctuary is invaded and reduced. An opinion clearly shared certain elements in Britain who sought to further their own ambitions by embarking on efforts to destroy the solidarity of traditional family life.

Headway towards these goals began with the careful courting of women, the legitimate justifications of certain reforms such as legislation on equal pay in 1970 soon corrupted by senseless fostering of antipathy over some imagined historic male conspiracy (the patriarchy). A convenient, if preposterous, claim utilised and adapted to justify all manner of later exceptions and bias. The spread of this divisive ideology gaining heavily from persuasions directed at impressionable young minds that sought to make out they could do as they pleased. An end encouraged by widespread denigration of men's traditional role as provider and protector, the State putting itself forward as the substitute.

As this sentiment spread it became the platform from which to question the old assumption that the traditional family, a married couple and their offspring, was an automatic good. Calculated efforts to erode the view that a father made a positive contribution to his family supplemented later by suggestions that a child's welfare was not necessarily served by full time parental care. It being feasible and equally beneficial for outside bodies, in this case government controlled, to sponsor child care.

This marked a fundamental shift from the immediate post-war days when society and its servants, the politicians, saw it as important to aid wedded couples by giving the married man an allowance against tax. The introduction of the family allowance supplying extra money for the second and any additional children. These quite modest benefits were supplemented in other ways, with priority for housing for example, all of which tended to give the average family independence and standing. Equally important was the special treatment of widows, while the few births outside wedlock often resulted in the adoption of the child, if care within the wider family proved impractical. All this was to change as Britain set about adopting policies that penalised those who lived up to their responsibilities and rewarded those who did not.

The legislative underpinnings of these new attitudes began with the 1967 Family Planning Act, a law allowing the authorities to provide contraceptive measures irrespective of marital status or grounds. A rule that would expand its remit over the coming years to the point where parents would be effectively excluded from playing any meaningful role in the control of sexual activity of their own children. The State, in a perversion of its own laws, ensuring that access to this advice and material was available to those who were below the legal age of consent.

Following this overture was the overturning of the distinctions between married and unmarried people. The Seebohm Report suggesting a special Social Services Department be set up to handle the needs of unmarried mothers, an idea leading to the creation of a National Council for One Parent Families. Initial steps to redirect benefits coming in 1969 when a proportion of the married man's allowance was awarded to what were called single parent families. Amended to include the whole amount six years later, by which time longer term aims saw benefits to children extended to the first child irrespective of whether the mother was married or not. Family allowance and tax exemptions being consigned to history in favour of universal child allowance, a flat rate for all children coming in 1978, with additional benefits for single parents being allocated three years later.

To begin with demands on the Treasury from these changes were not that large. After all, illegitimacy rates were still comparatively low, having declined from a peak of nine percent in 1945 to a low of five percent by the end of the Fifties. The rise from that point constrained to a degree by the growing use of abortion. Only later, when the restraint formerly applied by society fell away did the numbers of single parent households reach socially significant levels. Topping some 1.3 million by 1991, with never married mothers representing the fastest growing segment of this population. The number ramping on up to just under two million midway through the first decade of the twenty-first century.

Behind that rise, especially during the Eighties, was an awareness by young women that getting pregnant opened 'Pandora's Box' to a host of State sponsored benefits. Included was provision of housing, first made available in 1966, along with other grants, benefits and allowances. On the surface at least, it was an attractive option, have a baby without having to do anything tedious like working. Paying for this State sponsored generosity was everyone else, the tax burden shifting steadily down the scale since the 1950's, hitting low income married couples and their children. For those earning large sums this was not much of an issue, however more and more couples were coming to depend on two incomes to afford children. Those at the very bottom struggling to make ends meet because of tax demands they could ill afford.

One supposed response to this burden was the Child Support Agency, an organisation created by parliament in 1991 to assess and collect maintenance, usually from the father. Passing these funds in lieu of State benefits to the party caring for the child, mostly the mother. For a variety of reasons this proved far from easy, meaning that women who had children without the means to support them were entirely reliant on the rest of the population.

Not that these consequences affected attitudes which confirmed in the 1993 Budget the intention to remove the marriage allowance, something by then casually referred to as a fiscal anomaly. A plan implemented as part of the 2000 Budget, only those over sixty-five retaining it as a small addition to their pension. By then, the bulk of benefit was directed towards children irrespective of status, either via universal benefit or means tested tax credits for those on low incomes. The sums involved having become considerable, by 2003 for instance the money spent on supporting children had risen to over twenty-two billion pounds, more than twice the amount spent less than thirty years before. Equally predictably, lone parents are the primary recipients of much of this aid, by the end of the century over seventy percent of lone parents were receiving family credit or income support, more than half of whom also had access to housing and council tax benefits.

Concurrent with the eroding of financial incentives was the campaign aimed at undermining the legal status of marriage. Allies in the camp supporting this end included various fringe groups and influential bodies with direct access to government, which was itself receptive to pursuing such reform. Additional persuasion coming from the generally anti-family ethos of European elite's and the institutions they dominated. As a consequence it became the norm to hear open expressions advising that no notice should be taken of illegitimacy, views supplemented by the more radical views questioning whether the legal institution of marriage could be considered as serving any useful purpose. Thoughts that reached culmination in a 1988 report concluding there was no longer any need to support marriage over any other living arrangement.

These attitudes found expression in the various legal amendments that over time reduced the institution to a shadow of it former self. The most crucial step of all taken in 1969 when the Divorce Reform Act introduced a 'no fault separation clause.' The removal of guilt from marital breakdown was followed four years later by the Matrimonial Causes Act which introduced procedural changes allowing the granting of divorce by post. Further reform nine years was added by the Matrimonial and Family Proceedings Act which permitted the petitioning for divorce after just a year. A Bill also providing for the so-called clean break procedures which allowed couples to arrange for financial termination without any legacies. The later Children's Act (1989) put married and unmarried fathers on the same plain, effectively removing any incentive men might have in marriage other than tradition. Unmarried fathers finding themselves able to assume parental rights should they wish by making a Parental Responsibility Agreement with the mother. The further contortions of public policy illustrated when parental rights were given to homosexuals, a curious idea for a naturally barren arrangement.

Chapter 30

Consequences

In his book, 'The Welfare State We're In,' James Bartholomew spoke about East End of London families in the early 1950's, noting how materially modest lives in cramped terraced housing were nonetheless socially rich. The bonds between aunts, uncles and grandparents extending into the lives of their children and their children's children. A community of intermeshing generations that was demolished when the streets they lived in were bulldozed to make way for modern development, a well meant action that impoverished once rewarding lives.

What remains from that past is its attraction, the benefits still perceptively recognised and desired even by the most modern minds. The ordinary realising that stability and an enduring relationship give the best chance of constructing personal meaning. What they also appear to know is that their children do better while they remain married and living together, an arrangement whose stability improves the odds that their children will enter adult life well balanced and adjusted. Yet, since the 1960's the main aim of the influential here has been to deride the contributions of wedlock with all this meant to its offspring. It reaching the point where facilitating the breakdown of such a relationship has priority over any effort to support or protect it.

Reinforcing this ideology is the money that can be made from the wreckage of broken relationships. An influential industry having grown around representing the interests of one side over the other. Essential to its creed is employment of emotive appeals to influence the courts judgement. Allegations that are often difficult to substantiate, not only because of a lack of direct evidence, but also because what is at work in close human relationships often defies easy analysis by outsiders. Both parties capable of engaging in behaviour that includes all manner of physical and mental weaponry. Encouraging one or other to engage in confrontational behaviour invokes what is ultimately destructive to the cause of civil society. Something fully recognised by those who have sought to further these ends, aims pursued still further by trying to stack the odds in favour of one party.

It is no great surprise in the face of this hostility that the number of marriages has generally declined, nor is it any real wonder that the number ending in divorce in Britain is the highest in Europe. Both trends are mutually reinforcing as confidence ebbs and fears over what failure means grows. Inevitably, more people are, by preference or misfortune, living alone. While there are a complex of reasons for this, not least the demands of work which can be all consuming for both men and women. It is clear that many young men have assessed the attitudes of society, concluding that the burdens of marriage and family are not worth the risk to their financial or general health. Figures from the United States for example suggest that these numbers are as high as one in four or five amongst those of marriageable age.

One way around these perceived risks is co-habitation, a sort of trial marriage where a couple set up house together without formality. This provides a way of gaining the economic and social benefits of a married couple without the supposed problems of 'that bit of paper.' Both parties remaining free to act as they wish when they wish. The permanent existence of an easy out excluding genuine commitment, analysis showing that cohabitation is more vulnerable to collapse than those entering marriage without any trial period of living together. A reality knocking over one of the principle justifications for cohabitation, that living together first makes for a better marriage. In truth it succeeds while both parties find it convenient. As passions ease and the strains of proximity and perhaps children come into play, then the arrangement often proves too weak to survive.

As the numbers choosing this route have grown, so social campaigners sought to shift the law governing these loose arrangements by attributing rights formerly given to married couples to cohabitees. The Law Reform (Succession) Act of 1995 and the Family Law Act of the following year adjusted the situation regarding property. Further plans are now in place to create a situation where there are few actual differences between the two. With all this means to the division of assets in the event of breakdown, it is possible that this will further dissuade men from considering any form of social attachment.

It goes without saying that those most affected by this loss of social stability are children. Especially when the offspring are only connected biologically to one parent, it being common for a lack of interest to emerge, with one or even both adults taking it out on the youngsters with disastrous consequences. The spark to such a development often evolves out of a sense of competition for attention between the child and its natural parent and the other adult. Further complicating the situation is the resolution of disputes by violence, cohabitees are much more prone to throwing things or worse. Such examples seed problems that later stalk the child as it grows into adulthood. Equally worrying are those instances where the adults put themselves first, leaving the youngsters to care for themselves. There has been for some time a discernible trend amongst teenagers leaving home, either voluntarily or because they are forced out long before they are able to properly fend for themselves.

As it stands, the viability of single parenthood has only been made possible by the provision of financial inducements by the State. Surely a contributory factor to Britain's very high levels of teenage pregnancy, currently Europe's highest. While not all single parents turn our poor children, it is generally recognised that their children do worst, educational shortfalls, behavioural problems and high incidence of mental illness their frequent lot. A substantial portion of those ending up permanently stuck at the bottom of the socio-economic pile are the offspring of a single parent. Not that these problems are restricted just to the children, it is clearly no easy ride for the single parent to cope alone as the child grows, it can and does extracts a formidable toll.

The truth of the matter is that contemporary social policy has created a production line whose output is feral children. For many of these unfortunates, home is no loving refuge where mum and dad do their best, instead it is an empty place that leaves scars where no marks show. The costs of this national failing walk our streets, the angry frustrated young men and women ill adapted to the way life is, types qualified in inventive swearing, excessive drinking, fighting, drug taking and mindless sexual abandon.

While these comments present something of a bleak picture, credit must be given to those who continue to do their best despite the obstacles put in the way. The intrinsic attractions men and women have for each other still motivate plenty to take on the considerable demands of trying to establish a conventional and traditional family. During 2001 sixty-four percent of families with children were still married couple families. The majority of these working hard to remain as close to traditional boundaries as circumstances allow. The costs often imposing the need for both parents to earn, demands that lead to exhaustion and the destruction of self. The reason they do so are time honoured, for the love and commitment to each other, their offspring and the small world they try to create. Even for those who fail, often after enduring what ruins, the effort goes on to make amends as best they can.

Chapter 31

Sexual crudity and its price

Contributing to the division between men and women is the endorsement of sexual practice as nothing more than a meaningless liaison, frequently as one of a sequence. In this, women lose by failing to realise that come thirty most will have already lost what so attracts, while men, grow unfeeling. Finding only indifference in a life stripped of warmth and the rewards of emotional investment and constructive purpose.

The lurch towards this miserable outcome was part of world-wide phenomenon energetically taken up by young Briton's in the 1960's. Some of whom imagined they were blazing a new trail, half believing, the tongue in cheek assertions of the poet Phillip Larkin. Needless to say, the reality is more mundane, human sexuality nothing more than a basic drive that plays its part in every generation and culture. What could be seen as new was the freedom to indulge without pregnancy thanks to improvements in chemical and mechanical contraception, in particular the birth control pill.

Intriguingly this liberating capacity to control fertility has cast a shadow, for although sexual intimacy can be enjoyed by one and all, it has come at the price of isolating the act from its purpose. This is consistently sold as a good, one taken up and exploited by the visual media who play on its titillating aspects as a means to sell. Crude portrayal that robs intercourse of its mystery by turning private joy into a spectator sport. In Britain, as with elsewhere, this has brought about a coarsening in attitudes towards genuine intimacy, its crudest manifestation reflected in the sub culture of hooking up. Common to American campus life and perhaps here, social relations between the two sexes are reduced to meeting just for the purpose of sexual intercourse. There being no meaning other than the animal returns of the physical.

This loosening of restraint has unleashed predatory behaviours whose ugliest end has been the letting go of societal restraint on adult behaviour towards and in the presence of children. From a media that sexualises the immature to the sick malevolence of sexual exploitation by perverted adults, innocence is sacrificed. Government getting in on the act through its obsessive desires to impose adult responsibilities and understanding on the very young.

Mirroring this unpleasantness is the rise in the number of claims of rape. Something of a conundrum given the casual attitudes society now exhibits towards sexual behaviour and now common belief that women too share in these relaxed interpretations. Quite how legitimate these numbers are in what is a sordid business remains less certain. Adding to the distaste are distinctions in the protections the law supplies to those involved. Whether this has encouraged more women into making allegations, which by the very nature of this business are next to impossible to prove one way or the other in the aftermath, is also unclear. However, the confrontation this provokes fits in well with the agenda of those who object is social division. A philosophy that above wants to prevent the emergence of a world based on mutual responsibility between consenting, intelligent adults.

This sense of abandon cuts right across society. Unwanted pregnancies whose solution parliament seems to think can be solved by the repugnance that is abortion, matched by the forlorn idea that the answer to venereal disease is the condom. The subtleties of unchecked sexual licence evidently too difficult to be explored and assessed by that particular body.

What did for a time wake everyone up was the advent of what is known as Acquired Immune Deficiency Syndrome (AIDS). This disease, identified in the Eighties, carries a bleak prognosis for those exposed to the viral agent that is its cause. Although early predictions that we were all doomed have proved wildly inaccurate. In reality those who are most at risk are homosexual men, drug addicts sharing needles, the unborn child if the mother contracts the disease and early on a number of haemophiliac's who were given contaminated blood.

By the end of 2005 it is thought around 80,000 people in Britain have been identified as being infected with the Human Immuno-deficiency Virus (HIV positive), around a quarter of whom have succumbed to AIDS. Recent movement of the disease into the heterosexual community having more to do with those who contracted it elsewhere and brought it with them, mainly from Africa. A fact repeatedly denied by the authorities until evidence of this could no longer be refuted.

Recently, as the AIDS scare dropped below the radar, there has been a rise in other sexually transmitted diseases (STD's). Escalating numbers for example getting the generally symptom-less chlamydia, which if left untreated can cause female and, maybe male, infertility. This and other diseases such as gonorrhoea are often resistant to the antibiotics that at first prevented the spread of these unpleasant products of supposed sexual liberation.

Chapter 32

Facts about crime and the law

Nothing is more indicative of how things have changed in Britain over the last fifty years than the galloping growth of crime. The scale of this change can be deduced by reference to the records for England and Wales over the final decades of the nineteenth century and the opening twenty to thirty years of the last. For most of that era, the average incidence of recorded crime of all sorts was around the hundred thousand mark. The fundamental reason why it remained so low is down to the prevailing sentiment that existed within society. A moral frame obstructed those determined to break the law, a robust steadfast citizenry collectively frowning on law breaking, even if they did not actually appreciate the authority's that maintained it. That this attitude and what it meant largely survived the trials and profound hardships imposed by the Great Depression says much about the ethos and people of the time.

Signs of change can be seen by reviewing the years just before, during and after the Second World War. A time when crime rates crept upwards, although these increases were insufficient in themselves to alter the fact that life in these isles remained essentially peaceful and largely free of distressing, ugly incident. The movement towards new territory began in the 1960's, the latter part of the last century seeing a seven-fold increase in recorded crime. The apparent peak coming in 1992 when 5.6 million criminal incidents were logged against a population in England and Wales of around fifty million.

As with all such statistics, there is plenty of dispute over validity, the whole business muddied by differing methods of collecting meshing with changes in law that makes an action a crime in one era but not in another. Traditionally, the figures relied on what was reported and recorded by the police, a process that altered in 2002 following the introduction of the National Crime Recording Standard (NCRS). A procedural shift intended to make records more accurate, a change responsible for an apparent jump in the crime rate of about ten percent.

Operating along side these official numbers are figures derived from what is called the British Crime Survey (BCS). First run in 1982, this samples people living in private households about their personal experiences. This has limitations because it excludes crimes committed on those under sixteen years of age, just as it does not count sex offences, murder or incidents against commercial premises and vehicles, also leaving out shop lifting, fraud and drug offences. Despite these reservations, the BCS figures for 2003 totalled just shy of twelve million offences. Adding in the crimes automatically excluded led the Home Office to suggest that the probable crime figures were in the order of 22-23 million offences. A number subject to doubling or more if multiple offences are taken into account. Much of this crime is related to shoplifting, which has reached epidemic proportions with over one and half million cases a year. The primary motive of around ninety percent of those engaged in this activity is the need to feed a drug habit.

Where Britain fits into the international hierarchy of crime can be determined in part by reference to the International Crime Victim Survey (ICVS). Results taken from its 2000 survey which covered seventeen countries, suggests that England and Wales has become the second most risky place to live after Australia. Placing it significantly ahead of the US and France and just a smidgen ahead of the Netherlands and Sweden. When it comes to very serious offences, apart that is from murder, Britain tops the charts, indications of how violent things have become here over recent years.

Interestingly, as crime ramped up the numbers of those caught and subsequently convicted fell away. With only three percent of all crimes leading to an arrest, three fifths of which were dealt with by a caution. The Crown Prosecution Service and Judiciary being responsible for dropping or dismissing a further twenty five percent. A pertinent factor in this dismal performance was the surging involvement of juveniles in criminal activity, the 1994 audited BCS survey revealing that fully two-fifths of known offenders were under twenty-one.

Over the past few decades a great deal of effort has been directed towards identifying what techniques or methods works best in trying to rehabilitate repeat offenders (recidivist's). A good idea given that most crime is committed by a comparatively small number of individuals. Lots of different initiatives have been given a trial, including many experimented within the United States and Canada. Disappointingly, few show much more than marginal improvements, five to ten percent at most. While efforts to wean people off drugs or make up for educational failing, vocational and other social shortcomings clearly are the priority and must continue. The overall story is a poor one, figures for Britain suggest that only 3% of all remedial efforts to get people permanently off drugs actually succeeds.

A major handicap to effective action in recent years has been the intellectual aversion to locking people up. This resistance to incarceration makes it worth comparing jail populations with our peers. Unsurprisingly we have a comparatively small prison population vis a vis the crime rate. Home Office figures for the year 2000 indicate that for every thousand crimes committed we have roughly thirteen prisoners. The rest of Europe varies from a low of under five for Sweden to nearly fifty for Spain. France and Germany being similar to Britain, while the US has a whopping one hundred and sixty-six. In terms of actual numbers, the prison population increased from fifty-one thousand in 1995 to just over eighty thousand twelve years later, the maximum number that could be housed. A situation that seen the authorities releasing considerable numbers of detainees early, some of whom remain a danger to the general public as events prove.

As might be deduced, responsibility for this demoralising state of affairs has its roots in the liberalising of life. By attacking the institutions and traditions that interested and incited people towards respect for the law and each other, the socially progressive types who have dominated the world since the 1960's have actually brought about the very crime waves that now concern us all. This being a global issue rather than one unique to these isles. The State's actions guaranteeing that as more and more are added to the socially irresponsible, the situation will continue to remain poor, even if it does not get worse.

As most readers instinctively realise, unless that is they are from another planet, those who are culpable rarely admit their mistakes. Instead, as we have daily proof, the problems are denied using all manner of excuses, including ones that suggests the populace as a whole had become neurotic over fear of crime. That is, almost any answer except what the population wants and needs, more police on the streets.

Figures only tell part of the story of course, and while it is fair to say that most of the nation continues to make it through the week untroubled, there is a distinct change in atmosphere. A sense that the personal and collective security that once made life comfortable has gone. While most offences might be directed against property rather than people, the consequences are ugly enough to have seeped into the national conscious. For those unable to fund a move to a better neighbourhood, there is little doubt life can be a grim affair with plenty of mindless activity to put up with. Especially from wild out of control teenagers who have grown fearless in a country that has found itself unable to levy effective sanction against them.

The journey between the well understood regulation of yesteryear and the ineffective manias of today began with the desire to modernise. Part of that ethos was the belief that bigger is better. This view motivated the reforms incorporated into the 1964 Police Act, a Bill that merged many of the nation's small police forces into much larger units. Decisive in another way was parliamentary decision on the 8th November the following year to abolish the death penalty. Expectations of an explosion of violent crime pre-empted by a host of additional measures, especially those governing firearms. Penalties for possession of guns and ammunition in public places reinforced by an amendment that required a license for shotguns.

An interesting aspect of this intellectual eagerness to reform was the way it like to present itself as humane. One later product of this belief came to called care in the community. An end that saw many mentally unstable or ill people facing a future of indifferent treatment as the facilities that once had been there to take care of them closed down. Over the years since this idea took root, nearly eighty percent of all hospital beds for such patients have been done away with. Leaving many with nowhere to go except prisons, wholly inadequate places to handle those in need of specialist treatments.

The single most destructive step in this ratcheting of change however, was the sudden and swift decline in traditional policing. Something acted out when the pavement was swapped for the road. The 'Bobby on the Beat' replaced by the man in the car. Introduced in May of 1965 in the new town of Kirkby, just outside Liverpool, its immediate impact was to shift policing from prevention to reaction. The parochial life of the individual constable patrolling a neighbourhood he knew rapidly consigned to the past. The carefully won place as a known and trusted member of society, a human face to authority sustained by mixing and talking with local people surrendered. The architect of this plan, the urbane Roy Jenkins, Home Secretary between 1965-67.

Like minded reformers continued to push onwards over the coming years. Profound changes in the employment of sanction and the weighting of justice coming through a sequence of Criminal Justice Acts (CJA's). Novel penal and judicial reforms including the establishing of parole, suspended sentencing, majority verdicts for juries and other procedural changes and limits on the power of magistrates to throw out charges. One noteworthy measure that made it onto the statute books in 1972 reduced the age of eligibility for jury service, all eighteen year olds listed on the electoral role facing the call.

As the Sixties gave way to the Seventies, a deeper struggle evolved within Britain. One that to some extent mirrored what was a world wide phenomenon as various aggressive and violent elements acted out their fantasies. Here, this included a few trade unionists who willingly employed intimidation and thuggery as a means of pursuing wage claims, a few such disputes assuming frightening proportions. The struggles at the Grunwick film processing laboratory and the miners strikes cases in point, events that drew the police into ugly confrontations. Merging into this trend were riots that marred the Notting Hill Carnival, circumstances coinciding with an epidemic of street crime. The latter responded to by the police employing powers supplied by Section 4 of the Vagrancy Act to stop and search potential suspects. Excessive use of these authorities thought to be a factor in the Brixton race riots, events subsequently investigated and reported on by Lord Scarman. His findings feeding into the far reaching reassessment of criminal procedure that became the subject of a Royal Commission formed early in 1978.

The work of this body would lead to actions to constrain the hands of the police in favour of the offender. Not only was Section 4 repealed in 1981, but the whole issue of police procedure was revised under the terms of the Police and Criminal Evidence Act of 1984. A Bill laying out precise codes of practice and procedures for handling suspects, with mandatory tape recording of interviews, detailed record keeping and guaranteed access to lawyers before questioning (if requested). The rules regarding the admissibility of police evidence also being amended.

The impact was immediate, police work instantly becoming more administrative, multiple form filling leading to the ludicrous situation today where half an officers time on shift can be spent filling in documents of one sort or another. One unavoidable consequence was the reduction of police visibility, absence hardly helping the public's sensitivities and growing sense of distance. The setting up of an independent Police Complaints Authority and the Crown Prosecution Service doing nothing to close the gap. The latter established under the Prosecution of Offences Act of 1985 removed the authority the police had over whether or not to prosecute a case.

Missing by this time was any sense over what would reduce the accelerating crime rate. Indeed every action appeared to ease the path of the criminal at the expense of the law abiding. The entrenched aversion to prison leading to Home Office pressures on the judiciary to dissuade them from imposing penal sentences. A particular concern that worried was the escalating numbers of young people engaging in criminal activity. Treatment of young offenders the focus of the 1982 CJA, its measures dealing with partial suspension of sentences, early release conditions and other miscellaneous ideas. Further amendments coming in over later years when the issue and conditions of fines, custodial sentences and early release were introduced.

Damaging in an entirely different way was the strange provisions contained within the Occupiers Liability Act of 1984. This actually allows criminals in certain circumstances to sue property owners because they have been injured while endeavouring to rob the place. Equally strange is the obsessive attention to detail that leads to impossibly complex legalities. The 1988 Criminal Justice Act illustrates the point, its provisions ranging from aspects of extradition, suppression of terrorism, the provision of evidence for criminal proceedings, reviews on sentencing, statutory penalties, confiscation of the proceedings of an offence, money laundering, compensation for criminal injury and so on.

On a different level altogether were the actions of Michael Robert Ryan at Hungerford on 19th of August 1987 who shot and killed sixteen people, wounding fifteen others before taking his own life. In response to that insanity government passed the Firearms Amendment Act which banned ownership of semi-automatic rifles as well as restricting certain types of shotgun. Restrictions that failed to prevent a recurrence some nine years later when Thomas Hamilton entered a primary school in Dunblane, shooting fifteen young children and a teacher before turning the gun on himself. This saw tightening of what were already the strictest gun laws of any democracy. Not that this would do anything to prevent the spread of illegally obtained weapons over the coming years or the growing presence of armed police on the streets.

The first individual in a long time to make some impact on this dreadful situation was appointed Home Secretary in 1993. Michael Howard breaking the mould by using the slogan, 'prison works,' as indeed it does as anyone with any sense knows. The result was the first meaningful reductions in crime for nearly three decades, efforts that could be built on when he overcame opposition to get more prisons built. Not that this prevented interest in trying to find ways of controlling those likely to involve themselves in criminal activity without locking them away. The electronic tagging of offenders to monitor their whereabouts being pioneered in Manchester, Norwich and Reading.

Following this lead was a new government elected in 1997, one led by Mr Tony Blair. His public position already reflected a few years earlier by the cute phrase, 'Tough on crime, tough on the causes of crime.' These intentions translated into a comprehensive programme of reforms, some of which undermined the individual protections that had been incorporated into English Common Law over previous centuries.

Amongst the factors facing his administration were those related to the doubling or more of case loads. Overload contributing to the collapse in the numbers of crimes actually solved and brought before the courts. Legitimate public irritations over these failing were however little to do with the frontline officer. Policing the streets having become an ordeal as aggressive self righteousness and loss of respect for law took over many of the nation's citizens. Adding to the difficulties for the interested police officer was the bureaucracy, poor leadership, judicial failings and the ever present risk of interference by self serving politicians. It being little wonder that morale amongst officers continued its steady decline, something confirmed by a comprehensive survey in 1999-2000 into police sickness. Time lost amongst serving officers totalling one and half million days, with an additional 715,000 lost by its civilian employees.

In this atmosphere Labour's own efforts began with the Crime and Disorder Act (1998) which introduced Anti-social Behaviour Orders (ASBO). Its broader aims being outlined in 2001, ideas revised in 2004 and again two years later, by which time the effort was being greased by liberal amounts of money. In fact some two and half percent of the nation's GDP was to be directed towards criminal justice, more than any other nation in the OECD. A little more than sixty percent of this vast sum was directed to the police service, substantial recruiting raising police numbers to over 143, 000 (2007). Additional manning provided by nearly twelve thousand Special Constables and more than thirteen thousand Police Community Support Officers (PCSO), a near powerless, cheap police look-a-like. Supplementing this force were over seventy thousand civilian staff and of course the much loved Traffic Wardens.

If passing laws solve all these problems, then Britain would be crime free. Over the last ten years nearly fifty acts have been passed covering criminal, antisocial behaviour, policing, punishment and justice. Estimates suggesting that at least 3000 new criminal offences have been created.

A substantial part of the justifications for this flood related to the supposed need to combat terrorism. The Terrorism Act of 2000 and the later Anti-Terrorist, Crime and Security Act providing the police with wide sweeping powers to stop, search and detain. Initially this was without charge for up to forty-eight hours, extendable to seven days with magistrates approval. Authorities amended by the 2003 CJA to fourteen days and later up to twenty-eight under the Terrorism Act of 2006. Efforts to increase that still further are again before parliament as this words are written.

Also facing reform were the police, the Police Reform Act of 2002 detailing codes of practice for Chief Police Officers, how complaints and misconduct were to be handled and a host of other amendments. The broader intentions of improving police capability was the principle behind the formation of the Serious Organised Crime Agency (SOCA) in April of 2006. A unit intended to attack organised activity such as drug trafficking, immigration scams, individual and private sector fraud along with reclaiming assets earnt from crime.

Also seeing daylight over the last year or so are plans to bring into existence a compulsory National Identity Card, one associated with a National Identity Register. The unease provoked by this idea stirring widespread resistance, with much criticism aimed at concerns over data security in the light of recent mistakes that have seen personal information in governments hands going astray. Also under stiff challenge is the idea that this will help combat terrorism, an assessment that clashes with the reality that what really troubles the public is ordinary crime, not some unlikely terrorist event.

Embedded in the national psyche is the impression that criminals now routinely escape punishment for breaking the law, even when caught, which is not all that often. This has bred a deep rooted sense of dismay, even cynicism over government claims. Attitudes that keep their stranglehold because so few police officers are ever seen, despite substantial recruiting. Adding to the public suspicions are the obvious failure of tackle quite serious issues such as credit card fraud, which in 2006 alone ran to well over four hundred million pounds.

Equally unpleasant and sinister is the increasing use of technology to spy. The advent of closed-circuit television cameras (CCTV) and their use to look at public activity has continued to spread unchecked, with motorways, other roads, town centres, open parks, stations and car parks all coming in for permanent watching. There were a staggering 4 million cameras by 2002, a number that is incrementing steadily, their capability improving as the technology develops.

Like so many ideas, this has been thrust on the nation with few questions raised over whether this intrusion is beneficial. Although there is one area where this capability has proved useful, that of raising money. The London congestion charge would not be feasible without the development of number plate recognition technology, which is itself dependent on these cameras. Other justifications centre on the ability it offers to solve crimes, which on occasion it might, but then again, seeing a policeman might be more effective by preventing the crime in the first place. Little wonder many no longer bother to report criminal events.

Most dramatic of all is the shift from the police of old to something more representative of a paramilitary organisation. The land routinely patrolled by armed officers issued with automatic pistols and even submachine guns. A bewildering change amongst a population largely prevented from having or using any means of self defence.

While government can rightly claim reductions in some types of crime, this is mainly due to improved physical security and greater public awareness of the need to be alert, especially in the case of cars and homes. The other side of this story is one of crime blighting life, the peace of many ruined by thugs who are not afraid to kick someone to death in front of their children if they have a mind to. Types safe in the knowledge that however heinous the act, there are plenty with influence eager to excuse.

Chapter 33

Alcohol and Drugs

A major factor in day to day British life is the use of those various substances that induce inebriated, catatonic or pleasurable states. The commonest of these drugs is a fermented beverage of some kind, the original reasons for drinking such substances being entirely practical, water was usually unfit to drink. As far these islands are concerned, we know the Saxon's brewed ale, later Briton's taking to supping beer when it was discovered how it was brewed by the Dutch, its popularity later overtaken by cheaper and more potent gin.

Of course, partaking of alcohol has always had a useful social purpose, public houses acting as social centres and meeting places in both towns and villages. A drink or two acting as a social lubricant, the means to ease tensions or blot out the harshness of life. Today, with over sixty thousand places available where alcohol can be brought for consumption on site, there is no problem about access. Heavily advertised, drink is sold on the back of images that try to imply it is chic, cool, sexy and so on, persuasive aims whose real purpose is to separate the disposable, and sometimes non disposable, income of the drinker.

This has resulted in an atmosphere that has brought about excessive consumption by both men and women. One slaved, at least amongst the British, to a form of competitive desperation, as if imbibing to excess is a necessity, rather than what it should, just a means of easing tensions and allowing relaxed enjoyment. The fallout from this trait has created a reputation that follows Briton's where ever they go. One that sees individuals all too often descending into a condition where they have no idea what they are doing or why.

Whether the liberalising of the licensing laws in 2003 made much difference to these trends is hard to gauge, but the presence of large numbers of inebriated youngsters makes town centres potentially unpleasant at night. A disturbing indication of the scale of the issue, the thirteen thousand drink related offences committed each week. Outcomes that have seen a number of local authorities banning alcohol in public places in an effort to control its worst effects.

Excess consumption of alcohol has of course, a long history, so have formal and informal attempts to control its consequence. Societal pressures bringing legislative measures, the Gin Act of 1751, just one example. Later resistance growing around temperance movements, pressure groups that were behind the introduction of prohibition in the USA, parts of Australia, Norway, Finland and elsewhere during the latter half of the nineteenth and early part of the twentieth century's. More down to earth reasons have also incited limits, the restrictive opening hours of British pubs that applied over most of the twentieth century were defined by the Defence of the Realm Act passed in 1914.

The story of drug use cannot continue without considering the evolving attitudes towards another substance, tobacco. One that has seen the law impose itself on this habit, part of a campaign of vilification that attracted and then engaged the support of the elite's. The banning of smoking in public places gradually spreading across the Union, finally doing so in England in July of 2007.

First used by the Central American Mayan and Toltec civilisations, tobacco passed to the native tribes of the north who in turn introduced it to visiting European explorers. Having found widespread acceptance in Spain during the 16th century, its probable adoption by the English was down to John Hawkins or some of his contemporaries. The growing demand providing a cash crop that had a hand in encouraging the development of England's American colonies.

Methods of use have varied, early Europeans favouring smoking in a pipe, this giving way to a powdered form called snuff before cigars and then cigarettes took over. Social prominence snaring most people, its addictive qualities ensuring continued pleasurable use. It appears as if the potential dangers were recognised as early as 1912 when a Dr. Isaac Adler suggested a link between smoking and lung cancer. However its social context went unchallenged until the 1950's when the growing weight of evidence about what it could do to the health of the smoker gathered more weight. Contributing to this exposure was the work of Sir Richard Doll and Austin Bradford Hill who published their research in the paper, 'The Mortality of Doctors and their smoking habits.' While public tolerance of smoking has declined, it remains a resilient part of many lives.

Following a similar path are other substances, narcotics that have made a huge contribution to society through crime. Not that the usage of these mind altering substances is quite the radical departure some might think, opium for example could be brought across the pharmacy counter in Victorian Britain and was used by a small number who could afford it. While pain relief might have been the original purpose, many succumbed to its addictive qualities. Figures supplied in 1934 to the League of Nations suggest that there were only three hundred known addicts in Britain at the time. Cocaine was also freely available well into the second decade, it being a common ingredient in tonics and other patent medicines.

Amongst the concoctions popularised by hippies and other later fringe groups were marijuana (cannabis), Lysergic Acid (LSD), amphetamines, heroin and cocaine. Later, artificially created or altered products such as ecstasy and crack cocaine have opened up new spheres of experience. The long term disruptive affects of these chemicals is not always fully appreciated by those who willingly experiment. Especially amongst the trendy crowds advocating freer use of marijuana, a drug whose active toxicity has grown due to selective breeding of the plant from which it is derived. Its active ingredient, Delta-9-tetrahydrocannabinol (THC) disturbs concentration, also affecting memory, pleasure, thought, sensory and time perception besides compromising learning. Use leading to psychosis, anxiety and other personality disorders, with longer term influences including lung cancer should it be smoked.

These reservations can be extended to a greater degree to most of the other substances mentioned here, the highs they induce remain entirely out of the ordinary both in intensity and duration. Such experiences are known in some, if not all instances, to profoundly alter the potential satisfactions that might be gained from the normal events of human existence. A basis that can and does stimulate those exposed once to go on seeking these pleasures even to the point of self destruction.

A recent survey suggested that around a third of the British population admit to having used at least one of other of these illicit substances at some stage of their life, some 10% admitting to doing so regularly. These figures contrast with the BCS which suggests just over four hundred thousand were using prohibited Class A drugs (the most dangerous) while a further 1.6 million were using something.

The material point here is the understanding that these drugs can and will do harm, in some cases outcomes that are irreparable. This has a social context sufficiently important to persuade the authorities to attempt to restrict their usage. A stance that has long provided those criminally minded elements with the chance to make big money supplying the need. America is the obvious example, especially during the prohibition, when it became big business to truck in supplies of beer and other liquors. Organised gangs running very profitable rackets in the cities, while those out in the sticks survived well enough by distilling moonshine.

In a case of history repeating itself, the same situation has grown around narcotics, except that this time the dangers to society are more pronounced. Not only are the effects of these substances themselves malign, but the profits in supplying the need are substantially bigger. Highly organised and efficient trafficking ensures a steady flow of drugs into the main markets of America, Europe and elsewhere. An empire that employs tens of thousands whose living comes from encouraging human degradation. The money that changes hands not only funds the protective organisations that are murderously ruthless in their own interests, but provides a way of suborning those willing to take a payoff to look the other way. Corruption that reaches into every sphere of life, not least through the epidemic of petty crime that is so necessary for most addicts to feed their habit.

Chapter 34

Lawyers and their impact on society

Today, quite ordinary events and interactions are coming under the remit and scrutiny of official regulation that decides expectations or duties. Domestic and supra-national rule making is responsible for a mountain of paper that is frankly incomprehensible to the 99.99% of us who must live by common sense. Where it becomes necessary to unravel this labyrinth for some reason, most are driven to seek out those with specialist knowledge, typically a solicitor who might engage a barrister to supply a specific opinion on a point of law if required.

This has raised the profile of the legal profession to unprecedented levels, expert legal minds effectively presiding over every aspect of life, be it criminal or civil. The very high levels of intellect applied to such work cannot help but spot the loophole in badly written law or the opportunity for a nice earner based on some failing or other of business or judgement that results in an accident. The potential rewards attract the very best of talents, the dedication and commitment of those who reach the pinnacle earning millions.

As legal activity has expanded, so has the number of lawyers, most of them engaging in lucrative civil practice. Once the reserve of the very rich, almost anyone can now pursue remedy through the courts, often by using the 'no win-no fee arrangement.'

As far as criminal cases are concerned, its business as usual, two advocates, one acting on behalf of the crown and the other for the accused seek to achieve a favourable decision for their side in an open court where the evidence is tested before judge and jury (some complicated cases no longer involve a jury). The most skilful briefs adept at wringing every advantage from law and procedure, many who are the guilty gaining reprieve through minor transgressions of these complexities.

Lawyers here have also found it productive to copy their colonial cousins by encouraging litigation to pursue or resolve quite ordinary complaints. At the end of this legal rainbow is money, the so called compensation culture the thinking man's equivalent of the lottery win. Such activities washing much of the emollient of common sense out of life.

At the centre is the victim, a mainly artificial construct that suggests to the vulnerable and not so vulnerable that adverse circumstances are in fact transferable. That is, someone can be blamed for real or imagined difficulties. This plays on human frailty rather well, allowing many a subtle mind to devise a strategy that uses the heavy hand of the law to pursue retribution. A substantial part of Britain's population have fallen for this idea, competing to present themselves as victims, gaining through its hallowed status both sympathy and the recompense of a wedge of cash. One notable consequence of this activity is the rising cost of all forms of insurance cover, the potential for claims for whatever reason must be allowed for in the required premium.

The field of product liability is one area rich in potential for inventive legal brains. Commercial traders have learnt to be careful about giving anyone an opening that will expose them to litigation. One way of doing so is to put all manner of strange warnings on their products, an obvious example of what has become an absurdity includes cups of coffee that carry the advisory, 'Caution, contents maybe hot!' When they are caught out, it is not impossible for the costs of legal proceedings to force them out of business. Indeed the very threat of legal action leads some to settle out of court as a way of avoiding the larger costs of several days in court.

Besides the confrontational role the legal profession have assumed in divorce proceedings, especially for rich people. There is plenty of scope in using the British system of legal aid to fund cases against publicly owned or run services. Two illustrations of this oddity bring home the point. The Litigation Authority for the National Health Service reckons that clinical and non clinical negligence claims for 2005-2006 reached nearly six hundred million pounds, with a further £8.3 billion set aside for as yet unsettled claims. The second reviews the outcomes of the miners compensation scheme where some seven and half billion pounds was set aside to pay off claims for industrial injury and illnesses amongst former miners. To date some 3.4 billion pounds has found its way into the hands of those worthy of it, hundreds of millions ending up in the hands of lawyers representing claimants.

Chapter 35

The role of the media

We are all vulnerable to being persuaded by the artfully presented story or clever advertisement, those who claim otherwise are simply deluding themselves. Entire industries have after all developed around very clever folk who understand how to persuade or seed certain ideas. Capabilities that have reached unparalleled subtlety as ways to realise political, economic or social ends. Forces that are very powerful in the hands of both the scrupulous and the unscrupulous.

The pathway to this end is the culmination of a process that began with the invention of the printing press in 1468, its introduction into Britain eight years later providing the means of producing a newspaper, a way of spreading the same story to a larger number of people. The earliest surviving examples of these sheets reach back to 1588, the headlines of the day written during a year when the Spanish Armada made its way up the Channel. Slaking the growing thirst for information depended on for a long time on the growing numbers of papers and books until the advent of the telegraph, a device patented in 1838. This altered the form and speed of communication, what was urgent or vital could now be transferred from one point to another within minutes. The era of modern immediate communication really beginning with the invention of radio at the end of the 19th century. Film adding a visual dimension that saw important events captured and played back, giving people the chance to see and judge for themselves.

None of this could have really made headway if there was no human interest, fortunately (or otherwise) mankind hungers to know is going on. An instinctive need used by all sides during the First and Second World Wars, conflicts that helped propel the media to its current position. Its role during those times that of a conduit, a way of keeping the populace aware, helping to prevent rumours from running riot. While there was often an element of slant, even outright propaganda to the messages, few openly distrusted what was being said, especially when it was broadcast by the British Broadcasting Corporation (BBC).

This put unprecedented influence into the hands of those who wrote, filmed, told or presented the news. An awareness of that power reached maturity during the Vietnam war when public opinion was turned against involvement by television reporting. The very peak of this influence reached during the Watergate scandal when exposure of skulduggery by investigative journalists led to the resignation of Richard Nixon, the American President.

Helping the media towards cementing its authority has been the quality and speed of reporting, those involved becoming more daring and professional. The competition to be first with the story drawing out a relentless inquisitive spirit that meant few news worthy events escaped investigative focus. Its output has grown to a level able to support dedicated twenty-four hour news and current affairs channels where ongoing stories are flogged to death. Radio, newspapers and magazines filling in the gaps, leaving no stone unturned in the telling and analysis of what is current and hot. The impact of this expanding force multiplying as scientific and technical innovations combined to shrink the world, shortening the time between events happening in one part of the globe and an awareness of them in another. By the 1990's satellite links, computers, cameras and multi-function mobile telephones small enough to be carried by anyone have made it possible to see almost anything anywhere in real time.

Significantly this evolution has strengthened the tendency to define what is news, overlaying that with a presentation favouring the sentiments of the individual reporter or the organisation they represent. Concurrent with this retreat has been a decline in restraint, every form of media becoming much more aggressive, a reputation for intensity that is at times frightening. Every story and the actions of its participants capable of being held to the light where judgements can and are rendered, although whether facts play a part in that activity might be debated endlessly.

Boosting the role of the mass media has been the increase in leisure time. Some of the necessary diversions and entertainment's to fill these moments supplied by the output of television networks, film studio's and printing industries. Essential to its appeal is the incessant glamorising of life, a constant portrayal of the exceptional, the purpose being to excite. The endless exaggeration that accompanies this distorts perception, inciting discontent or worse in those who cannot detach themselves from this unreal diet.

The underlying themes of most forms of entertainment have been explored to their obvious limits, ends that are slaved to the constraints of human imagination. Early methods of boosting viewing leant heavily on sexual titillation, violence and coarse language to spice up otherwise standard plots. Hollywood building on this approach by greater realism, more explicit exposure and of course spectacular sets and scenes that make use of the latest computing technologies. One near standard feature is the improbable car chase and the obligatory ratcheting click of the automatic handgun.

Holding prime position in this production line of diversions is the soap opera. Programmes reliant on conflict orientated plots that feature people whose whole life lurches from one crisis to the next. The viewer being treated to a succession of miserable faces staring out from the screen, each suggestive of some extreme emotion, that is, as long as it's not happiness. The routine dialogue a sequence of platitudes and ludicrous comment about as close to real life as Andromeda is to earth.

Filling swathes of time are fillers about making someone a star or detailed records following the experiences of man D finding and building that dream house just down the road from who knows where. Rare now, are the intelligent home grown gem or something reasonable from the American networks, though they still come along from time to time. The social ramifications of this tsunami of twaddle includes the undoubted stunting of intellectual vitality amongst those who watch this stuff on a regular basis. Further inhibiting normal adult development is the conditioning that goes on as people are perpetually presented as helpless, beings somehow unable to surmount even modest adversity. A ridiculous state of affairs, but one that is having its effect.

Just about extinct amongst all the daily dross are programmes aimed at young audiences whose presenters do not find it necessary to hype every line or jump about as if sitting still and speaking calmly has been outlawed. Small wonder then that so many children cannot settle down to concentrate on doing anything quietly. A technique that is gradually intruding into features aimed at those who are older.

Other profitable avenues for the visual getting renewed treatment are the documentaries produced by people like Michael Moore and former US Vice President, Al Gore. Clever treatments of emotional subjects that help create the mass sensitivity necessary to allow that reaction to be used and directed for political ends.

The importance of the BBC.

Uncontested as the leading supplier of news and entertainment in this country is the BBC. An organisation funded via an obligatory viewing licence that furnishes approximately three billion pounds a year. Part, if not the sole justification for its privileged position, can be deduced from the wording of its Royal Charter which imposes a duty to operate without favour or bias to any group, organisation or individual. Free from having to worry about how to pay the bills puts the BBC in a very fortunate position, one free of commercial pressures.

A measure of its importance can be gained from the fact that around ninety percent of the domestic population derives some or all of its news from the BBC each day. Be this from its national radio network, various television channels or its prime position on the Internet. Elsewhere in the world, the BBC's reputation is such that many people use its services to find out what is going on in their own country. A position that ought to make it critical for those in charge to take the greatest care in ensuring that its reputation for even handedness remains intact. Disappointingly that is not necessarily the case.

Bias is common to all the world's major media outlets including the BBC. Part of the problem is that those attracted to the profession are more often than not conforming intellectuals chosen because they fit in. Unquestionably gifted and self confident, most of these types are instinctively drawn towards the rectitude of their own ideas. Attitudes that, subconsciously or otherwise, determine the what and how of reporting. There being little room for the uncompromising independent maverick who brought bite and honesty to the story, although remarkably, a few still make it.

What this means in practice can be culled from events in Rwanda during 1994 and the Congo over the years either side of the new millennium. In the former, hundreds of thousands of people were hacked to death or shot, while in the latter, a long running conflict resulted in the deaths of several million people, mostly through starvation. While these dreadful events were reported, filmed and discussed, it was done so in a manner that remained subdued compared to the hullabaloo raised over events at the Abu Ghraib prison in Iraq. The pointless humiliation of Iraqi captives by inexperienced and poorly led American service personnel openly portrayed as if it were the crime of the century. World-wide exposure and indignant condemnation indicative of the inability of western journalism and, pretty well everyone else it seems, to render moral judgement against absolute scale.

This loss of objectivity is also evident in the treatment of America. It being quite the norm amongst the BBC's correspondents to portray its people, culture and actions in a poor light. A choice victim in this pathetic business is its current President, George W Bush, a man nowhere near as stupid as the BBC and others wants us to believe, even if he is not the best reader of a script America produced. Sharing this harsh and unjust spotlight is Israel, a nation whose very survival continues to depends on eternal vigilance, necessity determining its responses. Difficulties that are often disguised, the impression sometimes suggestive of the view that only the death of all Israeli's will do. Indicative perhaps, that for some, the Holocaust remains unfinished business.

Further problems arise from the non reporting of events within the European Union. The BBC is noted for its one sided portrayal of this juggernaut and what its activities mean. Just as odd is the failure to offer any insight to the real situation in Iraq or Afghanistan. Indeed it is difficult to derive any understanding of what really is happening in those distant places from mainstream reporting. While important in another way is the contribution the BBC makes to creating and sustaining the hysteria about global warming. An horrendously complex and as yet, improperly understood issue.

Of course it is not all negative, credit must be given to the many documentary and natural world programmes that are produced by the Beeb (BBC nickname), even if some are now being used as the means to sell certain messages. This output has long been acknowledged as being amongst the world's, films that bring home the real wonders that exist in this world of ours. Sports are another quality component of the entertainment industry, great rafts of time filled with detailed coverage of everything from football, rugby and cricket to the more high profile events like the Tour de France and the Olympic games. Equally good and enduringly popular with domestic audiences are historic dramas that draw on the writings of Jane Austen, Charles Dickens and the Bronte sisters, products within their genre that are without peer.

Naturally dissatisfactions of one sort or another rise up periodically giving rise to criticism of the BBC and its attitudes. It's not unusual for politicians for example to express irritation and talk darkly about the need to reform. Such comments are frankly unnecessary if the organisation is doing its job according to the stipulations of its Charter. This document is quite specific, those who fail to live up to it can be held to account and dealt with without generating yet more paper.

Alternatives and conclusions.

For those who want to read their news and analysis, there are a bewildering array of newspapers and magazines, a spread of publications that covers every conceivable topic. Here, every form of reporting has its day, from the worst to best, writing that reveals the complex, the simple, the irreverent and the seedy.

Above all however it is the spread of cheap computers and its associated interconnecting communications technology that is making the biggest impact. As costs plummeted, interest rocketed in its product, the internet. Literally millions of sites supply information and opinion on every conceivable subject. A real bonus to this world wide network is the chance to get a world view from English language versions of newspapers from almost every country. This has spread understanding and helped break down the barriers of language and distance. This force for good offsetting the stranglehold gained by the traditional media, renewing the capability to expose the inconvenient story to the cleansing of public knowledge and adverse opinion.

One recent and surprising broadside at media as whole was delivered by the outgoing Prime Minister, Mr. Tony Blair. An individual uniquely qualified in most respects given that his time in office was closely associated with a masterly sense of control over the what, the how, and the when of reporting. While unequivocally supporting the need for a free media, he openly wondered about its behaviours, comparing it to a feral beast that tears into events and people. A view many Briton's may have sympathy with, even if they are perplexed by who said it.

Chapter 36

State run public services

Of all the hopes invested in Britain's post-war policies, none was more ardently pursued than the ideal of building world leading industries and services. The results of this endeavour were, to say the least, disappointing. Having sold off most of the industries to the private sphere, government is now left trying to run the health and educational services in the public interest.

Before the National Health Service (NHS) became a reality in 1948, individuals and families provided for themselves. Most belonging to some sort of voluntary savings scheme or, if they could not afford that, relying on being seen by a doctor or consultant for free, a common practice at the time. Hospital treatment was provided on the same broad terms, those unable to pay getting what was necessary via various charitable schemes. Despite the apparent limitations, there was no problem getting treatment. The medical establishment of the time was recognised for its pioneering efforts, placing it amongst the world's best. A foundation that relied on a system of rigidly run disciplined hospitals whose aseptic wards provided over 450,000 beds, often in small locally convenient units that did not impose the additional hardships of travel.

From the moment the NHS was established, it was dogged by funding shortfalls. Part of the problem was related to the fact that medical care had been provided by a mix of voluntary contribution schemes and cash payments supplemented by considerable philanthropic and charitable activity, a solution that hid some of the real costs. Demand was also checked by a general reluctance to bother the doctor, especially over what were perceived as trifles, after all, most had to pay. Compounding these legitimate miscalculations were the rapid advances in medical science during the Fifties and Sixties, efforts increasing what could be done if the money was there. The other important issue naturally enough was the enduring financial constraints on the Exchequer.

Administratively the NHS had been conceived with three divisions, community type services such as health visitors, midwifery, maternal and infant welfare clinics forming one, with the hospital services another and family doctors, dentists, pharmacist and opticians making up the last. Interest in improving this arrangement attracted early attention, the 1962 Porritt Report for example recommended it should be administered as a unified body. The later Cogwheel Report proposing specialist clinical divisions within hospitals as a means of getting medical opinion into the administrative decision making loop.

Major reforms were finally instigated during 1974 when Regional Health Authorities (RHA) were set up to manage all three parts. This was followed by a Royal Commission whose recommendations were embodied in the Health Services Act of 1980. Changes supposedly simplifying the set-up enough to allow delegation of authority through a new hierarchy. That this never really got off the ground was due to central government intervening on the basis that it was better qualified to find ways to improve efficiency and cost effectiveness. An opinion leading to the Griffith's NHS Management Inquiry which ended up concluding the service suffered from a lack of accountability. A vacuum it thought should be filled by the appointment of a single chief executive or general manager. An individual who would be tasked with raising the status of management, dragging in the clinicians as necessary to give them more of a voice.

In tune with ideas then prevalent, a 1989 White Paper titled 'Working for Patients' sought to introduce market concepts to improve NHS efficiency and cost control. This approach separated the purchasing of health care from those providing it, changes introduced via the National Health Service and Community Care Act of 1990. New financial arrangements seeing Health Authorities assume control for a budget they would use to purchase health care. General Practitioners or family doctors (GP's), also gaining the chance to own budgets with which they could purchase health care as they saw fit.

Having published a Patients Charter setting out a list of rights, or guarantees of standards of service, a further White Paper rolled of the presses in 1992. This took a more rounded look at the subject of health. Entitled 'The Health of the Nation,' it concluded the RHA's should be scrapped, an intermediate step in that direction coming from a reduction in their number to eight, a revision put in place under the Health Authorities Act. Following the change of government in 1997 the inherited structure was dismantled before much the same sort of organisation was reconstructed in its place. The cost of this fruitless exercise, about three billion pounds. As it stands in 2006, the NHS is divided into three parts headed by ten Strategic Health Authorities. Below are 152 Primary Care Trusts (PCT) with General Practitioners coming under what is called Practice Based Commissioning.

Having endured an existence in which it was usually stretched for money, the incoming Labour administration, having established its credentials for fiscal sense, began to substantially enlarge the NHS budget. By 2008 this largesse will have brought funding levels up to, or in excess of, that spent by Britain's continental peers. This capital infusion has allowed the employment of more consultants, family doctors, nurses and other health professionals. Its bloated administrative arm alone topping a quarter of million, of whom thirty thousand are senior managers. Total employment by the health service reaching a staggering 1.3 million people, making it the world's third largest employer after the American retail giant 'Wal-Mart' and the Indian State Railway.

For all its staffing, this monolith only manages to provide about four beds for every thousand people, the lowest number of all advanced countries. Of its continental peers, France provides seven and half and Germany eight and half. Equally critical is that Britain also has the fewest practising doctors per head of population, hardly surprising then that here, the prospects of surviving the various cancers, heart diseases and other common rectifiable ailments remains poor compared to its peer nations. Adding to the agonies are the lengthy waiting lists for routine non urgent treatments, figures that are subject to constant manipulation. Games that can even extend to the care of emergency patients being delayed so some idiotic statistical target can be met.

Adding to these well catalogued failings are the controversies that surround super-bug infections. While all countries experience such problems, Britain has a variable record in dealing with such outbreaks, lives being lost in circumstances that should have been avoidable. Events that raise legitimate questions over the practice of asepsis on the wards and more particularly the attitudes and training of staff in preventing its spread. Inevitably this querying leads to wondering why the proven apprenticeship based scheme that used to turn out State Registered and State Enrolled nurses the match of any was changed. The immaculately clean individuals that once staffed the wards were integral to the sense of confidence that surrounded standards of hospital care in bygone days. The modern nurse might be competent, but the appearance of some is less than inspiring.

This creeping shabbiness also came to include the partial rejection of human dignity, NHS patients sometimes facing up to placement in a mixed sex ward. A distressing situation for those already burdened by illness, a situation that remains with us in some hospitals despite political promises. Stranger still is the movement towards circumscribing access to a doctor, plans are already in place to replace or delay their involvement. It is now routine for example for a nurse to screen potential patients in casualty departments just because there are too few practising doctors. This diluting of competence cannot be good for the wellbeing of the patient.

Reactions to this overall decline can be seen in several ways, not least in dentistry where substantial numbers of people have turned away from State care. If only because they cannot find a dentist who actually works under the NHS, most qualified dentists preferring private practice. This trend is also being matched by increasing numbers taking out private medical insurance or, even pay for procedures themselves rather than waiting or running the risks of going into a NHS hospital. In both instances what this means is that patients are paying twice.

Contributing to these problems has been the growing and, at times, unreasonable, expectations of patients towards their local doctor. Overnight and weekend calls escalating to include trifles, over demand making provision unpopular. The instinctive response of doctors was to share the burden amongst themselves, a practical solution undermined by revisions to their contracts in 2004. A clause inserted into the new agreement allowing any GP to opt out of providing out of hours cover as long as they took a small pay-cut, unsurprisingly, nine out of ten practices elected to do just that. Inheriting responsibility for night and weekend cover are the PCT's, the costs of doing so much more than expected. Making matters worse were miscalculations by the Department of Health regarding salaries, changes that handsomely benefited the family doctor despite the reduction to their responsibilities.

A more recent shadow came from the debacle of the computerised Medical Training Application Service (MTAS). Thousands of newly trained doctors facing aggravating delays over employment because the system failed to work properly. Many expensively trained doctors concluding that emigrating was better than staying and putting up with what was a growing shambles.

Also stirring up controversy was the National Institute of Clinical Excellence (NICE). Its intended role was to investigate what drugs, methods and technologies were supposed to be the best as a way of standardising treatments and evening out the quality of health care across the country. These evaluations led to recommended approaches for all hospital treatments and procedures. Some of these conclusions have proved contentious, the need to contain costs seemingly the dominant consideration. Notable instances include the denial of certain cancer treatments and other expensive and difficult to assess treatments.

Amazingly, despite the huge increase in budget, the NHS entered a funding crisis late in 2006. A combination of monumental staffing costs, poorly negotiated Private Finance Initiatives, routine and unnecessary use of outside management consultants and the ridiculous situation that sees everyday nursing needs supplied through Agencies combined to absorb more money than expected. The solution was to reduce the number of available beds, slowing down access to treatments, cancelling various procedures, enforcing redundancies and other cuts. Measures that convinced even the Chief Executive Officers to admit that the patient care had deteriorated.

While these blunt assessments reflects general truths, it should not obscure the good that exists. Many after all still give their calling body and soul with all the good that this can bring. These bright spots do not however, alter the material fact that despite such efforts and the unwavering support of most people, Britain's system of health care no longer consistently delivers what its people expect.

The other service the State thinks itself uniquely qualified to administer is education. Over the first decade or so of peace, the basis of schooling in these isles had been constructed around the Tripartite system introduced by Richard Butler's 1944 Education Act. Its success reliant on a profession still respected both in and out of school. The method of the day reliant on streaming by ability followed by appropriate instruction under a teacher utilising the blackboard, suitable text books and other tried and tested approaches. The message or lesson being tested by verbal questioning and so on, the effectiveness of this learning enhanced by an environment promoting orderliness and discipline. Pupils usually sitting two to a desk facing the front where the teacher stood doing what needed to be done while the pupils did as they were told. The prevailing attitudes less tolerant of mucking about, many a wayward mind kept in check by fear of a rap on the knuckles or the cane.

This coherent programme ensured each child grasped the core requirement of later life, the ability to read and write. One whose fundamental was reinforced by numerical fluency, a requirement that covered some of the complexities of the Imperial system of weights and measures and our unique system of currency. Room existing for a little history and geography along with crafts, music, competitive games and sports. The culmination of this first phase coming with an examination called the Eleven Plus, those who passed, the academically inclined as it were, going onto what was called a Grammar School. Everyone else ending up in a Secondary Modern, or Technical Secondary Modern. Areas without sufficient pupils to allow such division attending a single school known as a Comprehensive.

Secondary school entrants faced an additional three years of schooling, soon to be four when the leaving age was raised to fifteen in 1947. From there, it was out into the adult world of work as a trainee or apprentice. Pupils attending Grammar schools were subjected to much sterner academic programme that sought to expand their intellectual horizons through exposure to the classics, sciences and other subjects. By the time they finished, most at eighteen, the cream might have had the chance to enter one of Britain's limited number of universities. Everyone else being assessed by the award of School or Higher School Certificate. The General Certificate of Education (GCE) at Ordinary and Advanced levels taking over in 1951.

In no other field were the resentments and jealousies evident amongst post-war British minds more at play than in education. Attitudes that flowed into an intense desire to level the opportunities, the selective system of education that had taken root drawing particular ire because it was seen as a way of institutionalising social division and disadvantage. Unfortunately the good that existed in the idea of a singular system never delivered, instead State provided education deteriorated into a vehicle that would largely prevent the best of talents from realising its full potential. It proving much easier for the overly politicised minds who assumed control of the educational establishment to create a system of growing mediocrity.

At the back of these views were some powerfully negative emotions. Something seen in Anthony Crosland who made the point during his time as Secretary of State for Education, by saying he wanted, *'to destroy every last f-----g Grammar school.* Although it is doubtful Mr. Crosland would have found pleasure in the subsequent decline in educational standards that became part of his legacy following the issue of Circular 10/65 issued during July of 1965 requiring Local Education Authorities to begin moving towards the Comprehensive system. At the heart of that slide was not so much the abandonment of selective education itself, but the coincident adoption of a mish mash of approaches where mixed ability groups tried to master subjects in an ill disciplined environment without being taught. An approach whose drawbacks were not corrected by raising the school leaving age to sixteen in 1972.

Amongst the well intended responses to the growing evidence that all was not well was the creation of a national curriculum. This was put together under the personal direction of Keith Joseph during his term as Education Secretary during Margaret Thatcher's tenure in office. The realisation that not enough time was being allocated to improving the ability to read, write and manipulate numbers addressed by central government deciding what should be taught. Central control of the agenda opening up a way later used by those hostile to strenuous teaching, especially of subjects that require disciplined rigour such as physics, chemistry and its necessary adjunct, mathematics.

Whatever good might have been achieved by this revolution was further confused by the replacement of the widely understood GCE O-level by the General Certificate of Secondary Education in 1986. An action marking the beginning of an obsessive quest to test pupils. The theory initially being that this would allow educational standards to be tracked, the reality has proved rather different, political objectives intruding, education, like health, becoming a political football. The results of all this testing routinely used as a way of showing the nation how well party 'A' is managing the education of the nation's children compared with the past results of party 'B.'

Amongst the other politically inspired changes that came and mostly went was that allowing a pupil able to pass the necessary entrance examination to qualify for an assisted place at a private school. Grant maintained schools was another venture, in this case a school, instead of being funded by the Local Authority, could opt to receive funding from central government. While further reforms provided parents with the right to choose which school their child attended.

Despite the national curriculum the numbers under-achieving continued to grow, especially amongst black and white children at the bottom of the socio-economic scale. With Mr. Blair making education one of his main interests, he sought to tackle the issue by resurrecting an idea proposed during Mrs Thatcher's time in office. The hope was that standards could be improved by involving local communities and businesses. If a certain sum could be raised locally this would trigger a government grant to enable the building of a school free from Local Educational Authority funding and control. Although of course it was still tied to the national curricula. These were originally to be called City Technical Colleges, but were renamed City Academies and later just Academies. The purpose was to provide more effective schooling, which in some instances they certainly have.

Less usefully during Mr. Blair's time at the helm has been the increasing distractions aimed at teachers and schools. None of these intrusions is more influential or taxing than the arrival of government inspectors. The individual taking the most pressure during this event is the head teacher, so much the key figure in making a school good and keeping it that way. Unfortunately the demands on the man or woman concerned have escalated to the point where many are retiring or resigning because of the administrative overheads and restrictive practices imposed centrally. Strains that became arduous when it was decided that the decay in societal behaviour should be dumped on schools. Consequences that include disruptive pupils and aggressive parents. Little wonder that so many teachers are also abandoning the profession, many citing a lack of respect from pupils, parents and government. Only the foolish would deny they have a case.

So worrying has education become for interested parents who cannot afford private school fees that they fight tooth and nail to get their children into the better run State schools. Those blessed with a well led staff who can still demonstrate what can be done, even with that common product of national life, the truculent boy and girl. A major determinant in this judgement is the posting of examination results. Itself a controversial idea where year on year improvements in the numbers are attributed to less demanding examinations and more lenient marking.

Comparisons between questions asked on old O-Level papers and the modern versions certainly bears out the point.

Of all the depressing statistics confirming the decay in domestic State provided education, none is more shameful than the one informing us that one in six of all children educated here struggle to read. What is truly perplexing about this fact is the refusal of the teaching profession to admit culpability. An obduracy that seems to centre on an irrational rejection of the proven, in particular that of phonic and rote, simply because they are out of fashion. The former, according to government sponsored report prepared by Sir Jim Rose, clearly demonstrates superior outcomes in developing this crucial ability.

Inevitably those who fail to grasp this essential skill will be condemned to struggle. One cannot imagine what life is like without having the confidence to read and write, with all this means when it comes to expressing yourself. Personal humiliations and embarrassments surely a factor in the aggressions of the inarticulate, as well as being a stimulus to truancy and wayward social behaviour that routes to crime. Contributing to these frustrations, especially amongst boys, is the inculcation of mental weakness by excessive emphasis on nebulous concepts such as fairness, equality and the suppression of a healthy, competitive spirit, especially in the physical endeavours of sport. A bias that to a degree is related to the wholly disproportionate numbers of female to male teachers.

As with health, the educational budget has also ramped up steeply over the past five years to over seventy-three billion pounds. Much of this funding directed towards expanding higher education. The motives behind this are again mainly political, it becoming a national objective to get around fifty percent of all school leavers into further education. An expansion made viable by increasing the range of possible subjects, both demanding and otherwise. Whether this is a good idea remains doubtful, as it appears to be producing an over qualified workforce. OECD figures confirming that already some 15% of the workforce appear overqualified for what they do. The recent decision to raise the school leaving age to 18 must also add to the problems schools already contend with, those bored at sixteen facing an extra two years, plenty of opportunity to become even more disruptive.

As with so many things, Britain needs a proper debate over its system of education. One possible way towards something better is to copy the

Swedish example, there, in 1992, they introduced parental choice, ensuring funding followed the child rather than going to the school. This decision has resulted in measurable improvements to both State and private sectors. Regrettably Britain remains dominated by something akin to the Stalinist mindset, types determined to micro-manage, even if they are no good at it.

Part of any solution must see a return to methods that teach effectively, which in itself implies those in the profession must be up to scratch. This means judging competence and rewarding the ones with the gift of getting the message over. Schools must also be given the authority to establish discipline as a first step towards providing an environment amenable to intellectual rigour, an atmosphere that gives each child the chance of unlocking their abilities. An essential element is the formation of sensible challenges that engage pupil interest. Essential to this is the teaching of subjects that are well understood and relevant, there is no room for half baked superficial treatment and propaganda. Nowhere is this more important than in the sciences, which have trivialised in pursuit of social and political ends.

It goes without saying that Britain basically depends on the raw talent entering its schools. These children must have the same basic potential as those who have gone before. Yet for all the world it does not look like it.

Chapter 37

A question of faith

Part of our essence as humans appears to encompass a need to believe in something. While this tends to be seen in terms of what is spiritual, a belief in God as it were, many now find such satisfactions in what is temporal, or worldly. Differences that do not alter the prime characteristic of faith, which above all else is defined by its passions, remaining at heart a manifestation of feelings whose strengths can stretch to the point where they defy logic and sense.

As this brief has indicated, Britain's history has swayed to such intensities, sentiment revolving around the perceived differences and importance of one form of spirituality over another. As the journey towards modernity continued, this particular interpretation lost some of its force in favour of concerns that placed man, his ideas and goals to the fore.

For the British historian wanting to chart this story, there is much in the way of records and documentation. Information that assists in the detailed examination of the great schism that divided the Catholic Church during the Reformation and the forces that came into play as Henry 8th schemed a division between England and Rome. An understanding that also helps in casting light on the effects of the Counter Reformation with its Inquisition and what this meant to life in Britain.

From this can be traced the intolerance towards those of the Catholic and Non Conformists faiths that saw a rough north south split settle across the land. Fierce devotions that ebbed gradually over the long years when Britain developed both economically and industrially on its way to assuming international prominence. By the mid point of the twentieth century it appeared as if active Christianity had peaked, although its ethos had thoroughly seeped into the bones of the nation, there seemed to little inclination to continue to overtly demonstrate its presence.

Despite that decline, many are still with us who regularly attended Sunday school, very large numbers of children gaining spiritual instruction during the 1940's and 50's and even into the early Sixties. However, as the national mood began to lighten, attendance fell away. Formal acts of worship for most people becoming limited to special occasions, regular church going the realm of a substantial, if dedicated minority. Understanding why this is so means considering the profound cultural and social changes that flowered during that time. The sombreness of high church services with its formality and subdued approach to worship losing appeal. A trend reinforced by the sense that the Church, especially the Church of England, was no longer as sure of God as it ought to be. A loss of commitment that appeared to affect much of its hierarchy, the attractions of the trendy social cause having greater appeal and, with it, the desire to meddle in politics rather than spreading the Gospel. Further division within the Anglican community coming later over involvement of females and homosexuals, divisions that would eventually threaten to split the communion.

These weaknesses gave strength to voices questioning the old virtues and principles. Voices eager to change the world by doing more than just expressing hostility to the Judeo-Christian ethics that is an integral part of our civilisation. Individuals openly contemptuous of the very idea of a God and dismissive of the thought that he would or could have sent a mortal son down to earth as a saviour.

Naturally this preyed on minds less than secure, casting them adrift to seek a new anchor around which the necessities of belief could be established. The retreat from traditional religion seeing alternative ideas flourish, almost anything serving as long as its certainties, real or otherwise, allowed for the same depth of feeling. A few identified it in forms of faith normally associated with other parts of the world, others developed the intellectual side, finding certainties in the sciences, relief coming from what can be seen and touched or made use of. Part of this saw the invention and gathering around new religions, one example being environmentalism. Its adherents advocating their own perspectives with all the radical fervour and more of the proselytising missionary. A group that became rather too eager to pour scorn on those who did not take up and repeat their mantra. Still more were to find what they wanted in the following of a particular sports team or political cause, extremes of devotion sometimes irrational in their intensity.

Associated with these trends, perhaps taking advantage of them, is the secular State, which has latterly become even more aggressive. Forcing its will on those whose faith takes them along certain lines towards beliefs that contest with modernity's cherished notions. A bullying reliant to some extent on propagandising that seeks to insinuate how religion has been responsible for much of history's bloodletting. A simple corruption of fact, the appalling death toll of the last century having everything to do with the human extremes of nationalism and socialism. Even where faith is wrapped up with killing, as has been the case within the Islamic world, it is not really belief that is the issue, instead it is means of exploiting its appeal for the worldly aims of gaining or perpetuating of power. Whether or not the world embraces a secular way of life will make no difference to this part of our nature.

In Britain today, most use Sunday as another Saturday. A day to be spent doing whatever, shopping, working in the garden, playing or watching sports etc. Yet, for all the distractions, the need for some way of assuaging the spiritual remains with us, despite material plenty. One who gave such a lead, at least for Catholics, was the late Pope, John Paul, an inspirational figure who expressed a clear moral message that brought a response from the faithful. Fresher evangelical approaches, rather easier on the mind and more cheerful in spirit than what is traditional, drawing in those seeking solace in worship.

Part of this revival incorporates Islam, a faith that only recently assumed world wide prominence. While the majority of British Moslems hold fast to its gentler persuasions, a few, born and bred here have been attracted by the radical interpretations emanating out of the Arab world. Culturally alienated men and women who have been persuaded to forgo their own humanity by embracing sedition, treason and the murder of people who have given them a home. That such individuals are often clever should not surprise, intellect quickly disconnects from what is real for the refuge of fantasy, that is true for all, not just the young fanatics of Islam.

Not that this country needs reminders or lessons about religious intolerance, the sectarian aspects that merged into the general conflict in Northern Ireland are far too fresh to think that. What it does need to be is on guard, a necessity prompted in part the ugliness arising out of a return of behaviour targeting Jews, their property and Synagogues.

Chapter 38

Collapse of law and order in N. Ireland

Casting a shadow over these isles for more than twenty years was the trauma of low level civil war. The expedient solution of partition in 1922 never squashing the conviction of some within the Republican movement that Ireland should be united. This underlying belief a contributory factor to the enveloping insurrection within the northern province that spread to the rest of Britain and elsewhere.

With partition had come ambitions by the Protestant majority to ensure continued Unionist dominance. Local reforms ending the system of proportional representation left in place by parliament, restricting voting rights to penalise the larger Catholic households and redrawing local boundaries in such a way that at the 1924 elections, only two of the eighty local councils ended up controlled by Catholic councillors. This political supremacy was steadied by the 1922 Special Powers Act that gave wide ranging authorities to the police. Security placed with the Royal Ulster Constabulary (RUC) and its reserve elements, the Ulster Special Constabulary (USC). Unionist control of the judiciary ensuring a sympathetic hearing for these forces whatever the circumstances.

Compounding this unfairness was the unequal distribution of economic wealth within the province, few Catholics making it into management or the higher paid positions. This however began to change when the Northern Ireland Development Council was founded in 1955, its ability to draw in new employers less constrained by sectarian considerations reducing the anomaly. An improvement that may have been instrumental in reducing the appeal of the Irish Republican Army's (IRA) guerrilla campaign initiated during that time. A lack of local support seeing it called off in 1962.

Not that this meant the cause of union between the North and South was dormant, its tensions remained just below the surface, economic reverse exposing its rawness. A situation only partially offset by increases in public expenditure instituted from Westminster. The means by which resurgent irritation found expression coming from the example of the American Civil Rights movement, a similar body being set up in the Province under the name of the Northern Ireland Civil Rights Association (NICRA). Its goals a mix of genuine grievance and overt political ends. The former seeing the call for universal suffrage, redrawing of the electoral boundaries and an end to discriminatory practice in employment and public housing, the latter demanding the repeal of the Special Powers Act and the disbanding of the effective B-Specials.

NICRA's opening gambit began in 1968 with a planned march that was banned on the grounds that the organisation was a front for the IRA (a possibility). Despite this decision, civil rights supporters sought to make their point, their presence resulting in clashes with the police. Heavy handed tactics by the authorities leading to adverse publicity that persuaded the NI Prime Minister, Terence O'Neill, to offer modest reforms, moves that were enough to tempt the Catholic Nationalist Party back into the local governing assembly at Stormont. These concessions, though modest, disturbed the wider Protestant community, causing a split in the ranks that affected subsequent negotiations.

As is so often the case, the perversion of legitimate cause based on historic grievance leads to increasing radicalism on both sides. Signs of this coming with the formation of the People's Democracy Party, it being they who organised a march from Belfast to Londonderry that set out on 1st January 1969. Its progress dogged by persistent abuse and attack by various ill controlled elements unchecked by the police. Events steering towards open division along sectarian lines that August when the annual march of the Apprentice Boys in Londonderry triggered open clashes in the Bogside area of the city. Violence spreading to Belfast, the growing scale of the disorder such that the Westminster government ordered in the British army.

Accompanying the rapid deployment of the military were hasty moves on the political front offering concessions that met most of NICRA's original demands. Overtures overtaken by events within the Republican movement. The IRA dividing over internal disagreements about how to respond to the situation in the north. The more radical voices of a splinter group that became known as the Provisional IRA (PIRA) winning local support by its advocacy of more aggressive efforts to protect the local Catholic communities. Attitudes that would end up in a violent campaign of murder and economic disruption that sought to force Britain's withdrawal from the Province as the prelude to union between north and south.

The descent into the maw of this organised campaign took a large step forward when Stormont resorted to 'internment without trial' for terrorist suspects in August of 1971. Use of British forces during this large scale operation that rounded up several hundred suspects for incarceration in the Maze prison compromising the goodwill initially shown to the British army by the Catholic community. What was left of it going in a volley of shots from the Parachute regiment that killed thirteen people during a protest march in Londonderry on 30th January 1972 (Bloody Sunday), it remaining unclear what it was that precipitated the shooting.

Despite the sharp intensification of trouble unleashed by the Provisional's during the early seventies, the resolve of the Loyalist community and the British public did not give way in line with terrorist hopes. Instead a sense of stalemate developed that encouraged secret discussion between the British government and the Provisional IRA, the outcome was the declaration of a cease-fire from February of 1975. An opportunity lost when hostilities resumed, the campaign becoming one of attrition based on indiscriminate bombing, random murders, kidnappings, extortion and political assassinations. Attention also given to economic disruption, use of propaganda to gain wider recognition of the political justice's of the insurrection and employment of guerrilla like strategies that sought to undermine the security necessary for civil government. Events that also motivated tit for tat actions along sectarian lines.

One of the most effective uses of propaganda during this period exploited internment. Following the removal of political status, over 500 prisoners refused to wash or wear prison clothes. This action was followed by a number going on hunger strike during 1981, seven IRA members and three of the splinter faction of the Irish National Liberation Army (INLA) starving themselves to death. The memory of Bobby Sands, the first to die, becoming a rallying point that saw him elected to the British parliament along with Owen Carrick, two others being voted into the Irish Dail. The success of this action not lost on the perceptive Sinn Fein leader, Gerry Adams, who was amongst the first to appreciate the possibilities of using the ballot box.

The toll of high profile assassinations began with the murder of the strong IRA critic, Ross McWhirter, who was shot at his home on the 27th

of November 1975. Four years later during March, the British Ambassador to Holland and the Conservative politician Airey Neave were killed in separate incidents. Lord Louis Mountbatten, his eldest daughter's mother in law and two teenage boys being blown to pieces when a bomb destroyed his boat in Donegal Bay, near his holiday home in 1979. The most daring of all these attempts, the bombing of the Brighton Hotel, where the Prime Minister Margaret Thatcher was staying during the Conservative Party Conference in 1984. While Mrs Thatcher survived, five others were not so lucky.

Indiscriminate killing using explosive devices started at McGurks Bar in Belfast on the 4th of December 1971, that bomb ended the lives of fifteen people, including two children. The following July saw twenty-two bombs going off in little more than an hour all over Belfast, the deaths of nine people leading to it being called the 'Bloody Friday' attack. Those south of the border were not to escape this miserable businesses, nine months later three bombs exploded in Dublin with another going off in Monaghan. In all thirty three people were killed, including children, an atrocity attributed to the Loyalist faction, the Ulster Volunteer Force.

On the 27th August 1979, the same day Lord Mountbatten was murdered, a carefully planned double bombing resulted in the deaths of eighteen soldiers at Warrenpoint in County Down. The first device killing six before a second hidden bomb claimed a further twelve as recovery operations were in progress. Sixteen of the dead belonging to the Parachute Regiment. A death toll increased by a further three RUC officers murdered near Lurgan. Eleven more names ending up on that ever lengthening list when a bomb went off without warning during a Remembrance Day Service at Enniskillen in County Fermanagh late in 1987. The worst single atrocity in this relentless campaign slaughtering twenty nine people, including nine children, at Omagh, County Tyrone during August 1998, the work of a Provisional splinter group.

Extending the use of indiscriminate bombing from Northern Ireland to the British mainland came just three weeks after 'Bloody Sunday.' A massive car bomb killing six at the Headquarters of the Parachute Brigade at Aldershot. The army being targeted once more in March 1973 when nine more were killed when a coach exploded on M26 motorway. A further bomb planted at the barracks in Yorkshire adding one more fatality.

Amongst the targets of choice were crowded pubs, two being hit within seconds of one another in Birmingham that brought the end to twenty-one people. The Guildford bombing added five more, while another in Woolwich caused two fatalities. This carnage continued with the detonation of two devices in central London that took out eight soldiers and seven horses engaged in ceremonial duties. While near the end of 1983 a blast at Harrods devastated six more families. The ongoing bloody business also striking the Deal barracks of the Royal Marines, ten dying at the time, another later succumbing to his wounds.

Although the campaign remained largely unsuccessful in terms of forcing political change, it did succeed in causing considerable economic disruption, especially the huge explosion at Bishopsgate in central London. These attacks continuing on into the twenty-first century by various dissident factions of the IRA.

Clearly fighting such a prolonged war, and war it was, requires money, and plenty of it. Crime was a fruitful source of these funds, robbery providing cash or goods that can be sold. Strangely, in the light of recent attitudes, a major source of PIRA funding came from contributions raised amongst the people of the United States. There being a huge constituency in America claiming Irish heritage who proved willing givers, money used to purchase much advanced weaponry, some of it American. Further assistance in sustaining and making the cause effective were informal links between the PIRA and various other terrorist groups including the Palestinian Liberation Organisation (PLO), African National Congress (ANC) and the Basque separatist organisation, Euskadi Ta Askatasuna (ETA). A willing supplier and the biggest backer of terrorism at the time, the Libyan leader Muammar al-Gaddafi. His country providing the facilities necessary to learn how weapons and explosives are used.

While periodic outrages took the headlines, the search for a peace formula rarely went away, amongst those who took on this arduous task were Margaret Thatcher and Irish Premier, Garret Fitzgerald. Their agreement in 1985 conceding a consultative role to the Irish Republic in the internal affairs of Ulster sunk by Protestant opposition. Nine years later, following the declaration of an indefinite cease-fire by the Provisional IRA, Sinn Fein participated in face to face talks during which it pushed for British withdrawal from Northern Ireland. The counter demand during these discussions seeing the Provisional's pressed to give up its weapons. The following February, co-operative work between British and Irish governments led to fresh proposals that directed attention towards self-government and the formation of cross-border bodies to handle joint concerns such as tourism.

Getting in the way of progress was the issue of arms, an intractable problem handed to the former US Senator, George Mitchell. His mediation leading to recommendations early in 1996 suggesting gradual disarmament during the course of talks. A proposal offering a way forward before a resumption of fighting saw Sinn Fein being turned away from the talks starting in Belfast on 10th June. Only the high profile intervention by the Northern Ireland Secretary, Mo Mowlem, helped restore both cease-fire and talks. The eventual product of those efforts being the Belfast or Good Friday Agreement that was declared on the 10th April 1998. All major groups, apart from the Democratic Unionist Party (UDP) led by the Reverend Ian Paisley, signing up to its terms.

Subsequently endorsed by referendums on both sides of the border, it committed its signatories to a peaceful and democratic path. Opening the way for an elected assembly in Northern Ireland with an all party cabinet with devolved powers. Other key aspects included surrender of territorial claims by the south over the north, conditional release of certain paramilitary prisoners, commitments to disarm and the decision to reorganise the police force.

Although progress was made, conflicting pressures saw Unionists seeking firm assurances on disarmament before the Executive was formed. Refusal by the Provisional's becoming a real sticking point and major headache for the leader of the Ulster Unionist Party (UUP), David Trimble. His statement at the end of November 1999 indicated how serious this was when he made it clear that if decommissioning had not begun by the end of the coming January, his party would withdraw.

Discussions that spring appearing to make headway when the Provisional's announced it would put its weapons beyond use under the supervision of International Inspectors. Although this allowed power to be returned to the Northern Ireland Assembly on May 30th 2000, Unionist suspicions were not allayed by vague assertions from the International Inspectors that 'substantial amounts' of arms had been stored where they could not easily be used. This increased pressures on David Trimble who faced accusations of making too many concessions without getting much in return. His response was to threaten resignation as First Minister, a promise made good on the 1st of July 2001. Not that this stopped the general erosion of confidence in his leadership hitting his party hard, dissatisfactions and uncertainties that found expression in the renewal of sectarian violence, especially in Belfast. Although re-elected as First Minister later that November, the situation remained tense and uncertain.

Elsewhere and, in line with the Belfast Agreement, policing in the Province was inherited by a newly constituted force, the Police Service of Northern Ireland (PSNI) from November of 2001. The necessity for all parties in the Province to support its role was to prove some years away, Sinn Fein remaining reluctant to put aside its reservations.

Making real political progression was increasingly tied to the Provisional's agreement to disarm in a way that could be verified. The international team tasked with getting them to do just that claiming such a formula had been devised, although once again exact details were scarce. Various manoeuvres by central government in Westminster and the different parties in Northern Ireland to circumvent this stumbling block once more heaping pressures on the Unionist leadership. Only when the international weapons inspectors were able to confirm in April of 2002 that more arms had been put beyond use did the a way of getting beyond the impasse open up.

The complexities of these arcane goings on did not help tempers on the streets, clashes between different groups of Protestants and Catholics becoming nightly entertainment, prompting British and Irish officials to call for urgent talks to cool things down. Despite the unexpected and surprising apology by the Provisional's for the deaths of some 650 civilians killed by them during the Troubles helping, the situation remained fluid with Unionist dissatisfaction high over the issue of disarmament. An exasperated First Minister and the other Unionist leaders once more backed into a corner. Hard nosed tactics eventually seeing the Executive and Assembly suspended in October of 2002 following suspicions of a PIRA spy ring at Stormont, none of the accusations sticking when all charges were dropped against the three suspects.

Fresh elections held during 2003 confirmed the shifting ground when Ian Paisley and the UDP emerged as the leading Unionist party following a campaign marked by demands for a re-negotiation of the Belfast Agreement. Mr. Paisley's role in a prolonged series of meetings between the various parties drawing to an end in December 2004 with what effectively a stalemate. Referred to as the Comprehensive Agreement, it really confirmed that future progress must be built on the principles written into the Belfast Agreement. In the lead up to and after these discussions, violence within the province remained subdued, if still nasty, it being possible that former terrorists distracted themselves by turning criminally inventive. Twenty-six and half million pounds being taken from the Northern bank in Belfast on 20th December 2004 in Britain's biggest robbery (at the time).

Helping to focus recalcitrant minds came strangely from the unexpected loss of grassroots support for the Provisional's following the brutal slaying of a Belfast Catholic, Robert McCartney, in January of 2005. Having admitted it was carried out by PIRA members, McCartney's sisters led a campaign that gained a high political profile, stimulating the flagging peace campaign. Conscious of this shift in attitudes, Sinn Fein leader Gerry Adams publicly called for the Provisional's to bow to the inevitable and renounce violence. Concurrence coming with a statement that in future the PIRA would concentrate on political solutions, a position reinforced later that year when it was announced that the last of its remaining arms were put beyond use. Not that this in itself ended the periodic beatings and other actions on the street.

Matters themselves coming to head during the 2005 General Election which confirmed the demise of the UUP, its leader David Trimble losing his parliamentary seat to a representative of the UDP. Against this backdrop of polarised support it might have been expected that hostilities would be renewed. Remarkably however, the principles set out in the Good Friday Agreement and reaffirmed by the Comprehensive Agreement, saw both sides meeting and establishing grounds for consensus at talks held at St. Andrews in Scotland during October of 2006. This truly historic change seeing Sinn Fein publicly endorsing the Northern Ireland Police Service. A decisive moment which resulted in the meeting and agreement between Gerry Adams of Sinn Fein and Ian Paisley of UDP to form an Assembly. The restoration of devolved power to Stormont coming on 8th May 2007 when Ian Paisley was elected as First Minister and Martin McGuinness of Sinn Fein gained the nod as Deputy First Minster.

Constraining armed insurrection imposed immense burdens on the British Army in Northern Ireland. Despite their prolonged presence and sacrifice, the death toll associated with the 'Troubles' topped 3500, a third of whom were killed in Belfast. The majority of these deaths were attributable to Provisional actions, including nearly 500 members of the British armed forces, with a further 600 being lost by the Royal Ulster Constabulary and Ulster Defence Regiment. The worst years came during the early Seventies, with 1972 being the single most bloody year. Added to this toll are the thousands who were wounded, many of whom will continue to face mental and physical difficulties.

Whether it is possible to quantify the cost in monetary terms is far from clear, it has obviously been immense. Maintaining levels of security that allowed some semblance of a life to go on was labour intensive and expensive. Damage due to bombing and subsequent compensation costs for loss and injury add immeasurably to the total. Much harder to quantify are the economic losses due investment scared off by the situation or forced to close due to bombing or some other act.

Chapter 39

Britain and Europe

Stimulated in part by US and British ideals as well as practical needs, the war torn continental nations of Europe in the late 1940's sought to resolve some of its early reconstruction problems by establishing cross border organisations. Pushed ahead by a developing Franco-German axis, the most far reaching of these was the formation of the European Economic Community under the 1957 Treaty of Rome. Independence of action and other worldly concerns were behind the reluctance of early post-war British administrations to take much interest in the development of these supra national ideals. Attitudes that had changed sufficiently by Harold Macmillan's Premier-ship to see negotiations start in 1961 with a view to joining.

Terms that would have made Britain a member were rejected by the French leader, Charles de Gaulle. A follow up attempt conducted during Harold Wilson's second term also vetoed by de Gaulle. The third set of talks embarked on by the committed 'Europhile' Edward Heath leading to agreement being formally accepted on 22nd January 1972. Accession to the EEC coming on the first day of the following year.

The re-election of a Labour government in 1974 saw it apply itself to resolving residual concerns left over from entry. Part of this related to higher food prices within the community, the product of what was called the Common Agricultural Policy. A complex and expensive scheme aimed at supporting prices via extensive subsidies and tariffs, the main beneficiaries being small French and German farmers. Leftover from this process was the enduring worry over the size of Britain's contribution to the Community budget, a concern that was only partially resolved in 1984 when Margaret Thatcher's government negotiated a rebate. The outcome of discussions by Wilson's government put to the test in a national referendum on membership held on the 5th June 1975, 67% of those who voted remaining convinced that membership was a good idea.

Progressing with the long term European designs were put before the Heads of State at a Summit held in Paris in early December of 1974. A consensus being reached on the setting up of a directly elected European parliament and establishment of a Regional Development Fund to disburse Community largesse. This meeting also accepting the principle of further economic and monetary union, work that took a step forward at the end of 1978 when the European Exchange-Rate Mechanism (ERM) was announced.

Behind this gradually emerging agenda were aims centring on the development of a fully federal structure. An idea formalised in a document produced by the Italian communist, Altiero Spinelli. The underlying thinking behind his work having taken place when Spinelli, Ernesto Rossi and Eugenio Colorni were exiled to the island of Ventotene during World War 2 by the Italian fascist authorities. Their hopes incorporated into the what was known as the Ventotene Manifesto, a document whose goal was a free and united Europe.

These principles were submitted to and accepted by the European parliament in 1984. Translation towards such ends taking a substantial step forward at the end of the following year with agreement to amend the founding Treaty of Rome via the Single European Act. A treaty signed into existence at the Hague and Luxembourg the following February opening the way for further economic, social and political integration. External manifestations of nascent European statehood coming from the adoption of its own anthem and flag.

Doubtless the most attractive feature of this growing European entity, at least to some, was the admittedly still distant opportunity to concentrate power. A desire that would eventually allow much greater influence on the world stage. Effectively re-creating the Old World, where a powerful Europe would be able to compete with the American's and the then, still extant, Soviet Empire. Unsurprisingly the most ardent champions of this cause were the French, a particularly enthusiastic advocate being Jacques Delors who had taken up the Presidency of the European Commission in 1985. Such was his confidence that he predicted around 80% of all decisions would be taken centrally within ten years.

It was the dawning realisation that on current lines this meant the creation of undemocratic system of government that incited the famous Bruges speech by the Prime Minister, Margaret Thatcher. Delivered on the 20th of September 1988, she chose to speak out for an alternative sort of Europe, one composed of independent democratic states co-operating freely to promote trade and commerce. Words whose importance would to some extent be lost in the tumult of other events. The Berlin Wall being torn down by exultant Germans, a prominent act in the collapse of the first communist order as Soviet satellites set themselves free.

With the end of the Soviet Empire came the decision by West Germany to assume the immense financial burdens of rebuilding its decrepit East German sister. The ramifications of this communicated itself across the rest of Europe through inflationary pressures and higher interest rates. Economic concerns reinforced by political worries over what the attitudes of a single unified Germany might become, concerns eased following the iteration of strong support for the European ideal by its Chancellor, Helmut Kohl. The wider implications of German unification being dealt with at a European Council gathering held in Dublin, Ireland, during April of 1990. Common approaches being devised to cope the German question and the requirements for assistance from the newly independent states of Eastern Europe. The European Bank for Reconstruction and Development (EBRD) created to handle the dispensing of monetary assistance. The growing attractions of the Community evident from other nations wanting in, including Turkey, Cyprus, Malta and Sweden.

What should be done next was considered in 1990 by a Council meeting in Rome, the nuts and bolts handed over to an intergovernmental conference to explore and resolve. The outcome of its lengthy deliberations were put before a follow on Council meeting in Maastricht. The draft treaty that would create the European Union being agreed when the respective Foreign and Finance ministers of the member states signed on behalf of their governments during February of 1992. A decisive moment in the furtherance of the concept of a European State coming from declared political objectives rather than just economic. Shifts confirmed by the change in name from the EEC to the European Union (EU).

It was at this juncture that the importance of not letting anything get in the way of the desired result became a little more explicit. Those responsible for this revelation were the Danes. The Maastricht Treaty facing the test of popular democracy via a referendum. A small, modestly funded group campaigning for a no vote squaring off against the might of the EU and much of the Danish government, winning a surprising victory. This however, was the wrong decision, the Danish electorate generously given a second opportunity to vote the right way. A few modifications and opt out clauses enough to be gain acceptance on the next vote.

Getting beyond the Maastricht Treaty brought into play monetary union. A complex undertaking that required time to implement. The main stumbling block the differences between national economies that were going to have to function under common rules. The organisation governing those rules was the European Central Bank, a body established in 1997. Monetary subservience to this organisation by interested countries taking a giant step towards other goals. Intentions helped by substantial investments via what was called a Cohesion Fund, money doled out to further the political ends of the community.

Suggestions of a submerging of national identities first gained expression through the introduction of the concept of a citizen of Europe. Portrayed at this stage as a complement to national citizenship, it is in reality difficult to see this as anything but a preparatory step towards a time when national identities as they are today become an irrelevance. A move that may well, at some future time, be accompanied by the adoption of a common language for all citizens.

Movement towards these broader goals was attained via the Schengen Agreement which came into force in March of 1997. Originally signed by Belgium, France, Germany, Luxembourg and the Netherlands some eight years earlier, this removed visa requirements, passport and border controls between these contiguous countries for all EU citizens. External visitors require a Schengen Visa which could be obtained from any of the consular offices of participating countries, this allowing freedom of movement across the borders of all Schengen signatories. Full harmonisation including co-ordinated external controls are scheduled to extend right across member and non member states by 2008, only Ireland and Britain looking set to retain some form of border control.

Awareness of growing gap between the centrist aims and the receptivity of the community's populations as a whole had been apparent for some time. Addressing this concern was part of the purpose of the 1997 Treaty of Amsterdam which became fact on the 2nd October after two years of protracted negotiations. Representatives of the fifteen member States hoped this lengthy document would rectify and defuse concerns that previous treaties were largely incomprehensible. A forlorn hope given that cloudy language is crucial to the European agreements.

Also integrated into this treaty were enhancements to the concept of the European citizen, extensions related to the idea of seamless European statehood and universal civic rights. Elsewhere hopes of remaining internationally competitive faced off with socialist interpretations regarding regulated full employment, sustainable development and so on. Statements tidied up by adding in words about obligatory social exclusion and anti-discriminatory practice.

Coincidentally the first moves were made to develop a frame around which a common foreign and security policy could be constructed. Confirmation of this purpose coming with the creation of a dedicated post, its first occupant, the Spanish politician, Javier Solana. The intention via this spokesman was to supply a way of elevating the EU's identity on the international scene. A co-dependent objective, the development of a common defence policy based on deployable European military force capable of being directed by the European Council. An issue that would wait until November of 2004 when a European Rapid Reaction Force of some 60,000 men was established, major contributors included Britain.

To make these ratcheting revisions permanent depended on institutional changes to many of the EU's sub-divisions, including its parliament, Council, Court of Justice and so on. The necessary consensus to these needs bolstered by outline thinking on future concerns, especially planning for further enlargement of the Union. Something that would require revaluation of voting rights and consideration of majority voting practice within the council and elsewhere. Circumventing the obvious drag imposed by reluctant member states like Britain and Denmark, provision was made for what was called variable speed integration. Those eager to get on with it could do so, leaving others to follow as and when.

Unsolved by the Amsterdam Treaty were some of the Community's more intractable issues, reform of the Common Agricultural Policy and the Structural and Cohesion Fund. Problems that went hand in hand with that evergreen question of who should supply money to the EU budget. Slowing economic growth, the impact of over regulation and the question of immigration bringing these concerns to the fore.

By the time the twentieth century had ebbed away the struggling economies of the former Soviet satellites of Poland, Romania, Slovakia, Latvia, Estonia, Lithuania, Bulgaria, Czech Republic and Slovenia were all striving to meet the requirements of membership. The primary incentive was getting their hands on the money Brussels dispensed and with it access to rich markets. Membership that would shift EU largesse away from its established members who had for some years been used to getting money to support the centralist agenda.

Foremost in the great changes in train as the century moved to end was the long awaited single currency, introduced on 1st of January 1999. Twelve countries opting to use the Euro from the word go, banknotes and coinage entering circulation on first day of 2002. Britain, along with the Danes, electing to remain outside of the so called Euro-zone, the latter getting a vote on the decision over whether to keep their own currency and with it greater control of their own economic direction.

Two months after the adoption of the Euro the issue of financial irregularities and other forms of corruption forced the resignation of the entire Commission, including its President Jacque Santer. Well for a few dramatic hours anyway. Followers of EU machinations were hardly surprised given that financial irregularities are part of the European Union's culture. Institutional corruption and its rewards serving as useful mechanism to keep people involved and in line by allowing those in it to help themselves from the money pot.

Preparations for further expansion of the Union brought government heads together at a meeting in Nice during the year 2000. Demanding discussions tying up diplomats in four important areas, the size and future composition of the Commission, the weighting of votes within the Council and an expansion of the principle of qualified majority voting. Resolution of these complex issues led to a number of compromises, most importantly larger nations faced up to giving up their second Commissioner, freeing up places that would then rotate amongst the other member States. The number of seats within the European parliament was also capped, while the Council of Europe faced up to revised voting arrangements that were re-weighted to take into account the intended expansion to 25 member states. The Council also adjusting the way its President was selected and the powers that individual could wield. New limits on the ability to veto measures within the Council were also applied to number of areas as part of a package of procedural changes.

It was ironic that once again it was a small nation that threw a spanner into the works, Ireland rejecting the Treaty in a referendum held in June

2001. The primary reasons for this rejection related to concerns over the treaty's economic impact and the influence plans for mutual defence would have on Ireland's traditional neutrality. Once again a second vote was called, a controversial decision, but one that allowed Irish voters the chance to deliver the agreement expected of them on the 18th October 2002.

Work on creating a European constitution itself began during February 2002 under the leadership of former French President, Valery Giscard d`Estaing. Its broad recommendations being presented seventeen months later, agreement on the text reached by June of 2004. Ratification dependent on the assent of all member states, something of a drawback given that it was rejected firstly by French voters in May the following year and then by Dutch voters a month later. Such an outcome is, as we have seen, an irrelevance to the political champions of the European project. The constitution being resurrected midway through 2007 by the German Chancellor, Angela Merkel, then holder of the rotating European Presidency. The so called Amending Treaty, containing about 95% of the previously rejected constitution.

Acceptance of the treaty coming in October of 2007 when the various Heads of State met in Lisbon. Gordon Brown signing on behalf of Britain, a decision taken after excluding the promised referendum on the decision. This agreement will supply the European Union with a legal personality in its own right. A decisive moment that will also see the position and powers of its President amended, an individual who may eventually be elected. Besides the setting up of self serving diplomatic service the powers of its foreign spokesman have been upgraded to the point where under certain circumstances the holder of that office will be entitled to speak for Britain in the United Nations.

The proposed adoption of qualified majority voting, further removal of the powers of veto and the introduction of the authority that will permit laws to be amended without calling an Inter-Governmental Conference (IGC). Easing the path towards future integration without vexing debate or reference to the electorate. Equally significant are plans to co-ordinate and harmonise financial, social and legal affairs including criminal justice. Extra authorities being given to European Court of Justice to adjudicate over the domestic affairs of member states in a range of areas. Proposals that extend towards developing a broader role for Europol, perhaps turning it into Europe's version of the American Federal Bureau of Investigation (FBI).

The triumph of this elitist and unrepresentative organisation was trumpeted by current EU President, Jose Manuel Barroso, who recently expressed his satisfactions that the twenty-seven members of the EU had voluntarily become part of what he called a post-imperial Empire. A celebratory note of something that remains intrinsically corrupt, a point confirmed when for the thirteenth straight year the EU's own accounts failed to pass audit.

Chapter 40

Immigration and race

In George Orwell's essay, 'Notes on Nationalism,' he discusses the underlying Anglophobia that tended to dominate intellectual life in 1930's Britain. While the reasons for this perversity lay beyond this book, it is an undercurrent that continues to reveal itself. Some having a need to express themselves by endlessly lauding other peoples, places and cultures over that seen as English. Apparently gaining through this weird practice some peculiar return at the expense of disturbing and frustrating a large number of the ordinary population. Wrapped up in what has become derision of average indigenous concerns is the question of immigration, a legitimate cause of public anxiety. Fully understanding the impact of this issue needs some knowledge of the last thousand years of immigrant history, facts that appear unknown to recent government ministers.

Following the arrival of the invading Norman's and a handful of Flemish weavers, the national mix remained unchanged until 1572 when the first of two batches of French Huguenots sought refuge. The largest of this group coming in 1685 following the Revocation of the Edict of Nantes, in all around fifty thousand settling in these isles.

Thereafter, at least for the next couple of centuries, the story was very much one of emigration, tens of thousands leaving these shores for all parts. It not being until the 19th century that the native mix was blended further by significant numbers from Ireland along with a small influx of Ashkenazi Jews who arrived towards the end of the Victorian period. A further seventy thousand, mainly Jews, arriving from Nazi Germany during the 1930's. Also preferring to stay on after the end of the Second World War were small numbers of East European's who found the idea of life under Soviet occupation less than desirable.

The first coloured immigrants in any number began to arrive in the 1950's, in the main from the Caribbean and the Indian sub-continent. People drawn in by the attractions of work. Arrivals from the Commonwealth soon topped seventy-five thousand a year, contributing to a total of around a half a million by 1962. This proved an unsettling experience for both immigrant and resident populace, rising tensions and other concerns seeing restrictions imposed via the Commonwealth Immigrants Act. From that point immigration and emigration roughly counterbalanced each other until the Eighties, when immigration increased enough to bring about a net inflow. Most of these were from the Commonwealth, although latterly people have arrived from all over, including Europe.

Current figures suggest the ethnic population of England and Wales is about 8%. The last ten years having seen an additional 2.7 million immigrants arrive, of whom around 2.2 million are of working age. This is increasing by about 160,000 a year, numbers matched to some extent by those leaving, especially amongst those retiring to the sun in France and Spain. Two thirds of this mass coming from countries other than the EU. Its reckoned that around six hundred thousand of this influx comes into the category of those who are highly skilled. Of the remainder, some eight hundred thousand are in the bracket of medium to low skills, at least capable of taking on work, the rest being dependant's or full time students.

While talented immigrants invariably contribute more than they cost, after all they are self motivated and would not come if it were not in their own interest. The problem really comes from assessing the contribution of those who are either mid to low skilled.

Before considering that point, it is worth noting that Britain did not have much of a labour shortage that justified an influx of this magnitude. What it did have was a growing mass who preferred not to take on what work was available. To be fair, where the work was and where the unemployed lived were often not the same, then there is always the mismatch between required and available skills. The real distortions coming from disincentives to work, it being financially punitive for many to take on a lower paid job when welfare payments provide the same or even higher income. These policies have influenced up and coming generations who often have no interest in engaging in productive life. In effect then immigration, especially of lower skilled workers has helped the country ignore problems created by its own social policies. At least temporarily.

Obviously favourable government and business opinion towards immigration is largely influenced by the economic advantages. There are several factors in play here, most beneficial of these is the supply of hard to find skilled personnel, talent that is often supplemented by a willingness amongst newcomers to be flexible in whatever way suits the job. This extends to the mid skilled bands for much the same sort of reasons, with the plus factor that excess numbers act to restrain wage levels. Immigration in general exerts downward pressures on unit wage costs, an outcome that is particularly influential among the low skilled jobs found in construction and the seasonal work associated with agriculture, hotels and restaurants.

All in all, these tangible benefits add up to make a positive contribution to the economy. Subtracted from this gain however is the tax overhead necessary to support those who cannot or will not work. Numbers supplemented by those unable to obtain employment because of changes wrought by immigration. Recent, rather muted grumbles suggests a dawning realisation of what this means, as Britain's business and other taxes creep upwards. For those interested in making comparisons, it is easy to sense déjà vu.

The impact on the indigenous populations of this unsustainable inflow is already unfolding in other ways. Increased demand for housing and greater strain on the essential supply of utilities in what is essentially a small island come to mind. As does the headache of transport, especially in the overdeveloped south-east and between the north-south axis of the main conurbation's. With some official projections suggesting the population may well increase by around six million by 2030, an increase that will see population density, already twice that of Germany and 12 times that of the United States, substantially increase. Life in these favoured areas is going to come under huge pressures, with all this means to the quality of life.

Rarely mentioned, although it ought to be, is what everyone takes for granted, the provision of food. While the domestic farming community have done wonders, it is heavily over-stressed and incapable of doing much more on the limited land that is available. It seem likely that increasing demands for housing must tap into space given over to agriculture, reducing the production of domestically produced food, making Britain much more dependent on imported foodstuffs. As world-wide demand for these supplies grows, prices are bound to rise, it being entirely feasible that as Britain falls behind in the future world economy then even modest disruptions to growing patterns and distribution may cause prices to increase beyond the national means to supply its needs. The consequence of such an occurrence is difficult to contemplate.

Adding to these concerns is the persistent refusal to implement policies that encourage integration. The dominance of an agenda opposing the development of a common consensus based on the existing way of life has over the past four decades encouraged some to live without relation to the surrounding culture. Whether this will over time lead to the growth of parallel societies, fragmented worlds that adhere to entirely different rules, is of course a possibility. A situation that will not prove easy to manage as and when economic difficulties prevent government from spraying money around as if there is no tomorrow.

As it stands today the national picture is something of a patchwork. The indigenous population endure what is happening. Tolerant as long as they can carve out a niche for themselves, sharing space with those here just to earn a bit of money before returning from whence they came, just as they have given room to those trying to settle down permanently. While most newcomers settle into a comfortable life, others are less than happy, surprisingly some are second and third generation children of earlier immigrants who feel alienated from what they see as depraved, greedy and self interested culture.

The answer to societal tensions related to race came early on via a legal frame that sought to govern the social and economic consequences. This first found its way into British life under the Race Relations Act passed by parliament in 1965. This made it unlawful in civil terms to refuse anyone access to a public place on racial grounds, also making it a criminal offence to stir up racial hatred. The Race Relations Board set up the following year to oversee this legislation focusing on conciliatory efforts rather than legal means. A role amended and broadened in scope three years later with the creation of the Community Relations Commission. Further legislative amendments were added in 1976, a year that saw riots in Notting Hill between black youths and the police. Extensions to the powers outlawing discrimination in housing, education, employment and so on were followed by a new body called the Commission for Racial Equality with wide ranging powers.

This approach did not prevent further racial trouble, riots in Southall during 1979 were followed by those in Brixton and Liverpool in 1981, and again in Brixton, Toxteth, Peckham and Tottenham during 1985, with more trouble in Brixton ten years later. The new century seeing outbreaks in Oldham, Burnley and Bradford, some of these provoked by local whites communities fed up with the perceived bias they detected in public policy towards immigrant populations.

The response to these and other issues has been the motivation behind several public enquiries, notably under Lord Scarman and Sir William MacPherson. The latter investigating the circumstances surrounding the murder of the black youth, Stephen Lawrence in 1993, where it was alleged that the police failed to apprehend the villains because they were an organisation whose actions varied according the colour of the victim. No evidence appears to have been found or produced to support this idea, yet various police officers were subject to disagreeable pressures in a public forum in which it was difficult for them to adequately defend themselves.

That the official face of the nation should sanction such behaviour was profoundly distasteful and unpleasant. A calumny that tainted us all. Guilt coming by association without a stitch of proof. Little wonder then that so much resentment bubbles below the surface.

Chapter 41

Done with Empire

The Anglophobic of the last few decades have enjoyed themselves. One cause that particularly attracted those eager to bash the English was the old Empire, an entity nearly always presented in negative terms. While its construction took centuries, its disposal was largely negotiated over a handful of years with, given the odds, comparatively little bloodshed.

Behind the desire for independence was a natural and entirely justified wish to run one's own affairs. Amongst some of the Empire's dependencies, this was already a substantive factor before World War 2, forces that gathered over the course of that conflict. These pressures were reinforced by early American hostility towards continued colonial possession, criticism that grew muted as the ideological conflict of the Cold War began to make itself felt. Nevertheless the dissolution of the Empire was to rapidly gather pace, its implementation often difficult as long simmering political differences within the colonies made establishing viable government problematic.

Most of these former colonies have found ways to progress, the exceptions largely confined to Africa where complex tribal affiliations have continued to divide nations established by European statesmen who did not consider such factors when they divided the continent amongst themselves. The resulting political turbulence combined with poor leadership meaning many such nations have struggled to the point that makes colonial rule seem less of an evil.

Following the formalities of Japanese surrender, it was India that most actively sought the right to go its own way. Indeed that country's loyalty during the war had to some extent been brought by the promise of independence. The stumbling block was finding a constitutional settlement tolerable to the majority Hindu Indian National Congress and the Moslem League. Sensitive to the risk of widespread bloodshed, a deal was brokered that partitioned the sub-continent in August 1947, forming Hindu India and Moslem East and West Pakistan. Law and order breaking down for a time in the aftermath of the agreement resulting in the deaths of more than half a million Sikhs, Moslems and Hindus.

It was in the Middle East that a struggling Britain found its next test amidst brewing tensions in Palestine. The understandable desire of surviving European Jews to get to their hoped for homeland at all costs creating an intense crisis. Direct British involvement in this land had only come about as the result of its role in defeating the Turkish Ottoman Empire in 1917. Military control of Palestine being extended and formalised under a League of Nations Mandate that authorised Britain to administer the area. Its policy during the 1920's and 30's broadly favouring Jewish immigration and settlement, a trend contested by the local Arab population. Nevertheless by 1939 nearly half million Jewish people had settled, despite increasing British restrictions on settlement and land purchases. After 1945 government policy sought to severely restrict further Jewish entry into Palestine, Jewish armed groups responding by conducting terrorist activities that made the matters worse.

As the situation degenerated Britain turned to the United Nations for an answer, the subsequent compromise partitioning the land between Arab and Jew on 29th November 1947. Tentative Israeli acceptance contrasting with outright Arab refusal. In the subsequent fight for its very existence the Jews won against heavy odds, declaring the longed for homeland of Israel on 14th May.

Elsewhere that year the momentum of events moved swiftly, Ireland choosing to become a republic outside of the Commonwealth while in the Far East, Burma (now Myanmar) and Ceylon (now Sri Lanka) moved towards independence with little trouble. A direct contrast to nearby Malaya where an insurrection by Chinese communists opened a long running campaign, one eventually defeated by shrewd British led tactics. The action itself making independence inevitable, the Federation of Malaysia assuming that step at the end of August 1957.

In Africa, the ending of interest began with conflict in Kenya, the indigenous peoples contesting with colonial settlers over the much favoured lands in the Central highlands. The response was a mix of concessions and the military stick that succeeded in breaking the rebellion, firstly in the city of Nairobi and then in the countryside. The justified demands of the local population met in part by a programme of political and social reform commencing in 1956.

Unquestionably these were uncomfortable years for Britain, no more so than in Egypt, where concerns over the strategically important Suez Canal led to conflict. The origins of this came from pre-war fears over Italian ambitions, a problem resolved by the Anglo-Egyptian treaty of 1936. In an agreement meant to last twenty years, Britain was allowed to base troops in the canal zone to guarantee its defence. Rising post-war nationalist sentiment throughout the Middle East saw fringe Egyptian elements agitating for cancellation of the agreement as early as 1949, eventually doing so unilaterally two years later. Britain however refused to give up its interests, its troops and assets facing a persuasive campaign of hit and run attacks.

Following the overthrow of King Farouk in July of 1952 by a revolutionary group of army officers that included Gamal Abdel Nasser. A series of tough negotiations were initiated between the two sides, Nasser himself directing Egyptian demands when he gained the top job. With British troop strength rising to over eighty thousand, hopes rode a roller coaster before a settlement was reached mid-way through 1954, the last British forces scheduled to leave during June of 1956.

Strangely, events then took a turn for the worse later that year when Nasser's interest in the economic benefits of damming the River Nile at Aswan fell foul of Cold War politics. Funding for the scheme, originally promised by the US and Britain, was jeopardised following Nasser's flirtations with Communist China and his decision to purchase arms from Czechoslovakia. Nasser reacted to the Anglo-American withdrawal of money by nationalising the Suez Canal, which was at that stage was still partly owned by British interests.

The counter to this decision coming from a series of secret meetings between Britain, France and Israel who agreed on a plan to retake control of the canal. The idea centred on an Israeli invasion of Egypt, which at some convenient point Britain and France would seek to intervene and instruct the combatants to withdraw their forces leaving France and Britain astride the canal. On October 29th 1956 Israel launched its offensive and in line with the agreement Britain and France offered to step in. Nasser's refusal led to military intervention anyway, which while successful, stirred considerable opposition from the United States already preoccupied with the Hungarian uprising. Strong pressure on the British pound providing a lever America used to gain compliance with a UN resolution for withdrawal. Action Britain acceded to without reference to its co-conspirators, denting both its prestige and independent authority.

One of the keys to the Suez crisis was related to its use as an artery for oil shipments to Europe, the growing role of this commodity motivating national policies of suppliers and consumers. This was clearly evident following the rise of local pressures in Iran that incited the nationalisation of the Anglo-Iranian Oil Company. Attempts to resolve the issue by compromise failing, behind the scenes moves to bring about a change in the Iranian government by supporting elements more favourable to what were seen as critical British interests eventually succeeding in August of 1953.

As if that was not enough the complexities of historic rivalries between Greeks and Turks beset British administration of Cyprus, where the largely Greek population sought union with Greece (Enosis). Beginning in the early 19th century this movement found political and martial stimulus under the Greek Cypriot organisation, EOKA. Skirting dangerously close to civil war from the mid-fifties, the deployment of British forces to counter giving way to negotiations that brought peace via the granting of independence in August of 1960.

Having spent a dozen years building up racial segregation into apartheid, South Africa found formal challenge on its own doorstep when the British Prime Minister, Harold Macmillan, spoke out in Cape Town during February 1960, noting the, *'Winds of change blowing through this continent.'* Words that acknowledged the moment was right for liberation, its start coming from the moment the Republic of Ghana gained its freedom after a ten year nationalist campaign. Nigeria, Sierra Leone and Tanzania (then Tanganyika) followed in 1961, before Uganda, Kenya, Gambia, Zambia, Botswana (then Bechuanaland) and Lesotho (then Basutoland) joined the ranks as the decade progressed. Tiny Swaziland finding its way to statehood during in September of 1968.

The hope for the future of each of these nations can best be summed up by what Julius Nyerere, then President of newly independent Tanzania, had to say, when he spoke about the joy of independence. Commenting that it was a victory that gave African's the right to construct their own future by their own efforts. Later appraisals of those hopes was often to disappoint both well-wisher and local. Tanzania itself having to wait until the twenty-first century when President Benjamin

Mkapa injected some economic vibrancy into Tanzanian life via privatisation and sensible market led investment.

Long important as a refuelling point of shipping bound for India, the British controlled port of Aden gained renewed strategic importance during the developing Cold War. Long an area of historic, arcane tribal affiliations, the status quo was disturbed by rising ambitions within the Kingdom of Yemen incited by the deployment of Egyptian forces. A coup developing into a full blown confrontation between British and irregular Arab forces, a costly crisis that lasted from 1962 until 1967 when British forces finally withdrew.

Maintaining the flow of capital from the Exchequer were events on the large island of Borneo in South East Asia, a place formerly ruled by the British and Dutch. Following the hand-over of the Dutch half to Indonesia in 1949, the three other territories of Sabah, Sarawak and Brunei remained under British control until 1963, when they were encouraged to become part of the Federation of Malaysia. A decision resented by the Indonesian President, Sukarno, whose ambitions were rather different. His supporters initiating an armed rebellion in Brunei and Sarawak, the British riposte being swift, if once again, lengthy. It not being until a change of leadership in Indonesia that circumstances provided for peace.

The road to full independence for the smaller Caribbean territories had its own headaches, the failure of the West Indies Federation in 1962 resulted in Jamaica opting to go it alone along with Trinidad and Tobago. Amongst Britain's smaller possessions, Malta became independent in 1964, declaring itself a republic in ten years later. While a plebiscite in 1967 saw Gibraltar's small population vote decisively to remain a British colony. Following into independent statehood was Barbados in 1966 and other smaller islands of the Eastern Caribbean in the Seventies and Eighties.

Running against this flow was Southern Rhodesia where Ian Smith led a white minority government into declaring unilateral independence on 11th November 1965. When protracted negotiations between 1966 and 1968 failed to provide a solution, Ian Smith's government declared Rhodesia a republic, the situation descending into armed conflict as opposition to white rule stirred. Although successful in its anti-guerrilla actions the political realties of sanctions brought the Ian Smith's government towards recognising the need to negotiate. Talks in London between all parties at the end of the seventies returned Robert Mugabe as the new leader of a fully independent nation. A bright future falling away as once more hopeless leadership reduced the incentives of those with the technical skills to stay and contribute. Modern Zimbabwe joining the pauper nations in what was a tragic waste.

Remaining under nominal British administration are tiny blobs here and there including Bermuda, the Cayman Islands, Montserrat, the Turks and Caicos islands, Pitcairn Island, St Helena along with its dependencies of Ascension and Tristan da Cunha. Closer to home the Crown dependencies in the British Isles include Guernsey, Jersey and the Isle of Man.

Chapter 42

British forces in action

Irrespective of its prolonged economic and social struggles, Britain has remained significantly involved on the world stage since 1945, partly because of its old colonial ties but, also because many of its political leaders have been outward looking.

Inevitably there have been plenty of occasions when its comparatively small military found itself deployed in distant parts on behalf of the nation, many of these actions having already been mentioned. Recent decades seeing the number and dangers of these engagements increasing. The following few paragraphs provides some background to what has been asked of British servicemen and women over recent decades.

The Falklands War.

Deep in the south Atlantic lay two more remnants of Imperial days, uninhabited South Georgia and the Falkland Islands, the latter settled by British descendants and administered as a colony. The origins of the dispute that led to war in 1982 related to the fact that both were claimed by Argentina, the Falkland's being called the Malvinas by that nation. The decision to use force came about from the circumstances then prevailing in Argentina, which at the time was controlled by a military Junta. Misreading the confused signals from the British government this unpopular group sought to exploit this old grievance as a way out of its difficulties. A misjudgement failing to take into account the possibility of an aggressive response by an equally unpopular Conservative administration.

The opening gambit in a difficult war came when a small number of men landed on South Georgia on the 19th March under the Argentinian flag. The lively debate that followed had not run its course before further armed forces landed on the Falkland's itself on the second day of following month. An intensive round robin diplomatic effort conducted by the US Secretary of State, Alexander Haig, failing to gain the withdrawal that would have prevented a clash of arms.

As those conscious of the history of these isles understand, a make do and mend approach so often characterises its endeavours. Something abundantly clear in the make up of the armada that left Portsmouth and elsewhere, heading south towards Ascension Island. Aboard the carriers Hermes and Invincible was the all important air support, the bulk of the ground forces embarked in commandeered commercial ships including the passenger liner Canberra. Protecting this vulnerable fleet was a mix of naval destroyers and frigates, a motley collection whose remit was to retake islands some eight thousand miles away in the face of approaching winter.

At the head of its early worries was the dangers of a submarine finding and successfully attacking the fleet while en route, a potential nightmare given the real difficulties of detecting a modern diesel electric boat. Fortunately this did not happen, the Argentine surface fleet, including the carrier, Veintecinco de Mayo, later taking itself out of consideration by staying in harbour following the sinking of the cruiser Belgrano. A controversial incident given that it was just outside of the total exclusion zone declared by the Britain.

Action on land began with the retaking of South Georgia, a tense affair when a mix of special forces and Royal Marines overcame bad weather, the dangers of submarine attack and an Argentinian detachment that luckily surrendered without British casualties. By dint of good planning and the element of surprise, getting the troops ashore on the Falkland Islands was also achieved without heavy casualties. Success made possible by the steadfast presence of the Royal Naval ships in San Carlos Water, the effectiveness of the Sidewinder missile equipped Sea Harrier combat air patrols and the crucial decision by the Argentinian Air Force to concentrate its attacks on the military ships rather than the all important logistics fleet. A strike against the Canberra for example was certain to have caused catastrophic loss of life and possible abandonment of the mission.

The very real dangers of accurate missile and bombing attacks by the Argentinian Air Force exposed the vulnerability of the navy's ships, the early loss of HMS Sheffield preceding the later loss of Ardent, Antelope, Coventry and the RFA Sir Galahad. Losses that could have been much worse if the bombs or missiles that hit Antrim, Plymouth, Argonaut,

Broadsword and Glasgow had done their work. As it was, the later loss of the Atlantic Conveyor proved a serious blow given that she carried the vital Chinook heavy lift helicopters.

As ground strength rapidly built up it became possible to make use of the early diversionary raids and intelligence gained by elements of the Special Forces. Aggressive operations by these units having already destroyed some of the dangerous Pucara ground attack aircraft based at the Pebble Island airstrip. The deployment and use of this main strength making its first impact in a difficult action at Goose Green and the surrounding area.

Subsequent movement by reinforced elements across the island towards the defended approaches of Port Stanley had to be made on foot following the loss of airlift capacity. Part of that build up seeing units put aboard two ships, the Sir Galahad and Sir Tristram, with the intention of ferrying around the island to offload in the area of Port Fitzroy and Bluff Cove. While offshore and still loaded with troops an effective attack by Argentine aircraft caused many casualties. Losses that did not alter the outcome as difficult, but nevertheless successful actions brought tactical victories on the cold windswept slopes of Mount Harriet, Two Sisters, Mount Longdon, Wireless Ridge and Mount Tumbledown.

The strategic end coming when all Argentine forces surrendered on 14th of June in what was a win against all the odds. Victory earnt by the collective effort and professional attitudes by all the forces involved. The guys on the ground facing arduous physical conditions against a foe that at times proved itself well able to hold its own. As all the commanders have subsequently admitted, it was a very close run thing.

The First & Second Gulf Wars.

Saddam Hussein's decision to invade Kuwait on 2nd August 1990 also involved substantial British forces as part of genuinely multinational force drawn from the America's, Australasia, Europe, the Middle East and the Indian sub-continent. Warned to withdraw, the Iraqi army chose to dig in, beginning a two hundred and seven day occupation that ended with its annihilation by a massive American led air and ground assault whose opening salvoes began when hundreds of cruise missiles were launched on 16th of January.

After thirty-eight days of intensive air attack and naval bombardment the ground forces, led by what was left of the Kuwaiti Army crossed the borders. Major British armoured units sweeping into the northern part of the occupied territory to engage elements of the elite Republican Guard. Allied progress was rapid on every front, most Iraqi units already knocked out psychologically, either surrendering or trying to flee under heavy pressure from ground attack aircraft. While resistance stiffened in and around Kuwait City the issue was never in doubt. The ongoing ferocity of the allied attack leading to a breakdown in Iraq morale and collapse of its ability to function, the headlong attempt to flee north exposing to relentless aerial attack.

British Special forces played a role during the conflict when they operated inside Iraq, seeking out communication assets and mobile scud launchers targeting Israel. Saddam's strategic sense recognising that provoking an Israeli response might widen the conflict and weaken the consensus amongst the allied forces and its Arab contingents. Other complications during this campaign saw the use of hostages, mostly foreigners based in Kuwait who were captured during the invasion. While the explosive destruction and setting on fire of over seven hundred oil-well heads was environmental vandalism on a grand scale. Oil also being released into the Gulf where it drifted south contaminating much of the shoreline.

By using overwhelming fire-power casualties amongst the UN contingent were kept down to low numbers. Overall fewer than five hundred coalition deaths were reported, Britain sustaining forty seven. Estimates of the number of Iraqi servicemen who died for Saddam's dreams are difficult to determine with any sort of certainty, one figure frequently quoted is nearly one hundred thousand, this appears excessive. A low of around thirty thousand has also been found, unfortunately, as with so many western sources, the studies are often compromised by domestic points scoring rather than simply presenting facts. It seems probable the real numbers will never be known.

One of the consequences of the First Gulf War was the survival of its leader, Saddam Hussein. His use of power, long despotic, continuing to blight the lives of those he did not favour, including the Marsh Arabs, Kurds and the Shiite majority. The imposition of the UN embargo providing a useful propaganda tool for Saddam to continue his rule by exploiting the humanitarian plight of most of the population. Following the anxieties raised by the attacks on America in 2001 and the endless artful games pursued by Saddam Hussein. Tolerance of the situation lessened in the influential circles surrounding the American President, George Bush, and the British Prime Minister, Tony Blair. Both stepping up demands for clearer confirmations over the various questions relating to the possible Iraqi possession of chemical, biological or nuclear weaponry.

It was this impenetrable fog of concerns and hyped up pressures, flimsy and uncertain reasons at best, that saw war restart on the 20th of March 2003 with heavy air attacks on military targets in Baghdad and elsewhere by the predominately American and British coalition. Ground forces joining in within days, the British armoured thrust aiming for Basra, which after a few sharp engagements was largely secured within the week. The main American effort pushing rapidly onto Baghdad, overall operations concluded with general cease-fire on April the 10th.

To begin with resentments directed at British and American forces were muted, attitudes were almost welcoming, although that was not to last long. The vacuum created by the deposing of the dictator and his regime quickly filled by the desire for revenge amongst those who had long been abused. Perhaps nothing would have prevented this, but the lack of a strategic plan to rebuild the nation once the fighting was over certainly did not help. Although work to clear the port of Umm Qsar was quickly accomplished, allowing humanitarian aid to flow in, the scale of the task was clearly well beyond the uncertain efforts with which reconstruction began.

Reinforcing this outpouring of hate was the reactions of fringe elements in wider Arab world who blamed America and to a lesser extent Britain for their own national failings. As these dissatisfactions grew, the momentum towards chaos gathered, feeding off nearly a quarter of million tons of looted arms and explosives that disappeared when the old regime collapsed. Malcontents drawn to the Al Qaeda flag arrived by the hundred, invaders who established strongholds in places like Fallujah and Ramadi, where they mistreated the local populations rather more badly than Saddam Hussein had ever done. Their only goal, the chance to take a pop at the American's and British and anyone else who was in the way.

Suicide bombings, shooting and barbarous beheadings amongst competing militia's and fanatics jockeying for position and power, a nightmarish scenario exploited by Iran and everyone else eager to get rid of difficult young men. Latterly this has abated, helped by the killing of a substantial majority of the Al Qaeda acolytes and the realisation amongst many militias that in a battle of attrition with the American's they lose. With as many as two million Sunni's having fled, Sunni militants are becoming more conciliatory, realising perhaps that once America and Britain have gone home they will be at the mercy of the Shiite majority.

Despite these incredible difficulties, the ordinary people of Iraq showed that having the chance of a say meant something. Elections have been held and courageously supported to the disappointment of the western media experts, most of whom are not remotely interested in the fate of ordinary Iraqi's. A government, however corrupt or shaky was formed, one that struggled to cope with low level civil war. Only the Kurdish north escaped the mayhem, mainly because it was more ethnically homogenous and had benefited from the stability provided American and British aerial protection in the preceding years.

Hindsight's certainties have suggested that one of the many coalition's mistakes was the disbanding of the old Iraqi Army. The training of a reliable replacement along with an honest police force having proved more difficult than expected. Nonetheless progress is being made, although it has been costly in terms of human life. The United States forces taking on the bulk of the fighting, its willingness to learn, the application of innovative technology and the sacrifice of its soldiers helping many Iraqi's realise that the future belongs in their own hands.

Of uncertain significance to militia attitudes facing the British in and around Basra was the calamitous surrender of fifteen Royal Navy personnel to Iranian forces at the end of March. It seems possible that, for a time at least, it helped convince those against the coalition that the British were feeble. Pressures by Shiite militias backed by Iranian forces made life next to impossible for small British force stationed in Basra over the course of 2007. While experienced and disciplined tactics certainly imposed heavy losses on these forces, a lack of boots on the ground and uncertain political will in London made the sort of action necessary to suppress the insurgency beyond the British capability. As it stands, over one hundred and seventy British service personnel lost their lives in this far off place, it must be hoped this sacrifice has benefit.

Although this is uncertain, matters now being in the hands of the Iraqi's themselves. May they succeed.

The Balkans.

Yugoslavia was at best an artificial creation, its unity owing much to the ruthless ambitions of Broz Tito. Careful management of the historic antipathies between its six ethnic groupings an achievement undone by his own death in 1980 and the later collapse of communism and the Warsaw Pact. Economic strains and conflicting ambitions finally breaking apart this unlikely alliance during the final decade of the last century. The fate of its union a complex affair due to the mixing of populations, differing territorial claims, sectarian aspects and conflict aggravated by long memories and the desire for revenge.

Slovenia led the way towards fragmentation, voting for independence at the end of 1990. A short war with the Yugoslav army failing to prevent its successful secession midway through 1991. Croatia, made its own bid for independence at the same time, a sterner task due to internal resistance from its Serbian minority. Assisted by the Serbian dominated Yugoslav national army these forces overcame the sparsely equipped Croatian forces, most of central Croatia falling under Serb control. The worst of this fighting brought to an end early in 1992 by the Vance Peace Plan, an agreement that failed to contain the ancient antipathies between Croats, Muslims and Serbian's that led to civil war in Bosnia and Herzegovina.

With these old hatreds came atrocity and what became known as ethnic cleansing, people being driven from their homes as all sides sought to create homogenous regions. These actions were beyond the capacity of the British army and other peacekeepers to prevent. Only the later aerial involvement of NATO and the success of the Croat offensive that reclaimed much of its lost territory created the conditions allowing peace to be hammered out between all sides under the Dayton Agreement in November 1995. The force that was to secure this treaty was called the Implementation Force (IFOR), which at its height included ten thousand British troops, this number halving by 1998 when the Stabilisation Force (SFOR) took over.

Irritations associated with Serbian influence infected ethnic Albanians in Kosovo. Tensions that saw violence erupt, the situation propelled by a ready supply of arms following the collapse of Albania. As the guerrilla campaign spilt out into open warfare during 1999, NATO aircraft were used to target Serbian Belgrade and the units of the Yugoslav army under its command in an effort to compel acceptance of terms on the government led by Slobodan Milosevic. Inevitably these actions were accompanied by movement of the various populations trying to get out of the way of the fighting. Eventual acceptance of terms by Serbia seeing the effective division of Kosovo and deployment of UN forces (KFOR), some thirteen thousand troops from Britain making up its largest single detachment.

Not left out of this catalogue of Balkan woes was Macedonia, tensions between ethnic Albanians and the Macedonian authorities seeing confrontation and peace keeping by NATO forces during 2001. One particular hot spot, the Presevo Valley in southern Serbia, an area settled by ethnic Albanians.

As it stand today, the situation in the Balkans remains uncertain. There are unresolved issues in Kosovo at the time of writing raising fears of a renewal of hostilities in a bid to force a political solution. Bosnia and to a lesser extent Macedonia also remain tense. Islamic radicals and arms smuggling have been at work creating a volatile partnership that is drawing a response, known malcontents being thrown out by the Bosnian authorities sensible enough to know that they do not want the trouble these types bring. Whether these tensions will lead to political rearrangements remains to be seen, attitudes amongst the Big Powers tending to vary in what they deem as acceptable.

Afghanistan.

Following the murderous attacks on the United States on 11th September 2001, the organisation America most held as responsible, Al Qaeda, with its charismatic figure head come spokesman, Osama Bin Laden, were sought out. Various means determining that this organisation and Bin Laden himself had found shelter under the wing of the then Afghan government, the Taliban. This knowledge sparked a campaign to oust the Taliban, so denying a safe haven for Al Qaeda terrorists. While that end was soon accomplished, subsequent efforts to stabilise affairs have proved much more awkward.

Here again there not much evidence of a coherent strategy to build up the region economically. Most of the money is currently derived from opium production (95% of the world's supply comes from Afghanistan), ideas about replacing this are scarce. The early opportunities to make an impression, so much the important ones, generally missed. About the only common interest amongst all sides comes from trying to clear the mine strewn landscape.

British forces were deployed to southern province of Helmand, where they continue to slug it out with the Taliban and the highly profitable drug gangs. The terrain and proximity of the Pakistan border along with the historic suspicions of Afghans to any interference make the situation fluid and the outcome uncertain.

The need for realism.

If the history of these engagements reveals anything at all, it is that modern generations are as capable as their forebears in proving themselves in the face of adversity and danger. Success that is owed as much to their innate qualities as to any training or equipment they may receive. Clearly however, as the experiences in Iraq and Afghanistan have demonstrated, the dangers are formidable, sufficient to expose any technical or human shortcomings. Amongst those that are obvious even to the outsider, is the use of inadequate vehicles, a lack of organic aerial support and other failings related to the shortage of electronic countermeasures and specific technological aids.

The deployment and continued use of the Land Rover has been a major blunder. While fine for sheep farmers, this is not a satisfactory vehicle when faced by fanatic A's several pounds of explosive on the end of his rocket launcher. The result has been deaths and severe injuries that might have been avoided had the troops been in something designed to withstand the effects of explosive attack. While the message has percolated, it is rather extraordinary it took so long for something better to find its way into operational use, especially as that something has been around for decades. Equally perplexing is the lack of airlift capacity to exploit tactical circumstance, arrange logistic supply or get casualties away to hospital. Quite why it has taken so long to rectify is once more the pertinent question.

Unquestionably those involved in facing up to the realities of insurgent warfare in these places fully recognise the benefits of what is available to help them. It does not matter if we are talking about bomb proofing, electronic countermeasures, guns that can take out incoming mortar rounds, multifunction robots that can search and watch without endangering the vulnerable soldier or unmanned air vehicles that can patrol day and night. These difficult campaigns been the mother of all manner of inventions, solutions, even if they are partial, to unavoidable dangers. Equipment that Britain has a duty to identify, buy and get into use in sufficient quantity as quickly as possible.

Although the building of the Armed Forces Memorial in Staffordshire is a welcome sign of national awareness of the sacrifice of the 16,000 thousand members of the British forces who have lost their lives since end of the Second World War. Stone memorials are no answer. It's better for the guys we send out in our name to come home at the end of their duty uninjured and not in a box borne on six shoulders. For those who sustain the terrible injuries of modern warfare, all we can do is everything we can do, for them and their families.

Chapter 43

Mirroring the nation. The monarchy

On the face of it the monarchy appears to be one of the few things unchanged over the years this book concentrated on. Yet the attrition in respect towards all of the nation's institutions has compromised much of the mystique formerly enjoyed by Britain's royalty. The loss of reserve and deference that once insulated king or queen from over familiarity fell away, something indefinable being lost. This was made possible by technology, the camera allowing intrusion into the corners of Royal life, something that was at first welcomed and encouraged by the Royal Family. A decision it would have cause to regret as interest grew beyond what was good for either side.

In retrospect, the personal fortunes of Queen Elizabeth the Second during her long uninterrupted reign followed those of her kingdom. While the Queen herself has remained gracious and resilient to what must be a strained existence, three of her four children struggled to find the private contentment that helps make life in the public eye bearable. Misfortunes that reached their peak in the early nineties, the Queen herself referring to this time thus, *'1992 is not a year on which I shall look back with undiluted pleasure. In the words of one of my more sympathetic correspondents, it has turned out to be an Annus Horribilis.'* What prompted these comments was the divorce of the Queen's daughter Anne and the separations of Andrew and Charles during a year when the God's extracted further toll, fire destroying significant parts of Windsor Castle.

Most affected was her eldest son Charles, the Prince of Wales, heir to the throne, whose marriage to Diana Spencer was to deteriorate and end in ill advised public revelation. The intense build up of hopes that surrounded their courtship and marriage held a desire for a fairy tale ending. Expectations as unfair as they were unreal, the frenzied media attention the photogenic Diana consistently attracted leaving little chance of hiding the strains on them both. The mutual love they shared for their children insufficient to overcome what led to alienation in which an attentive public took sides. Never was this more apparent than at the funeral of the Princess of Wales some years later following her tragic death in a road accident in Paris. The distinguished behaviour of her sons at that sad time a sharp contrast to the ostentatious zeal of public grief and the calculated rudeness of other participants.

It is not unreasonable to suggest that from there the only way was up, the dedication of various members of Royal family to good works has continued, slowly rebuilding favour in a atmosphere that has reverted to a more restrained examination of its role and place in the nation. Here, almost uniquely in the modern British experience, events have taught lessons that have been learnt, vital has been the realisation that flirting with the media is a double edged sword. The rebuilding of the House of Windsor owing much to the low key attending to ceremonial duties without actively courting public exposure. Long may this endure for their sakes.

Chapter 44

The face of Britain

The population we know about on these overcrowded isles is made up of just over twenty-nine million males and about thirty-one million females. As with most advanced countries, we are living longer, women having an average life span of eight-one years, five more than men. Recent analysis indicates that ninety-two percent of this population is Caucasian (white), the rest a collection of Africans, Asians and those from the Caribbean. Recent influxes drawing in additional numbers of African's along with substantial numbers of young people from all over Europe and elsewhere.

Government and political representation.

Britain remains in theory a constitutional monarchy whose parliament sits at Westminster. Of its two representative Houses, the Lords remains a non elected assembly composed of appointed life peers, hereditary peers and a number of clergy while the Commons continues as a fully elected body with 646 Members.

Sixty years ago it could be said without contradiction that parliament was the repository of political power and influence. Now, in common with our continental peers, Britain is on a journey towards an uncertain political future. Domestic democracy eroding as parliament devolves into a satrap (a local ruler or subordinate), A decline essentially brought about by the ceding of authorities to that supra-national burgeoning entity based in Brussels. EU rules, directives and laws being incorporated directly into British law without examination or debate no matter what their influence. Inevitably this has compromised both the status and independence of the nation, although not to the degree that would prevent parliament from asserting its authority in the peoples name if it had to. Nonetheless, seventy to eighty percent of all domestic law is now the by product of that un-elected and unaccountable entity, a process that is binding successive parliaments, which is itself contrary to the historic tenets of the British constitution.

Taking this still further was the new British Prime Minister, Gordon Brown, who on the 18th of October 2007 initialled his acceptance of the proposed EU Amending Treaty. As subsequent negotiations did not alter the content, what is being put before parliament is a constitutional agreement that must, when fully implemented, further reduce the roles of national government. In effect substituting elected authority for centrist powers presided over by un-elected officials whose interests will not be subject to any recognisable means of democratic restraint. Further cementing the growing separation of the ruling from those who are ruled, ensuring, as it has done throughout history, that at some point in the future somewhere in Europe (including Britain), forces will develop that will contest in the only way it can, by violence. Any such threat to the powerful may see the nascent European Gendarmerie Force, which is intended to have authority over local police forces, being used as the means of compulsion. Alas, modern Europe is returning to its roots, forgetting its own history and the warnings expressed by the American philosopher, George Santayana, who said, *'Progress, far from consisting in change, depends on retentiveness. Those who cannot remember the past are condemned to repeat it.'*

Along with this seepage of power there is also a discernible drift away from internal political integrity. The historic Union between England, Wales, Scotland and Northern Ireland gradually relaxing, preparation perhaps for the later developments that will see Europe divided into regional entities. Of the old partners, Scotland has made the most progress towards pseudo independence, regaining its own parliament and certain self governing rights in 1999. Wales having agreed to its own independent assembly with more modest authorities a couple of years earlier. While the Northern Ireland Assembly is also taking on its own internal affairs.

At the moment Britain's traditional first past the post electoral system continues to determine the makeup of parliament and with it the government. Declining levels of support for the two main parties failing to prevent the fact that they continue to take the bulk of the seats. Joining Labour and Conservative MP's in Westminster are the members of the Liberal Democrats and those who represent the specific ambitions and interests of Scotland, Wales and Northern Ireland. Reinforcing these ranks is an occasional independent, someone who normally gains office because of a burning local issue where emotions are enough to get people to abandon party allegiance, an event usually reserved for a mid term by-election. Out on the margins are various pressure groups and would be political parties that draw modest support, but not enough to gain access to parliament.

While the degree certainly varies, all the main parties are essentially left of centre socialist entities that reflect the general post-war desire of the British to have a society that panders to its needs. This remains the undisputed centre ground of British politics, although gradually this consensus has been fraying. Not because of any change in the desire for a cosseted life, but because more people are realising that those in authority are unable to deliver what they like to pretend they can.

Further indications of the haemorrhaging of parliamentary authority can be seen in the increasing public profile of the Prime Minister and the Executive. Even Ministerial appointment to the Cabinet, once considered the peak of public office has become diluted. What counts now is keeping in with the PM and his personal coterie, meeting the demands required by the Oath's of Office or public interest seems very much a secondary consideration. This shift marks a major change in another way, for instead of the PM being first in a Cabinet of equals, the role has become much more Presidential in style and substance. An outcome that reflects the growing role of the media and the issue of personality rather than administrative competence. An end that fits in well with the declining sense of reason that has steadily distorted public life and debate, something unlikely to get better given that politics no longer attracts the best of talent.

Equally beholden to the narrow interests of those who define national policy are the local authorities tasked with administering the counties, boroughs and cities. Power over what they do the result of control of funding, fully three quarters of local budgets being supplied by central government. A longer term threat to their role coming from the expectation that as power is accumulated by the EU, its regional authorities will assume some, if not all, of the responsibilities currently discharged by domestic local government.

Adding to elected officialdom are those who stand and gain office to the European parliament. Here the electorate is more brave, voting in a wider range of opinions, strangely including those who against the EU itself. Essentially toothless, these Members of the European Parliament (MEP) are paid out of the large capital transfers Britain and the other major nations make to fill the EU coffers.

A surfeit of Law.

Respect for justice and the law means distinguishing and adjudicating between those who live and act within its constraints and those who do not. Unfortunately modernity has sought to apply fresh interpretations to this tradition, almost seeking a kind of neutral system that arbitrates between differing segments of society. This is at odds with the bulk of the population here, which continues to think in terms of the way it used to be, even if they no longer assume it is so.

This change in attitude has grown during an era when life has found itself overwhelmed with formal regulation, rules, demands and advice that cover most, if not all eventualities, in overlapping and onion like layers of confusion. This overbearing tide involves itself even in day to day things once left to common sense. The result is a growing sense of distrust within society, at its root is the failure to understand what is impossibly complex.

Just how ludicrous this has become can be deduced from an exercise conducted by a body called 'Open Europe.' A group that set itself the task of counting up all the pages that dealt with law from the official journals of the EU. Concluding that in all there were 666,879 pages printed since the EEC itself was established in 1957 (to mid point of 2007). Just over a over quarter of these pages are still active.

As far as Britain is concerned, more than thirty-two thousand statutory instruments have been introduced that brings EU law into British life. A bewildering figure reaching into every area, business in particular facing an arduous series of measures and directives that brought even the EU Commission itself to recognise that it is suffocating enterprise under red tape. Home grown Bills simply add to this complexity that reaches far beyond the comprehension of any single person.

The job of making sense of this swollen mass belongs to a legal system that in theory, remains as it was, an elaborate construct built out of statutes, ancient Common Law practice and other traditions. An independent judiciary functioning through a layer of courts, its highest domestic body being the House of Lords. Beneath it, the Courts of Appeal, both civil and criminal, the High Courts, Crown Courts, County and Magistrate Courts. As with parliament, the traditional right to interpret in accordance with English law has been corrupted by the need to meet external criteria set by other bodies. The most important of these is the partisan European Court of Justice, also relevant, the European Court of Human Rights and the International Court of Justice, based in the Hague, Holland.

For all the imagined protections provided by these courts, there is little doubt that the traditional liberties and protections that surrounded the individual are being eroded. Afoot are moves to make English Common Law conform to an entirely different base, that used by the Continental schemes. The ratcheting attacks on the Law of Habeas Corpus evident, as are erosions to the right to trial by jury. It is only reasonable to assume that in time the presumption of innocence, the protections of Double Jeopardy and the right to silence will also be squeezed out. Immeasurable losses, especially for those who fought to keep these very rules intact.

As it usually the case, such suggestions are denied, however, as Gijs de Vries, the Dutch delegate to the European Convention and the European Anti-Terrorism Co-ordinator pointed out in the Daily Telegraph as long ago as the 31st of May, 2003, there was going to be an obvious requirement to harmonise national criminal law at some time in the near future. The means to justify steps in that direction are coming from the issue of terrorism, yet, such activities are hardly a new phenomena to these isles. Effective means have always been found to handle what threatens our way of life without introducing draconian measures that seek to alter the entire basis of English law. The reality is that this country faces no threat it cannot handle without modest strengthening of domestic laws and some common sense. Yet today, government has a different agenda, one as attracted to subverting our way of life as it is to protecting it.

The economy.

Britain has a trillion dollar economy, one that grown over the last financial year by 2.7%, the forecast for the current year being much the same. Equally heartening is the performance of that former bugbear, inflation. Although having been held in check at around two percent for around ten years, a mix of internal and external factors caused the Consumer Price Indices (CPI-is the common international measure) to inch upwards, reaching 3% by the end of 2006. This trend drew the Bank of England's Monetary Policy Committee into raising interest rates, a sequence of successive quarter point rate rises bringing the CPI rate back to 1.8% by the mid point of 2007.

Of the total workforce of just over twenty-nine million, eighty percent provide a service of some kind, be this in the private or public sectors. The largest single employer is the State itself, just over seven million people being paid out of the public purse. The money that allows government to employ so many people coming from the efforts of the private sector whose most profitable segment is the highly specialised financial service industries that provide banking, insurance and those other expert services that facilitate domestic and global business. About one in five of everyone economically active is involved in this industry.

The heart of this activity is in London, its old financial centre, known as the Square Mile, combining with new expansions in the dock-lands development known as Canary Wharf. Behind this massive organisation is a long legacy of expertise in financial matters that was reinforced by the liberalising of the Stock Exchange and the globalisation of the world's economy. Timely coincidences that boosted the city's importance as a provider of sound monetary management. Helping make it so are some of the world's most astute financial judges, individuals from America, Canada, Australia, South Africa and elsewhere. Talented people drawn to London to forge an alliance with domestic minds in the quest of making money. Well known financial institutions generating significant profits include HSBC, the Royal Bank of Scotland, Barclays, Prudential, Legal and General etc.

As discussed at length earlier, British industry has taken a pasting, although it still contributes to earning our way in the world. Manufacturing employment has declined to twelve percent of the total, although now its productivity is amongst the best thanks to investment in modern plant, new industries and up to date techniques. Better management and a healthier attitude amongst workers now complement each other, helping make more of our traditional remaining strengths, those of creativity and design.

In all manufacturing contributes nearly a quarter of the national GDP, its main strengths lay in chemicals, plastics and pharmaceuticals, Bio-technology and drugs, aerospace and automotive engineering, electronics and communications. Newly important is textile production based on up to date machinery, clothing and footwear, paper and printing and, even remnants of traditional industries boosted by inventive and fully modernised practice's, efficient steel making, ship building and repair are examples. The largest single sector in the manufacturing is that supplying food and beverages, over half a million employees working in more than 30,000 related businesses.

Amongst the world leading organisations that have production capacity here, even if they are not wholly British owned, include Imperial Chemical Industries, British Aerospace, British Telecommunications, Cadbury-Schweppes, GlaxoSmithKline, QinetiQ (a spin off from the old Royal Aircraft Establishment), Rolls Royce Aerospace and Unilever. Other major employers include international firms such Ford, General Motors, Honda and Nissan. Mixed in with these global leaders are a host of specialist firms operating in niche areas who continue to compete internationally. Britain's main export markets include the United States, Germany, France, Ireland, the Netherlands and Belgium, while the bulk of our imports arrive from America, Germany, France and of course the Far East, in particular China.

Retail, logistics, hotels and restaurants collectively form an network that supports some six million jobs, the second largest employer. A vital part and contributor to the domestic economy is tourism, now the sixth largest industry in terms of earnings. Whereas once retail meant a row of small specialist outlets, often manned by the owner, the scene today is dominated by multi-department or chain stores. It's rare to find a High Street without the same shops or stores, a scene repeated in the shopping mall. Supplementing this layout are retail parks where huge barn-like structures house high street brand names such as Marks and Spencer, Debenhams, John Lewis, Tesco's, Sainsbury's, Halfords, B&Q and Curry's amongst others in the fight for trade.

Over two million people earn a living in the building industry, either as designers, architects, skilled tradesmen or unskilled labour. Driving this surge is an increase in the demand for housing as well as prestige projects such as the site of the 2012 Olympic Games. While the bulk of those engaged in the industry are self employed or work in very small firms, often on a subcontract basis, growing numbers are itinerant workers from overseas, competition that has seen some domestic builders losing out. Abroad, British firms compete for a share of the construction boom that is seeing many huge and ambitious projects underway.

Critically important to any modern economy are utilities, the running and maintenance of these networks keep two hundred thousand busy. Major players include National Grid Transco, one of the largest suppliers of electricity and gas in the world, along with operators such as Southern Water. The energy that helps keep the country warm and industry running comes from a combination of sources. Nineteen percent is derived from nuclear power plants, another thirty-seven percent from gas fired stations with a further third supplied by those fed by coal. The balance coming from expensive renewable resources such as wind power.

Although Britain still has reserves of coal, natural gas and oil, its future power needs currently faces obstacles from impractical individuals and organisations obsessing over man's supposed contribution to global climate change. With less than one percent of the world's population and an insignificant industrial base, Britain is relatively inconsequential, however this intensive fear mongering appears capable of derailing the implementation of affordable solutions. It is hard to see the British people thanking these committed souls should the lights go out at some future point because the wind does not blow on cue. Never mind the nation finding itself with the power costs that make industry un-competitive or heating costs unaffordable.

Of the remaining workforce, a little more than one percent of it is engaged in agriculture. Farming uses about quarter of the available land, highly mechanised intensive methods making it efficient, at least by European standards. From this, about sixty percent of the nation's food is home grown, around two thirds of production given over to livestock, with the other third producing arable crops such as wheat, barley, potatoes, fruit and vegetables.

Insensitive attitudes and ignorance continue to threaten this success. The destruction of the domestic fishing industry is just about complete, the result of the failure to stand up against predatory foreign interests that over fished home waters, bringing about the collapse of local fish stocks. Further authoritarian influences are encouraging the diversion of grains to facilitate the production of bio-diesel and ethanol. This will increase food costs for staple foods such a bread and meats, the latter depending on grains for feedstock. Indications of this were seen recently as demand across the world increased, the spot price for wheat topping ten dollars a bushel for the first time. Further threats to livestock farming coming from the spread of diseases such as foot and mouth, blue tongue and others.

Official unemployment figures throughout Europe are much higher than governments like to pretend. Such is the case here where at the end of July 2007 it was reported that 1.65 million were out of work. At the same time some 2.7 million people are reportedly disabled or sick and unable to work. The likelihood that nine percent of the working population are unfit to labour being wholly improbable. The truth is that many pretend to access the various State benefits. Even more odd are those young men and women aged twenty five and under who are not in full education or seeking work, but somehow escape being counted. What this means is that the real unemployment rate is at least four million, with some estimations suggesting the number of those who are economically inactive is up around eight million.

Taxation and public liabilities.

Over the last decade government has increased the proportion of money it takes from the national income to about 43%, a jump of about 2.4% since the Labour government was elected in 1997. The largest increase amongst the G8 group of leading nations, most of whom have been working towards reducing the tax burden.

Using HM Treasury figures for the last financial year (2006-07) revealed that government expected to raise £516 billion in revenue. Income tax providing the largest single slice of that sum, generating £144 billion with National Insurance adding another £90 billion. Value Added Tax, Corporation Tax and Excise Duties drawing in £76, £49 and £40 billion pounds respectively. Other tax raising measures such as Council Tax, Business Rates, Inheritance Tax and Stamp Duties meeting the balance. Over the same period the Exchequer expected to spend £552 billion, or £9,200 for every man, woman and child in Britain. The main areas funded are the various forms of social protections at £151 billion, health at £96 billion and education which accounts for £73 billion. Other major areas of expenditure include Scotland, Wales, Northern Ireland, local government as whole, the judicial service, defence, transport, the BBC and capital transfers to the European Union. All of these figures continue to grow year on year as the British government reverts to the belief that it is best qualified to decide spending priorities.

Estimates for this period suggested the Exchequer expected a deficit of about 36 billion pounds, a shortfall that is met by borrowing. This gets added to the overall national debt which is estimated to be around 572 billion pounds, the interest on this coming out at about twenty-seven billion pounds per year.

Ominously, Britain faces, as do other nations, major worries over how it is going to meet future pension liabilities. The source of this problem reaches back to 1945 when plans to provide a satisfactory pension were compromised by the failure to develop a long term investment strategy that would fund the commitments. Further complicating the picture is an ageing population and the volatility of investment returns. Past efforts at reform, all well intended, have turned the whole thing into a complex and inefficient system that provides both flat rate and earning related payments funded by a mix of taxation, private business and voluntary contributions.

The promise of the current government to rectify these short comings have fallen short. Indeed the abolition by the Chancellor, Gordon Brown, of the dividend tax credit hit pension funding at the wrong moment, falling stock market returns seeing many private industry schemes run into serious under-funding. This has led to most private occupational plans, especially those based on final salary being closed off to new members. Expensive rescue plans have recovered the situation to some extent, but attitudes have changed as have expectations. This means the public purse faces additional liabilities in the future, not least from its own public sector promises. Increased employment by government is costing the nation a further forty billion pounds per annum just to meet its pension needs. When all these debts are factored in together, public sector debt soars to well over a trillion pounds.

With such large sums at stake it would be rational to think that great care would be exercised in ensuring the money collected was spent wisely. Yet as pointed out earlier in this book, investigations demonstrate that public spending is poorly controlled and wasteful, with substantial fraud and overspending without proper accountability. Making matters worse is escalating personal debts, made up of mortgage liability, outstanding credit card debt and personal loans. It being estimated we collectively owe nearly 1.38 trillion pounds, the average unsecured debt being twice that of the rest of Europe. If mortgages are taken into account, then each household owes over fifty three thousand pounds.

A measure of the distress this is causing can be gleaned from a BBC article that mentioned those seeking professional help via the Citizens Advice Bureau average just over thirteen thousand pounds of debt. Surprisingly, well perhaps not, given the bias of advertising and inclination, women are the biggest spenders. Females making up more than three fifths of all bankrupts, many more struggling with mountains of credit card debts. Only recently have checks on borrowing in Britain come into play, it being far too easy for too long to borrow substantial sums, people even borrowing to pay off existing debts.

Transport and housing.

Britain has problems with overcrowding, intense pressures being exerted on space for housing and industry, never mind the means that will allow movement between the two. The working population chokes road and rail routes during the daily ebb and flow into and out of the big cities and towns. Nowhere is this more apparent than in the south-east, the area dominated by London, although the scenario is familiar enough to those who live around the other great conurbation's of the Midlands and the old industrial North.

Across the land the main mode of travel is by car, the primary means of moving goods, the lorry. The major routes then are provided by motorways and an elaborate network of inter-linking lesser roads. Yet despite the pressures on these highways experimentation to encourage greater use of public transport saw special lanes set aside to speed up coach and bus services. Other efforts to try and get cars off the road in crowded places has led to a number of schemes, the most controversial was the introduction of congestion charging. An idea trialed in London, its success (in raising money if not reducing traffic) is likely to see it being taken up elsewhere. Even more radical plans have been aired to charge for road use, vehicles being tracked electronically and against a scale related to time and distance billed for use. Trying to impose restraints on personal movement will only add to the resentments that are building over high fuel costs, the impact on the economy bound to negative as it drives up the necessary costs of living.

That the general public resist blandishments to use public transport is entirely rational, it is both expensive and inconvenient. While all road movement is balanced on the knife edge of gridlock due to weight of traffic rail travel remains limited by the number of lines, rail width and bridge height. London is the hub of the network, the lines reaching out towards the other major cities and industrial centres. Movement within the capital is dependent on the underground system, the world's largest. The trouble is, despite sky high fares, virtually all rush hour train services are jam packed to bursting. What adding millions more people will do can only be imagined.

Britain's housing problems are in part the consequence of its social policies as well as its expanding population. The encouraging of the singular at the expense of the family, a splintering exacerbated by the obsession with the internal combustion engine and personal mobility. Strands that have done much to disperse the population, making daily travel a necessity. In combination these patterns have moved life away from the compact self contained communities. Small towns and villages whose narrow streets could have been retained and moulded by sensitive development instead ruined by road widening and demolition. Reconstructing such a heritage by salvaging old buildings and blending the new around them might see a return to the communities of old, reducing the pressures for huge spaced out development that consumes limited land and perpetuates today's problems. Concepts that are possible now the post-war planning mentality Britain borrowed from the Philistine's has lost much of its grip.

One partial solution to the shortage of living accommodation has been the conversion of old disused buildings into apartments. Although most end up as expensive properties, especially in London. Notable examples include the old dockside warehouses, largely unused since the advent of the container ports. Another trend is the development of odd corners, space snapped up to cram in a few new dwellings, older large houses on big sites are also being targeted, after purchase they are often knocked down and replaced by large number of smaller dwellings or an apartment block. Whatever is done is certainly complicated by decisions that see permission for housing to be built on flood plains. The wet summer of 2007 and the winter of 2008 leading to widespread inundation of the south-west, the north and low lying mid-eastern counties.

The Commonwealth.

This historical legacy endures as the Commonwealth of Nations, a voluntary, non-political organisation of equals made up from fifty-three member states representing nearly a quarter of the world's population. Britain still having a few dependent colonies by virtue of them being too small to exist as viable independent states.

On a regular basis the Heads of State of these nations gather to discuss common interests. The broader aims of this partnership tries to find consensus that will further economic co-operation, as well as inspire interest in the ideals of democracy and human rights. Helping to serve these ends are several organisations, a permanent London based Secretariat, the Commonwealth Foundation and the Commonwealth Business Council.

Foremost in maintaining the bonds within this group is sport, the most obvious example being the Commonwealth Games, which, like its Olympic cousin is held every four years, attendance making it the second largest sporting event of its type in the world. Equally important is that quintessentially English game of cricket, which figures highly in keeping alive links between the West Indies, South Africa, Pakistan, India, Sri Lanka, Australia, New Zealand and latterly Bangladesh and even Zimbabwe.

Inevitably there is an ebb and flow to the strength of these relationships, Britain itself, or at least through its elite's has tended to focus more on its continental neighbours, reducing Commonwealth ties. Economic interests are also changing for other nations as well, drawing attention elsewhere, whether these forces will pull it apart is unknown.

Chapter 45

As we have become

Although there is little left of the class structure that once presided over national life, it is still possible to divide the population along broad socio-economic lines into three groups. A layered society whose attitudes and opinions have diverged from the certainties of yesteryear when what one thought and spoke of was closely aligned to social position. Today, there is a jumble of outlooks that do not necessarily have anything to do with personal status.

Societal division

The upper strata, or elite, is a much broader based and numerically larger constituency than was once the case. While its intellectual cream is supplied by the top ranks of academia, business and the professions, its most important couplet continues to be drawn from the political hierarchy and news media. A symbiotic entity that largely defines the national agenda through the exercise of legitimate elected authority and the use or misuse, of the power to inform.

Surrounding this core, even if they are not necessarily tightly bound to its ideas, are a host of others who are attracted to the notion of importance. Most prominent are celebrities, people whose success in the world of entertainment or sports brings considerable financial rewards and, for those who actively court it, a great deal of publicity and the chance to be seen as a trend setters. Less obvious, but nonetheless having a major impact are the expanding numbers that make and spend fortunes, entrepreneurs as well as highly paid members of big business.

Spread out below is the rest of the nation, a majority made up from those who make a decent living, even if they have to work long and hard to get it. This savvy group includes what is left of the old middle class as well as much of the former working class. Its ranks drawn from all walks of life including the middling tiers of teaching, banking, law and medicine along with professional middle managers, administrators, engineers and various types of technicians. Its spread reaching out to bring in those people who are in skilled and even unskilled productive work, individuals who collectively contribute to the national output.

Underneath are that gradually expanding mass unable or unwilling to engage in an economic or socially constructive life. Not that this means they want it that way, anymore than it means they are stupid. Nor does it necessarily imply they are consigned to some penurious poverty, the generosity of welfare diverts substantial resources that ensure reasonable living. That is, as long as one excludes the affects of moral decay, lack of purpose and personal emptiness. Mixed up this group are all manner of folk, including indigenous whites as well as a smattering of those from both old and new immigrant communities.

National traits.

Most of the men and women of my youth were identifiable by their steady, calm and well mannered demeanour, qualities contributing to domestic tranquillity and international admiration. It made for a gentle place, one whose glories have now been pushed aside in favour of an almost desperate irreverence.

Not that this means everyone has fallen by the wayside, principled character hangs on against the odds amongst all age groups, including the young, who are not all shameless or ignorant. Despite such modest consolations, there is little doubt the general premise is true, the land has become contaminated by those who do not know how to act. Unthinking rudeness and petty aggressions winning out, the hardened overcoat most put on to insulate against its abrasive rub indicative of behaviour with few redeeming features.

Of all the consequences, none is more damaging than the souring of social relations. The hoped for world with its free dialogue between equals with common goals less in evidence than petty one-upmanship and clever disparagement. Trends encouraged by a media that delights in confrontational presentation and belittling. Aims that subvert the essential dignity that belongs to us all.

There are other losses to contemporary life, not least the decay of moral persuasion, that way of establishing what is right or wrong and acting on it. Conscience, both individual and collective, which is so essential to the long term survival of a decent society has lost support. Instead, individual interpretations dominate, a selfishness that divides the nation, on one side those who conquer its lusts, on the other those who surrender to them, a split that leaves us all vulnerable.

Grinding its bottom out on these rocks is another of those precious qualities, privacy. The obsessions of making public what is best left private has become nauseating. Its most loathe-some example at the time of these words provided by the public inquiry into the death of the Princess of Wales. Besides subjecting her sons to further pain, it also insults the French authorities who conducted the original investigation. A crassness that reached its miserable peak through the revelations of personal and private letters, a diversion that has little to do with the causes of an automobile accident.

Although individual British talent and skill continues to make its mark in various fields, collecting the able and translating whatever potential they have into a large endeavour often seems beyond the reach of those born to these isles. A failing that has much to do with a recalcitrant parochial attitude and a reluctance to take responsibility. There is always plenty of talk about what should be done, committees and other forms of talking shops permeate the fabric of national life, what is often missing from their deliberations is realism, understandable action and good judgement.

This has infected all walks of life, far too much effort ending up in failure for comfort. Besides the catalogue of poorly run private and public industries this book discussed earlier, these weaknesses get in the way of sporting success, especially at the international level where getting to the top is always difficult. An apt example of this can be traced from the aftermath of England's rare win in the 2003 Rugby World Cup. For whatever reason, the primary managerial architect of that triumph, Clive Woodward, did not continue as Head Coach. Equally odd was the immediate decline of the national squad, the team struggling to rise above the clutches of average. Naturally, those assembled to defend the trophy in the 2007 tournament were given little chance, a point apparently proved when they were taken apart by the eventual winners in the group stages. Yet strangely, out of nowhere, the team suddenly found that they could play after all. Reaching the final by defeating both

Australia and France against the odds, contesting a consecutive final, a fifty-fifty game which they only narrowly lost.

What this confirms is the extraordinarily contrary attitudes that exist amongst the native peoples, sentiments that range from defeatist weakness one moment to near miraculous spirit that defies logic the next. Which is perhaps evidence that we are as we always have been, largely an individualistic race, one that is both inward and outward looking at the same time. Frequently ambivalent to danger, it takes a dire situation and impossible odds to spark a prickly stubbornness. Forces that bring unity, which under the right leadership can endure almost any challenge. Although to do so means overcoming the national affection for self delusion, the putting of the collective head in the sand which is often preferred to facing up to the truth.

Societal variation.

Collectively, modern elite's might be seen as the new royalty. It being a fair bet that many see themselves in this light. The trappings of power, the desire for titles and privilege along with what is, in some instances, obscene ostentatious living, matches anything that could be attributed to the old aristocracy.

Anchoring its political core is the idea that 'we know best. Which translates in practice to big government plus big budgets equals utopia. An arrogant fantasy with a pronounced aversion to common-sense and learning from experience, something no longer fooling most ordinary people. The response of the politico-media machine to decaying trust has been to adjust what it tells in favour of sophisticated manipulation. Aided and abetted by an easily distracted populace, those with influence and authority have largely escaped critical scrutiny. Even parliament yielding to the temptations of privilege by implementing special tax rules, generous expense provisions and superior pensions for itself. Whatever is genuine about this activity fouled by denying adequate information through the gagging its own laws (the Freedom of Information Act). While there are those of us who feel this is some sort of new low, accept the solace provided by the words of Sir Thomas More who wrote centuries ago that those running things had become, '*a conspiracy of rich men procuring their own commodities under the name and title of a commonwealth.'*

These attitudes have contaminated impartial and honest governance. A dishonouring that sees the routine denial of solemn promises and other gimmicks that are trundled out to keep the public in the dark. The rejection of a promised referendum over the latest ratcheting of the European project just the another act in this demoralising process.

Willing helpers in this game are those whose role in life ensures their opinion will be heard. Whether it really was Lenin who referred to people like this as useful idiots is one of history's uncertainties, but it's fair comment to say that some celebrities have become just that. Exploited individuals who willingly or otherwise act as flag carriers for ideas that that are not necessarily beneficial to themselves or society as a whole. This sordid business achieves its aims by exposing the happenings of personal lives, the more turbulent the better, satisfying diversions for an audience obsessed with the trivial goings on of starlet X or Y. Individuals whose lives are all too often slaved to theatrical gestures, senseless speech and ridiculous self destructive behaviours as a means of keeping themselves in the public eye.

Away from the triumphs and disasters of the elite are those who might be called the doing OK, if not great, part of society. Many of whom concentrate much, if not all, of their energy on managing their own affairs. It is here that the old middle class strictures are strongest, with all of its decencies, desire for stability and concern for independence. Most of this group centres its effort on the family, the fretting and anxiety that is an intrinsic part of loving and protecting their young long enough to allow them to take their place in the world their great achievement. At the other end of the scale, but still a part of this group, are those who live by pursuing the transitionary luxuries of modern life to the exclusion of all else. If there is any grounds for unity amongst this bulk, it comes from the growth of cynicism, especially over public life, many adopting electoral passivity as a measure of their contempt.

Much less fortunate are those scavenging a life at the bottom. Far too many in this group enter the university of the street where graduation comes from displaying prowess in alcoholic consumption, violence, drug taking, meaningless sexual activity and criminality. Any spark of interest they might have had in something more out of life ruthlessly suppressed by a diet of televised garbage that would turn Albert Einstein into a vegetable. Their ranks slowly increasing as those with influence continue to deny the importance of a stable and loving upbringing in the opportunities for a successful life.

How we look.

The majority of Briton's no longer display any particular affection for looking good. Change that have little to do with social status or wealth. The individual who tumbles out of an expensive house into an equally expensive car hardly different in appearance from the inhabitant who slouches away from a run down east London tenement to catch a bus.

Painfully obvious here is the clear lack of regard amongst growing numbers of the population for their own wellbeing. The rapid increase in those whose dietary intake exceeds that needed for healthy life a case in point. Virtually unknown in my boyhood, it has become common to see overweight people on the street, sights contrasting with those at the other end of the scale who are obsessive about what they eat. A good example of this are the so called supermodels, emaciated beings whose frail and sickly appearance influences a wide audience, especially pre-teen girls.

Even amongst those who might be considered as having little need to be concerned, the question of body image can still be all important. So much so that if diet and exercise regimes do not deliver what they seek, more and more are willing to gather at the door of the friendly plastic surgeon. All manner of procedures are now performed, adding or subtracting bits from various parts of the body. All with the apparent aim of rectifying some particular shortfall of nature, a trend that is very much a growth industry. One infecting ever younger people who eagerly mimic their elders by announcing dissatisfactions over variations in shape and size that are entirely normal to any healthy population.

Curiously, despite this modern turn of events with all of its fascination with individuality, there is a remarkable regimentation to dress. A uniform of jeans and T-shirt, an ensemble often accessorised by trainers. For reasons that defy logic, jeans are often deliberately torn or artificially faded, while the T-shirt is usually crumpled, advantageously dirty or embellished with some meaningless message or image. Variations to this modern sartorial elegance come from trousers of varying length and volume, some with a collection of pockets and bits that hang off whose purpose is obscure. The only advantage that can be seen is the availability of space to secrete that vital ingredient of urban survival, the bottle of water. Concessions to the onset of winter made by adding more layers, a mish mash of ill fitting oddments whose visual impact is suggestive of colour and pattern blindness.

While dress and grooming for work is, for some at least, an improvement, the overall societal trend is suggestive of pauperism. The few who stand out in the classical sense, supplemented by handful of others who at least wear things that are co-ordinated and of tolerable fit and quality. Remarkably these trends have been embraced by all ages, societal obsessions over youth seeing the mature abandoning decorum in an effort to be seen as with it, whether it is appropriate or not hardly seems to matter.

With men and women largely dressing along the same lines, differentiating between the two is sometime difficult. The widespread adoption of the decollete and even the bare midriff have partially solved this conundrum. Areas where the tattooed artwork or pierced flesh are often visible, an ugliness that is hopefully already past its peak.

Personal grooming and hygiene are another casualty of changed attitudes, the clean and tidy short hair of yesterdays man as rare as the carefully coiffured artistry of yesteryears fashionable woman. The opportunities for the skilled hairdresser limited to the unkempt, or windblown style. Men finding a different path in a renewed eagerness to dispense with the waiting for alopecia by having their hair shaved off, others encouraging the onset of natural loss by going in for inappropriate and aggressive treatments that help it fall out. The unshaven look, enjoying the justifications of that inventive comical label, designer stubble.

The nation's children.

The example any population gives to its children is critical, Britain, along with other western nations has peeled away most of the protective layers of childhood. What is left provides physical wellbeing while imposing demands that assault the forming mind in its immature frame with adult concerns. A world of mixed messages imposing burdens on youngsters expected to cherry pick their way through what seems appropriate. The distinct lack of moral guidance all the more complex and confusing given the various forms of propaganda put out by those with twisted ambitions. Difficulties exacerbated by the political gamesmanship that has turned schooling into a marathon long on testing and short on effective teaching. An environment often dominated by the pretence that the world and life should be fair, when everyone knows that it is not and never will be.

This has altered and extended teenage life, long a trial anyway, into an period whose boundaries are largely defined by the actions and attitudes of like minded peers. One isolated from wider experiences as modern households evolve into realms of individuals rather than homogenous families who share and interact around common aims and shared interests. Pressurising adolescents still further are the demands to conform to the latest trend or fashion. Surreal film and computerised games furthering the distance between normalcy and fantasy.

Overwhelmed with demands, many become old before they are grown. The necessary time available for their character to evolve and develop adult security, time essential to forming the rounded maturity that enriches simply denied. Little wonder so many form a flinty exterior that is not always receptive to reason. The modest step of smoking a cigarette as a sign of rebellion or early adulthood, replaced by destructive seductions of too much drink, the commonality of the expletive and the discarded condom.

The lucky ones are those with interested parents, adults who hope that what they do will leave its mark so that when the time comes to let their children find out for themselves, they will hold back from fateful leaps. When the mistakes come, as they do for all of us, there is fortune still in a home where a shoulder is there to cry on, the priceless bounty of an unconditionally loving mum and dad.

What people do besides working.

Shopping is the most important recreational activity in modern Britain, vast sums put down on every conceivable product, with women far and away the most influential half of the population in deciding spending priorities. In fact going shopping has become a ritual act, the mall a modern temple. Weekend attendance at these places is phenomenal, people of all shapes and sizes milling up and down aisles burdened with produce of every kind.

With home so much the centre of life, improving it has become a way of exercising the practical skills denied by the average working life. The realm of Do It Yourself (DIY) activities the cheapest way of realising ordinary aspirations for a better something. A vast industry supplies every possible variation of need, the huge DIY stores supplementing endless television programmes replete with ideas to go with the books and magazines on how to do this and that. Matching that interest is that of gardening, long a British passion, growing plants and vegetables a sanctuary from other duties.

Centring life still further on the home comes from exploiting technology, comparatively cheap wide screen televisions, projectors, sound system and the DVD players making a domestic cinema come game playing centre a common part of using up the social hours. The advent of digital services adding the potential for home entertainment by a substantial increase in the number of television channels to go with the role the internet. The tiny MP3 player providing a way of further insulating oneself from the hubbub of daily life, it ubiquitous presence represented by the I-Pod and the internal headphones.

Sport is an important leisure activity, providing a social as well as physical avenue to get away from life's pressures and frustrations. Large numbers take part in football, rugby, cricket, tennis, cycling and so on. More attractive to most however is spectating, both as a means of entertainment and a way of gaining some sense of belonging in a culture that lacks it. Competitive football leagues draw huge crowds every week, some fans wrapping their life around it. This has become very big business with vast sums being earnt by the top players. Gate receipts and clever merchandising of the brand making a top team a potential money spinner. Owning a Premier League football club the ultimate symbol of the super rich.

Socialising has evolved, the ascendancy of career and the reduction in the importance of the wider family reducing the circle of people one meets outside of work. This is a problem for all age groups, the young at least getting around it by flocking to the many high street bars. Many, rough and ready places, desperate looking saloons that remain so until full of people. By then they are noisy as everyone strives to talks at once against the backdrop of the ubiquitous big screen television showing the latest football match. Technology has also sought to capitalise on the obvious social emptiness, the internet opening up ways of finding friends via chat-rooms and services that offer the chances to meet someone.

Eating out as both necessity and social purpose has burgeoned over recent years as restaurant of all kinds vie for trade with country pubs that rely on providing food to draw in trade. Less attractions for all age groups include theatres, cinemas and live music events.

Adult education in Britain is also well entrenched, providing through it various channels both social ends and ways of learning. One very successful experiment is the Open University, where a degree can be earnt through spare-time study. Other government sponsored facilities such as night school offer courses in that range from flower arranging to modern languages.

Chapter 46

The world of which Britain is a part

When it comes to wielding influence in the world today, no matter what the sphere, the United States remains uncontested, although there is much uncertainty about how long this can endure. From the overall perspectives of what has best served humanity, America's post-war role has generally been a force for good. A lustre tarnishing recently over misgivings created by the Patriot Act and other legislative measures the US government introduced following the 911 atrocities. The compromising of civil protections accorded to its own citizens has raised reasonable anxieties that it to is undermining what it seeks to protect. Concerns bolstered by the high handed and questionable internment of terrorist suspects at Guantanamo Bay. While the justifications for these actions are based on the legitimate desire to prevent further terrorist activity, two wrongs are no way to make a right.

America's friends have undoubtedly been disturbed by these moves, even though they recognise that hard decisions must be made in a prickly world whose ranks include those who will target someone simply because they are an American, a Jew or an Englishman. It can be difficult, if not impossible to negotiate with such types, however the search for common understanding and grounds that will support mediation must go on, lest man's fickle and awkward nature continue to give into unreasoning violence. Naturally judging what might work best in a particular situation is, and will remain, a black art, one that goes wrong even when the right decisions are made. It is a search that can only be made more difficult if the United States is perceived as being indifferent to what the rest of the world thinks.

Economics and western hegemony

The foundations of political and social stability today are increasingly tied to meeting material needs. The last two decades having seen a spreading awareness of what life can offer amongst the world's populations, those who do not have a share, wanting it. Trends brought about by the amazing advances in modern communications which have made it difficult for governments and ruling regimes of all kinds to insulate their people from wider knowledge.

The need to respond to these understandable desires has penetrated the political conscious all around the globe, helping bring tacit acceptance of the efficacy of the free market economy no matter what the political structure of power might be. The threat to the autocrat coming from their need to contain that natural outcome of economic freedom, a desire for a share of power. Sensitivities that if poorly managed can derail progress and lead to repression. The resultant instability in one place able to communicate itself freely to neighbouring territories as people move to escape chaos.

For all the reservations and obstacles, the last couple of decades has seen rapid expansions in global productive capacities in some unlikely places. Exposing the established nations of Australia, Europe, Japan North America and others to pressures that go beyond simple loss of influence due to declining market share. Growing wealth introducing strains that are influencing the unequal debates that have been the norm in the world's forums for years, voices previously ignored or silenced, voices that must now be heard.

Realistic observers of this trend already know that America, in fact all the advanced economies rather singular interpretations are on the wane. Although doubtless their role will continue to be substantial because of the persuasions supplied by momentum of established position, entrenched wealth and unmatched military might. Forces supplemented by their significant role in many of the world's supra-national organisations. Even so, change is afoot and the need to identify and keep reliable allies will grow in a world of fading and emerging power blocs. Entities whose differing agendas will offer competition to the traditional hegemony of the last half century.

The most obvious of these impending changes is likely to come from the shift that will see the centre of the global economy moving towards the populous Far East. As this develops further, it will put Europe and, to a lesser extent North America, on the periphery, forcing complacent westerners who feel that what happens in the world will continue to be determined by politicians in Berlin, Canberra, London, Paris or Washington to think again.

Such a fundamental shift might do more to expose the vulnerabilities that have taken root in the western sphere, countries that have corrupted the necessary means by which individuals find a sense of purpose and contentment within modest lives. Instead, everyone is forced to endure a confrontational culture where unity is prevented by the endorsement of a multi-cultural agenda. Conditioning whose divisive outcomes lay the foundations of future instability. Should any reminder be needed of the elemental forces of difference, then the situation in the Balkans over the past ten to fifteen years clearly reveals the ongoing importance of a means to lubricate away natural frictions.

The only country to tackle this reasonable successfully is the United States. There, several contributory factors reduce the impact of ethnic difference, not least a common hope amongst all for a share in the good life. Space also helps, America is a big country. Equally significant is a common interpretation of what it is to be an American, one taken up by recent immigrants who face a host of persuasions whose purpose is to inculcate a sharing of this vision. Although quite how this unity will stand up to economic dislocation is open to question, even for the America. Current resentments amongst the resident communities over illegal Mexican immigration suggests there might be limits to its tolerance.

It is hard in the circumstances to see much sympathy for any western nation getting into trouble coming from those who derive strength from homogeneity and rising ambition. After all these are largely self induced predicaments, the consequences of foolishness as much as arrogance. The emerging nations might well reflect on past humiliations, inwardly celebrating in the struggles of former masters.

Further strains on traditional western hegemony are evident, some emerging from within its own ranks. Leading the pack is a hopeful Europe, the power grab of its elite's engineered in the hope of creating a base on which it can dominate. One reliant not so much on military or economic strength, but more on its assumed sense of moral superiority. Russia to is regaining strength, its decline from superpower status rankling with its leadership and people, sentiment that is underwriting strong motivations to climb back up into the reckoning. The way it might do so coming from the exploitation of raw material and energy reserves plus more aggressive marketing of arms. Potentially more powerful (perhaps) in the longer term is China. Its huge population and rapid economic growth providing the means on which it can base its own bid for influence. Vigour that may well be artfully employed to further the divide between America and Europe as a way of gaining greater authority for itself.

The aggregate provides potential for a great deal of future disagreement in a world that is becoming more interdependent. One can be sure that some of the aggravation will be based on fresh interpretations of historic antipathies, but there are certain to be new sensitivities as nations and emerging power blocs jockey for position. Using human natures variability as a guide suggests there will few principles on which unity can be forged for long other than advantage, international relations remaining something of a lottery. In this old game, opposing sides will continue to try and manage each others feelings by diplomacy and sometimes by brinkmanship, those interested in neither will exploit violence as they always have. Where this will all end up is anyone's guess, the misstep only dangerous because material wealth has been used to produce weapons able to kill millions.

Supra-national ideals.

Most small nations face an uphill struggle to make their voices heard against the major movers and shakers of the world. They are simply not important enough unless they have something the major powers want or are scared of. Oil fits the bill in the case of the former, an atomic bomb in the latter. However, all this has its limits, the modern era demonstrating the constraints that affect even the big players.

The solution to the problems that haunt relations between big and small were meant to be resolved by the activities of various voluntary supra-national entities, of which the United Nations (UN) and its affiliated bodies are the most important. The founding principles providing for a forum where difficulties could be discussed and a consensus arrived at, or at least ameliorated to allow negotiations and cool heads to prevail. Seemingly plausible and achievable ends given the goodwill at the time.

Unfortunately the UN and it various sub-agencies such as United Nations Children's Fund (UNICEF), the United Nations Educational, Scientific and Cultural Organisation (UNESCO) and the UN Human Rights Council (UNHRC) face a struggle to remain effective. Not least because internal scandals, national attitudes and changes in policy are often at odds with the founding idealism.

The hidden past of one former Secretary General, Kurt Waldheim, as damaging as the recent suggestions of complicity of another in the corruption and embezzlement of funds generated by the Iraqi Oil for Food programme . Something that has included suggestions that the then Secretary General, Kofi Annan, was conscious of some elements of malpractice. Recent investigations have also revealed corruption amongst the peacekeeping operations, a huge undertaking involving over 100,000 people at a cost of over seven billion dollars a year. However, getting at the facts is always made awkward given the UN's own internal audit source documents are often withheld.

Destructive in a different way is the recent strategic shift in the activities of bodies such as UNICEF. Focus distracted away from ensuring children survive in favour of objectives that serve feminists and social engineers. The inexplicable diversion of attention and precious resources away from providing essential food and medical care in favour of concerns over rights is simply bizarre. It is a distortion of purpose that has spread to other areas including the Human Rights Commission, or as it is called now, the UN Human Rights Council. A body that freely criticises Israel at every opportunity but routinely ignores other nations known to compromise human dignity.

As high hopes have given way to disappointing modern realities, even its greatest champion, America, has begun to lose interest. Given that the US provides 22% of the total UN budget, this loss of enthusiasm holds real worries. The new Secretary General surely has his work cut out as he tries to restore confidence and prevent corruption destroying this vital organisation.

International Security.

Internationally, peace is usually in the hands of diplomats adhering to well defined protocols that govern what can be done legally. Where such mechanisms break down, arbitration by a third party may resolve the dispute, only rarely do circumstances lead one nation to slugging it out with another. Within this frame every country, big or small, seeks to protect itself by forming a police force and military arm. Internal problems are usually resolved by police action, although they can be backed up by military forces in extreme circumstances, external threats usually seeing the reverse.

Globally, international security after 1945 was mainly the result of the balance of forces existing between the world's two superpower's and the support they offered to the UN. Away from the machinations of these opposing camps and those they favoured, most places managed their own affairs. The biggest problems most faced related to internal breakdown that usually saw some group of malcontents killing at random for a particular political goal, actions that tended to end up disrupting economic life. Actions of this sort seeing the antagonists referred to as freedom fighters or terrorists depending on the perspectives of the observer.

The last sixty years has seen a surfeit of killing along these lines for a raft of reasons that can sometimes be understood and sometimes not. Over the last decade or so this has assumed even wider dimensions, mainly because of the attacks on the US on 11th of September 2001. Two thousand seven hundred and fifty two people being killed following the deliberate crashing of two aeroplanes into the twin towers of the New York World Trade Centre. Two other hijacked aeroplanes also going down, one demolishing part of the Pentagon, where the death toll reached three figures, the other crashing into a field in Pennsylvania when passengers bravely took on the hijackers.

There are many explanations advanced for these outrages, its modern manifestations emerging from the plight of the Jewish people and the formation of Israel. Ongoing Arab resentments to this small nation and the fate of displaced Palestinians merged into a resurgent international movement by events in Afghanistan following the Soviet Army's intrusion. Mujahideen fighters drawn to the fight dividing following the Soviet withdrawal, the resultant civil war seeing power eventually falling into the hands of a radical group called the Taliban. It was they who extended hospitality to the various radicalised extremists with far reaching objectives whose standard bearer is Al-Qaeda.

Behind this movement are a curious blend of dissatisfactions and resentments brought about by their own interpretations of what was right. The domestic situations in certain Arab nations, events in Palestine and the role of the United States as well as Christian's in general combined to fire religious zeal and hatred. Multiple grievances exploited by those who called upon the Islamic nations and the Moslem Diaspora to rise up. Whilst the vast majority of Moslems are not into killing anyone, this divided house and its two sects, Sunni and Shia, have indulged in a no holds barred bloodletting, mainly by killing each other.

The finger might usually point to Al Qaeda, however prominent support is provided by Iran, a nation funnelling aid to anyone that suits the aims of its theocracy. Primary recipients include the Taliban in Afghanistan, Hezbollah in southern Lebanon, Hamas in Gaza as well as the various Al Qaeda cells and Shia militias in Iraq and elsewhere. Also involved is Saudi Arabia, its strict Sunni beliefs (Wahhabism) furthered by substantial investments in the facilities to push its own brand across the world.

The tensions spread by radical clerics is a danger to many nations including Pakistan, where tribal sensitivities and military rule have kept the atmosphere charged. Worries that this will spread to Kashmir keeping alive the chance of further confrontation with India. Elsewhere the impact of Islamic scripture has led to murdering in Thailand and the Philippines, nearby Indonesia avoiding the worst of the extremes. Events on the other side of the Indian ocean in Africa showing others as less squeamish, radical faith a factor in troubled Somalia, Sudan, Nigeria and elsewhere.

There are dangers enough in all this without the Iranian President, Mahmoud Ahmadinejad, publicly calling for the destruction of a sovereign State and fellow member of the United Nations, Israel. The goals of the Iranian theocracy include seeking the nuclear gun, although as Neils Bohr, the Danish physicist presciently saw more than six decades ago, possession offers little actual security once the other side has it. Not that killing large numbers of people matters to certain fanatics, which is of course the background worry to all modern terrorism. Particularly what those stripped of any kind of conscience would do should they gain access to a nuclear, chemical or biological weapon with all of its potential to kill large numbers indiscriminately.

International dependency.

Of all the long shadows cast over the human family, none is more miserable than that which rests over Africa. This vast continent of eight hundred million souls has, for the most part, made little progress other than meeting very basic needs and, not always that. The solution to its misery, at least in the forums of world power is always the same, more money. Yet, surely it is a legitimate question to ask what good has the billions and billions Africa already swallowed actually done.

This giving, whose origins lie in human compassion, has it a long history, formal aid as an international act coming as early as 1812 when the US passed the 'Act for the Relief of the Citizens of Venezuela.' Britain busying itself with the concept for its colonies during the 1870's. This mix of generosity and self interest continued after both World Wars, America for example supplying vast quantities of surplus food to Europe to prevent mass starvation.

Recent figures (1997) indicate the most generous donor in terms of percentage of GDP has been Denmark at just under one percent, Britain supplying a quarter of one percent, while the United States is slowly retreating from past generosity by furnishing a lowly 0.08%. Although of course that remains a huge amount of money given the size of its economy. Nearly two-fifths of these loans and grants, excluding those related to military requirements, end up in Africa. Part of vast international effort that supports about forty thousand aid funded workers on a variety of projects.

Amongst those voicing opposition to this flood of international aid is the Kenyan economist, James Shikwati. While choosing not to question the motives behind the giving, he outlined the corrupting affects during an interview with the German news magazine Der Spiegel in July of 2005. This, shortly before the G8 leading industrial nations committed themselves to increasing the sums given. As James pointed out, those who received the most money always ended up the worse for it. Illustrating his points by noting how money or food aid ends up distorting local economies and markets, undermining the incentives to develop and advance. The whole thing becoming a lucrative racket that sees money siphoned off into the private pockets of the powerful and front organisations. A point proved in his own country where nothing much gets done unless someone is paid off.

Africa today effectively shares the fate of the western underclass, lives corrupted by moral decay brought about by welfare dependency. If it is to escape from this trap it must take the path that leads to economic development. Suggestions that African's lack the intellect, ingenuity or energy to do so is ridiculous, they are just as capable as the ordinary of India and China who have already begun this journey. What is needed is leadership, African leadership. Those genuinely interested in the welfare of these peoples as the whole must encourage this talent, which alone will drag this backward continent forward into modern times, giving it the confidence and self respect they are capable of earning. Pouring in money as a salve to a misguided and tortured western conscience has, as James Shikwati rightfully understands, achieved next to nothing of which Africa can be proud.

Hints that there are those willing to try come from the efforts of the Ethiopian economist, Eleni Gabre-Madhin. Her interest in trying to establish free market ideas in the hope of increasing the efficiency of local farmers by allowing them a better return for their produce is one that will hopefully flower.

A new basis for power.

There can be no argument with the view that the world is a long way from getting a handle on providing everyone with a reasonable standard of living. It is a task that is going to get harder if that broad western based coalition who have taken it upon themselves to save the world succeed. These agitators depend on raising fears of a catastrophe, any kind will do as long as it supports elaborate central control and repression of economic growth and development.

None of these various concerns has proved more useful than the idea that human activity is perturbing the climate. A belief whose basis appears founded primarily on the emergence of technologies allowing scientists to monitor the weather in detail. Analysis of data concluding that average temperatures appears to be rising. A result that ought not to be seen as remarkable given the earth is always warming or cooling for one reason or another. However this has lent itself as an ideal vehicle to those who delight in telling us we are all doomed. Such is the importance of this issue that a brief examination is advantageous as a means of illustrating for the last time in this book, the dangers that are inherent in a loss of human reason.

At a very basic level we can assert that our climate is determined by the earth's rotation, its tilted axis and geometric alignment to the sun, fundamentals completed by the orbital distance between the two and the varying radiative output of our star. Subtlety begins by considering the solar wind and the influences of cosmic radiation, interacting components whose climatic role is swayed by the earth's magnetic field and the competing strength of these two streams. These ever changing factors interacts with the gaseous atmosphere, surface topography and oceanic masses. The resultant dynamic determining the varying cycles of global temperature and the earth's shifting patterns of precipitation.

What makes the atmosphere so critical in this ever changing arrangement is its makeup. The different gases contributing towards an ability to absorb and trap some of the sun's heat. In so doing it keeps the surface temperature high enough for water, well most of it, to remain liquid and, it must be said, for our own and other forms of life to exist. The most important of these gases is water vapour, perhaps as much of 95% of the entire warming effect is related to its presence. The influences of carbon dioxide (CO2), nitrous oxide (N2O), methane (CH4) amongst others are important, but comparatively minor. A vital component in the overall equation are atmospheric clouds, which directly influence the earth's reflectivity or albedo.

As part of a general increase in scientific activity, specialist investigators assembled a record of the earth's temperature that reaches back tens of thousands of years using what are called proxies. Methods that allow astute judgements to be made about the prevailing conditions in the past, one such approach using ice core samples. This revealed that temperature and precipitation levels over the earth have been in constant flux over both long and short periods. Its extremes are the cyclic ice ages whose primary cause is thought to be related to long term changes in the geometric relationships and orbital distance between sun and earth. The less dramatic, but still significant, interglacial variations are put down to regular fluctuations in the sun's output and other complex effects such as atmospheric contamination caused by volcanic eruptions. What all this work illustrates is that our climate is constantly changing all on its own.

Modern interest in working out what was going on raised concerns, at least prior to the early 1970's, that the earth was cooling, the last fifteen or so years seeing the opposite view take hold. Since then politics has intruded and assumed control of the debate and the use that can be made of it. Always eager for a way to control, those in positions of influence have unleashed a flood of concerns that specifically target the release of carbon dioxide (CO2) into the atmosphere through man's use of fossil fuels. The general premise stating that release of additional CO2 will lead to the earth's atmosphere trapping more heat with catastrophic outcomes. One particularly convincing advocate of this line is the former Vice President of the United States, Albert Gore, who circles the globe by private jet to deliver expensive predictions of impending disaster. Persuasions heavily reliant on constant media propaganda that employs every resource at its command to this end.

Part sponsors of these worries include some of the scientists making up membership of the United Nations International Panel for Climate Change (IPCC). It is they who reported that the earth's global mean temperature has risen by about 0.6 degrees Celsius plus or minus 0.2 of a degree over the last hundred years or so. The bulk of this rise occurring before 1950, well before atmospheric levels of CO2 levels began to climb. Such modest figures lie well within the remit of natural variability and, as such, are a weak basis for the dramatic actions desired by ardent environmentalists.

The solution to this quandary has been twofold, any event suggestive of change gets a banner headline. A hammering of the conscious with reports about it being hotter than normal, colder than normal, too much rainfall or too little and so on. Incidents that are, given our capacity to scour the world for what is unusual, comparatively easy to find. Conclusions that seek to inculcate anxiety with all of its irrational consequences. The second important tool is the use of prediction based on computer simulations of future climate. Scenarios that are taken as the Gospel, despite science being unable to accurately model the way it is at the present.

This has led to the partial corruption of science through the ludicrous idea in some quarters that CO2 is some sort of poison, rather than what it really is, an essential adjunct to all earthbound life. A further oddity in this mania is the fact that man's activities are only responsible for about four percent of the total global emission of this gas. Which begs the question. Is this a problem? The honest answer is of course that no one really knows. Some scientist are convinced, others are a great deal more circumspect.

What we can say is that the production and absorption of this gas is part of an endless natural cycle whose potential for damage is constrained by certain factors. The most important of which is that gases of this sort act logarithmically, which means that accumulating levels of the gas act on a reducing scale until it reaches a point at which it saturates. At that stage additional quantities do nothing. While that threshold has not been reached, it is getting closer.

This leads us to debating what, if anything should be done. As it happens there is. We need to do more research. Not the sort of investigations that bend to political objectives, but work that allows the scientists the freedom to report their results and conclusions based on the facts. If concrete judgement is not possible, or is contrary to the desired view, then it must be accepted as such. There is no place in this for malevolent personal campaigns against those whose findings do not support the agenda of over zealous environmentalists.

It is an examination that should be bolstered by realistic economic strategies. It makes little sense for a small country like Britain to tie itself in knots trying to return to the stone age while China, with twenty-two times the population, continues to commission coal fired power plants by the dozen.

It is possible these concerns have validity, but that is at the moment speculation, not proven fact. However, given the time it takes to achieve anything meaningful, today's efforts should be directed towards the development of better technologies that reduce our real impact on the world. Squandering vast sums on carbon trading scams and other zany ideas is a diversion of resource that serves no useful purpose. What it might do however is arrest human development and give rise to extremes that might lead to conflict. The resentments of the less well off who will have to bear the brunt of this exercise might not prove controllable, which will not do any of us any good.

Chapter 47

An end

What is left to say at the end of this convoluted journey is not much. The Britain of my boyhood has largely gone, in its place are fragments that remind and a modernity that leaves me cold. Yet it is not all gloom, for our history has shown before there comes a time when the mood of the people changes and they realise at the eleventh hour their folly. Should this be so this time, undoubtedly all will find common cause with the sentiments expressed by the late Ronald Reagan, fortieth President of the United States, who said, *'government is not the answer to the problem, it is the problem.'*

Recommended reading

Obviously this brief summarising of so much could never stand on its own. Progress towards a wider understanding could begin by considering these works. The first is highly recommended for anyone trying to get to grips with the social deterioration of modern Britain.

The Welfare State We're In.
by James Bartholomew
The Death of Common Sense.
by Phillip K. Howard.
Crime and Civil Society.
by David G. Green, Emma Grove & Nadia Martin.
The Rule of Lawyers.
by Walter K. Olson.
Londonistan.
by Melanie Phillips.
Can we Trust the BBC.
by Robin Aitken

Finally, at some stage in life reader, if you have never read one, take up a comprehensive history of Britain by a proper scholar (most book stores stock one or two). Do not live on in ignorance of rich and proud history.

Limited Index

C.

D.

E.

T.

U.

V.

W.

Y.

Printed in the United Kingdom
by Lightning Source UK Ltd.
127175UK00001B/16-48/P